AF580890

THE COLONIAL ENCOUNTER

THE

COLONIAL ENCOUNTER

A reading of six novels

M. M. MAHOOD

ROWMAN AND LITTLEFIELD
Totowa, New Jersey

First published in the United States 1977
by Rowman and Littlefield, Totowa, N.J.

ISBN 0-87471-915-1

First published by Rex Collings Ltd
69 Marylebone High Street London W1

Printed in Great Britain

CONTENTS

ACKNOWLEDGEMENTS

In order to keep this book as readable and as vendible as possible I have dispensed with almost all footnotes, and the only references in the text are to the book under discussion in each chapter. But I do not want to dispense with my gratitude to the many scholars whose work has helped me to order my ideas on novels of the colonial experience. I have tried to record my debts to them, and to give readers the opportunity of checking my statements, by means of the Notes on Sources to be found at the end of the book. In case my omission of much literary criticism should seem churlish, I would like to stress that these notes are not a bibliography. I have enjoyed reading many critical essays on the six novels here discussed, but like my favourite V. S. Naipaul character, I have been obstinately determined to paddle my own canoe.

In this place, I would like to thank, first, the Librarian of the Beinecke Library at Yale University, the British Library of Political and Economic Science, King's College, Cambridge, and the Library of Congress; and then the many friends and colleagues who have been unfailingly helpful in response to my queries and to requests that they should look over portions of manuscript: Roger Anstey, Edwin Ardener, E. Bojarski, David Brokensha, Keith Carabine, Anthony Copley, G. K. Das, P. N. Furbank, Albert Gérard, Margaret M. Green, Robert Green, Ian Gregor, Eloise Knapp Hay, Lyn Innes, Mark Kinkead-Weekes, Dipak Nandy, Zdzisław Najder, Ben Obumselu, John Ramsaran, Iain R. Smith, Jean Stengers, C. T. Watts—so bald a list seems poor return for so much kindness. I am grateful also to a small group of students at the University of California at Santa Barbara who asked many pertinent questions; and to those fellow-members of the University of Kent, undergraduate or otherwise, whose interest in Third World Studies has been a constant encouragement. Parts of these essays have appeared as 'Amritsar to Chandrapore: E. M. Forster and the Massacre' in *Encounter*, 41 (1973) and as 'On Not Shooting an Elephant' in *Twentieth Century Studies*, 10 (1974), and are here reprinted by permission of the editors of those journals. The care, speed, and interest of Muriel Waring, assisted by Freda Vincent, have greatly smoothed the book's passage from script to print.

M. M. MAHOOD

Canterbury 1976

For Freddy and Jan Bateson

INTENTIONS

Readers whose response to the proliferation of books, especially books of literary criticism, is the same as that of the Preacher have cause to be grateful that this is one book and not six. If life had been longer and art shorter I would have enjoyed writing at leisure on each of the novelists whose names head the following chapters. As it is, I have limited myself to the study of one novel that I consider the masterpiece of each writer, with the possible exception of Conrad. Most people would consider *Nostromo* that writer's greatest novel, but 'Heart of Darkness' is so seminal a work that inevitably it presented itself as the subject of the first of this series of critical essays.

My first intention then is to offer the reader an affectionate scrutiny of six novels by writers I particularly admire. I have called these studies 'readings' and their method is mainly exegetical. This has brought me face-to-face six times over with a naive-seeming but persistent problem: how much of the story to re-tell? Partly because not every reader will have these novels fresh in his or her memory and partly because a slow-motion playback of parts of the story seems to me a useful critical strategy, I have risked the patience of other readers by a fair amount of recapitulation. I have been more apprehensive about the harm this method might occasion to the books themselves. The critic's besetting fear is that of being a parasite, of crawling ivy-like over the structure of a loved and admired work until the beauty of its form is obscured. And I should greatly deplore having done this, because form has been my chief concern.

At the same time, these are not formalist essays. The image that most of us carry of the purely formalist critic is, I suppose, of the connoisseur who appraises with eye and hand some perfect example of the potter's art: the object as in itself it really is. But in these essays I have acted upon my belief that such appraisal is much more complete and durable if we know something of the clay from which the pot was made, if we have watched the potter throw and fire the pot, and if we can compare this particular pot with others from the same hand.

When I write of pottery my mind goes immediately to a small town in Northern Nigeria where for some years a famous English potter worked alongside the local craftsmen to whom he introduced the potter's wheel. A pot by the Englishman Michael Cardew and a pot by the Gwanki woman potter Ladi Kwali—they can both be found in international museums—are alike in the pleasure that each can give to the beholder. There is an analogy here with the relationship that these six novels bear to one another. The art of story-telling is universal, though the special form of it that we call the novel probably developed its highest *technical* competence in Europe early in this century. Other countries have since learnt these techniques, but this fact does not render their novelists derivative from, still less dependent upon, the European novel. My second intention in this book has been to put some of these novels from new literatures alongside some of the best English novels of the twentieth century and by close and appreciative readings to establish their parity. Much attention is currently being given, in universities and elsewhere, to the literature of what we awkwardly call the Third World, or the developing world; and by its catholic acceptance of everything published as 'literature' this attention sometimes does a disservice to writers who take their art seriously. Twaddle in print is as common in developing as in developed countries; distinction is as rare there as here, but when it appears it is certainly not of a second order. I should be very happy if my juxtapositions did something to persuade the guardians of the pure English tradition of fiction that we do not need to change our criteria in approaching Third World novels. So I have put my six novelists together as if they were all writing in the great circular room envisaged by E. M. Forster. After all, the resemblance to the Reading Room of the British Library becomes the closer if some of those 'approximated by the act of creation' are from tropical lands.

Not that these novels have been selected on the grounds of quality alone. There is another feature they have in common, and I am afraid it is one that would earn me Forster's disapproval, for he considered classification by subject matter 'sillier still' than classification by chronology. But in choosing six novels which are all concerned with the experience of colonial rule and its aftermath, I have been guided by an interest which Forster would certainly have understood, though he would have deplored its pompous name of inter-disciplinary studies. It is an interest that has existed whenever historians, critics, philosophers, and others have talked together in coffee houses and bars and common rooms. But only in the last decade or so have academics encountered the real difficulties of inter-disciplinary studies, as they have struggled in new universities to bring the methodologies of the various subjects into relationship for those who have not yet been made at home with any one methodology. It is in this teaching situation that the pitfalls of falsification, and in particular the distortion of history into the raw material of literature, or the debasement of literature into the mere documentation of history, become most dangerous. I have tried here to give both disciplines their due. I have tried, that is, to find ways in which historical thinking on imperialism and on the relinquishing of empire, as distinct from the mere chronicling of imperialist rule, might shed light on the traditional and central concern of literary criticism: the work of art as the figment of a particular sensibility. That has been my third intention. And since we are shortly to meet in the figure of Conrad's Kurtz an awful warning of what happens to the more grandiose human plans, perhaps enough has now been said of intentions.

IDOLS OF THE TRIBE

CONRAD'S 'Heart of Darkness'

1

The autumn of 1898 began for Joseph Conrad 'a time of great tranquillities'. The phrase is Ford Madox Ford's, and the tranquillity—a relative term in Conrad's anxious existence—was in some measure Ford's benefaction. After months of wrestling with an unfinishable novel, from which he had earlier in the year contemplated running back to sea, Conrad accepted with relief Ford's offer to rent him his Kentish farmhouse. There, abandoning *The Rescue,* he began to enjoy the company of various writers who, like Ford himself, had settled in that corner of the country, and in December 1898 started to write a story he had conceived in the late summer: 'Heart of Darkness'.

Such tranquillity invited the strong and creative recollection of emotions from Conrad's earlier life: above all, of the profound disillusionment and disgust he had experienced when, as a steamboat captain in the employ of the Société Anonyme Belge pour le Commerce du Haut-Congo in the year 1890, he had found himself implicated in what he was to call 'the vilest scramble for loot that ever disfigured the history of human conscience and geographical exploration'. This revulsion is most strongly remembered in the first part of 'Heart of Darkness' when the narrator Marlow goes ashore at a port which is recognizably Matadi, and finds various evidence of the civilizing mission at work: the carcase-like railway truck with one wheel off, round which the Africans, whose burdens it was brought here to alleviate, have to carry their head loads; then the appalling chain-gang; above all, the Grove of Death:

> They were dying slowly—it was very clear. They were not enemies, they were not criminals, they were nothing earthly

> now,—nothing but black shadows of disease and starvation, lying confusedly in the greenish gloom. Brought from all the recesses of the coast in all the legality of time contracts, lost in uncongenial surroundings, fed on unfamiliar food, they sickened, became inefficient, and were then allowed to crawl away and rest. These moribund shapes were free as air—and nearly as thin. I began to distinguish the gleam of the eyes under the trees. Then, glancing down, I saw a face near my hand. The black bones reclined at full length with one shoulder against the tree, and slowly the eyelids rose and the sunken eyes looked up at me, enormous and vacant, a kind of blind white flicker in the depths of the orbs, which died out slowly. The man seemed young—almost a boy—but you know with them it's hard to tell. I found nothing else to do but to offer him one of my good Swede's ship's biscuits I had in my pocket. The fingers closed slowly on it and held—there was no other movement and no other glance. He had tied a bit of white worsted round his neck—Why? Where did he get it? Was it a badge—an ornament—a charm—a propitiatory act? Was there any idea at all connected with it? It looked startling round his black neck, this bit of white thread from beyond the seas (pp. 66-67)

The anger of this passage, all the more effective for being kept in check by the wry personality of Marlow, can be felt not only in the sardonic reminder of anti-slavery propaganda—'free as air—and nearly as thin'—but also in the sustained and controlled rhythm, emphasized by the repetitions of 'slowly': an effect which Conrad's manuscript shows to have been deliberately and even painfully sought. Physical dissolution is suggested in the way unco-ordinated human features emerge from the shadows: *the* black bones, *the* eyelids, *the* sunken eyes, *the* orbs, *the* fingers. Thus depersonalized, the Africans take on a representative role; this group of contract-labourers stands for a whole culture which is being exterminated. We are witnessing the process foretold by Lord Curzon, then Under-Secretary of State for Foreign Affairs, a few months before 'Heart of Darkness' was begun: 'from the necessities of politics or the pretences of philanthropy, the living nations will gradually encroach on the dying'.

This is magnificent protest writing. Before it is anything else, 'Heart of Darkness' is an exposure of colonial exploitation. Yet even as we recognize the primacy of this aim, we are met with a problem of origins. On the one hand, Conrad himself described the tale as 'experience pushed a little (and only very little) beyond the actual facts of the case' (p. vii). On the other, Norman Sherry, in his sober and systematic investigation into Conrad's Congo experiences, convincingly shows that in 1890 Conrad was embittered far more by his own exploitation at the hands of Camille Delcommune, acting manager of the S.A.B's station at Kinshassa, than he was by European exploitation of Africans. In replying to a letter from Kinshassa, his uncle Thaddeus Bobrowski refers to Conrad's resentment at the Belgians' 'exploiting' him (*wyzyskiwać*); and Jessie Conrad maintained that Conrad felt 'cheated all through' at not being given command of one of the company's steamboats. The vessel in question was to take part in an exploration of the Congo tributaries as far as Katanga, as part of an expedition led by the acting manager's brother, Alexandre; presumably Camille Delcommune, who becomes 'the Manager' in 'Heart of Darkness', prevented Conrad's participation. Nothing illustrates more clearly the shift in Conrad's attitudes between 1890, when he worked in the Congo, and 1898, when he wrote his story, than the transformation of this expedition of Alexandre Delcommune, which he longed to join, into the Eldorado Exploring Expedition of the novel. There it becomes an exploit carried out by 'sordid buccaneers' whose sole desire is 'to tear treasure out of the bowels of the land'.

The bitterness which informs and shapes 'Heart of Darkness' is, of course, much more than a cry of sour grapes. Yet it is hard to find evidence that in 1890 Conrad witnessed much brutality and oppression, though plenty of slovenliness and incompetence offended his seaman's eye. At that date, the activities of the Congo State, which were to arouse such fierce criticism early in the new century, had barely begun to impinge on the interests of the various trading companies. Conrad's diary records only one encounter with a State official, though that was sinister enough: 'Met an off[er] of the State inspecting. A few minutes afterwards saw at a camp[g] place the dead body of a Backongo. Shot? Horrid smell.' His experience of the ivory-trading heartland above Kinshassa was limited to a very rapid voyage to Stanley Falls and back, on which there can have been little time for shore exploration. The one direct reference to atrocities in Conrad's correspondence tells us very little. In 1903 he wrote to Roger Casement, with whom he had shared a lodging at Matadi, that during his time on the upper

Congo he had 'never heard of the alleged custom of cutting off hands among the natives. . . . Neither in the casual talk of white men, nor in the course of definite enquiries as to the tribal customs, was ever such a practice hinted at.' This is not a denial of atrocities; Casement, just back from his fact-finding mission as British Consul in the Congo State, had no need to ask Conrad about those. Rather Conrad's statement is offered to Casement as confirmation that mutilations of a kind State officials were known to condone in 1903 had not been indigenous practices thirteen years previously. It affords, however, no positive evidence that Conrad, in 1890, had knowledge of such European malpractices.

What this letter to Casement does tell us is that while he was on the upper Congo Conrad kept his 'eyes and ears well open'. Especially his ears; a great deal must have come to him by hearsay. He learnt, for example, of the fate of his predecessor Freiesleben—an incident skilfully placed near the beginning of Marlow's narrative—from the Danish steamboat captain Duhst, with whom he travelled overland on his return to the coast; and Duhst, we know, had strong views on the character of one of the State officials, Lothaire, whose native name was 'Murderer for ivory' or 'One who practises witchcraft for ivory'. Roger Casement, who was to extricate himself from the civilizing mission in the following year, must have had grim stories to tell Conrad; and among the traders and missionaries of the epoch were several who in course of time spoke out about the brutalities they had witnessed. While Conrad was at Kinshassa a meeting in London was told—rightly or wrongly, but at any rate 'on the testimony of Europeans on the spot' such as Casement's friend Herbert Ward—that the State was bartering Africans for ivory: the very theme of Conrad's first African story, 'An Outpost of Progress'.

Herbert Ward had been involved, in 1887 and 1888, in Stanley's Emin Pasha Relief Expedition. This catastrophic undertaking was the subject of angry controversy in Africa and Europe at the time of Conrad's employment by the S.A.B. Already, during his previous, unemployed months in London, what H. Fox Bourne was to call, in a bitter book, the 'other side' of the expedition was beginning to reveal itself in the English press. In a letter which reached *The Standard* in November 1889, Stanley insinuated that he had been let down by the rearguard of the expedition, five Englishmen who had been left in August 1887 on a tributary of the upper Congo with instructions to follow the advance party through the forest as soon as they were able to obtain porters from Tippu Tib. These the Arab chief failed to produce, and the rearguard waited for over a year. Their commander Barttelot became brutal to the point of insanity in his treatment of the party's African followers. In addition, scores of the men died of disease and malnutrition, until the camp at Yambuya became, as Ward's diaries show, a veritable grove of death:

> The campfires are flickering low, the greater number of our men have gone indoors, but there are still a few lingering round the dying flames. As I pass along their attitudes change somewhat, and their dull and weary eyes peer hopelessly into mine. How the dark faces are lined with their misery and suffering as the red light flashes upon them! What a world of hopelessness and agony in their glance! . . . Thirty-nine graves now in our little God's Acre, and six months gone! Good God! will these porters never come? Must all of us lie down and rot and die?
>
> . . . .
>
> Another poor fellow dead. (Fifty-one graves). There are about thirty men who are simply skin and bones, unable to walk, and to see the poor dying wretches, their great hollow eyes staring at vacancy, sitting naked on the dusty ground, propped up by their elbows, with drooping heads, gradually dying, it is a hard sight.
>
> . . . .
>
> This eternal waiting is awful; day after day passes; we see no strange face, we hear no news; our men are daily growing thinner and weaker, except in a few cases. Poor wretches! they lie out in the sun on the dusty ground, most of them with only a narrow strip of dirty cloth a couple of inches broad. There they lie all the livelong day, staring at vacancy, perfectly aware that they will never live to leave this camp. . . . Almost as many lives will be lost over this philanthropic mission as there are lives to save of Emin's people.

Such aspects of the Emin Pasha Relief Expedition contrast strongly with the views of it held in Brussels. These are well represented by the smooth account written by A.-J. Wauters, a friend of Conrad's relation Marguerite Poradowska and probably the man responsible for Conrad's appointment as steamboat captain. When Conrad arrived in Brussels for his final posting in April 1890 the city was still *en fête* for Stanley's triumphal return. At the celebratory banquet, each end of the hall was decorated with a pyramid of flowers from which protruded the tusks of four hundred elephants.

This astonishing crudity recalls Fox Bourne's insistence that one objective of the expedition, which cost so many hundreds of lives, was the wish of Stanley and his royal backer Leopold to deflect to the Congo Emin Pasha's alleged hoard of ivory. The charge was untrue; Stanley was only looking for a means of defraying the expenses of relieving the Pasha. Nevertheless, it cannot be forgotten that the disastrous bargain with Tippu Tib, for the porters who never came, was struck with this ivory in view.

2

The process of imaginative recall was once likened by Wordsworth to the experience of looking down into shallow water where glimpses of plants and stones on the lakebed are mingled with reflections of the cloudscape overhead. Conrad appears to have remembered his Congo experiences in much this way. Across his sharpest recollections of things he had heard and seen in Africa there moved a turbulence of recent protests about the mismanagement of affairs in King Leopold's private empire.

The agitation started the year that Conrad settled down to shore life as a writer. It began with an incident made famous in a thousand news items and articles as 'the Stokes affair'. Charles Stokes, an Irish ex-missionary turned trader, was summarily executed in the Eastern Congo in 1895 by order of Lothaire, on the pretext that he was supplying guns to a powerful Afro-Arab slaver. When news of the execution reached England there was a public outcry which pressured the Congo State into paying an indemnity to the British government and bringing Lothaire nominally to trial. Not every newspaper regarded the affair as a Jenkins' ear; some felt justice had been done to a dangerous gunrunner. But many journalists presented Stokes as an exemplary character who had been forced to abandon his vocation as a missionary in order to ensure the future of his eleven-year-old daughter. Whatever the rights and wrongs of the case, it had the effect of alerting the whole British public, and not just the members of the Aborigines Protection Society, to the arbitrary nature of Congo State rule.

Conrad was impressed by the Stokes affair, which recalled the atmosphere of ill will and suspicion to which he, another British subject, felt he had been exposed in the Congo. In *The Inheritors,* a novel attacking the Congo State in the thin disguise of *le système Groenlandais,* which Conrad wrote in 1899 in collaboration with Ford, there is a confrontation between a *système* governor and a French traveller called Radet, who is in part Conrad himself but in part also, I believe, the French explorer turned English journalist Lionel Declé, who was a leading defender of Stokes. 'You did not talk like that out there!' 'No—*pas si bête*—you would have hanged me perhaps as you did that poor devil of a Swiss.' One of the two main characters in Conrad's first story about the Congo, 'An Outpost of Progress', has become a trader in order to earn, like Stokes, a dowry for his daughter. And in 'Heart of Darkness' Stokes's fate is seen as the possible destiny of the 'Harlequin', the young Russian adventurer whose presence as a freelance trader is savagely resented by the Manager. Marlow overhears the Manager talking to his subordinate about

> some man supposed to be in Kurtz's district, and of whom the manager did not approve. 'We will not be free from unfair competition till one of these fellows is hanged for an example,' he said. 'Certainly,' grunted the other; 'get him hanged! Why not? Anything—anything can be done in this country.'(p.91)

Later, when Marlow finds the Harlequin's manual of seamanship and remarks 'He must be English', the Manager mutters darkly 'It will not save him from getting into trouble if he is not careful.'(p.100) The danger of which Marlow has to warn the Harlequin was real and topical in the eyes of Conrad's first readers.

The Harlequin's casual disappearance into the bush also recalls, as Norman Sherry has shown, Conrad's memory of Roger Casement's ability to travel light. Here we have perhaps an example of farther memory mingling with nearer reading, the clouded sky imposed upon the sunken stone, to form one of the emotional foci of Conrad's tale. Casement in 1890 was, like Stokes, an Irishman who had for a short time been a missionary. Now, however, he was in the State's employ. Conrad liked him immensely when they met at Matadi, and when Casement renewed the acquaintance thirteen years later Conrad invited him to Pent Farm for a weekend, praised his work for Congo reform, and wrote warmly to Cunninghame-Graham in his commendation. Conrad's admiration was unaffected by Casement's deviancy, of which he was well aware. And yet according to an American journalist Conrad said much later, after Casement's execution, that his first sight of Casement was 'sinister' and that he 'remained always mysterious' to him at Matadi. This could have been misreporting on the journalist's part, or hindsight on Conrad's; but it may be that Casement from the start seemed to Conrad an enigmatic personality—like Stokes.

We shall see that the Harlequin is much more than a memorial blend of Stokes and Casement. But the fact that Stokes was in Conrad's mind when he invented the Harlequin suggests that public agitation over the Congo State did much to move—in Dryden's phrase—the sleeping images of things, including the ambiguous image of Casement, towards the light.

The hostility aroused by the Stokes affair was fanned into new life at the end of 1895 when an American Baptist missionary, J.B. Murphy, charged the Congo State with various atrocities. Murphy was the first to assert that State officials authorized their soldiers to bring in the right hands of those Africans whom they had shot for failing to produce the required rubber levy; his assertion was supported by Lionel Declé. Disclosures such as these appalled many people in England who had sincerely believed, at the time of the Berlin Conference, that in repudiating the Anglo-Portuguese treaty which would have given Portugal control of the Congo mouth, and instead entrusting it to King Leopold's Association Internationale du Congo, Britain was furthering a great work of philanthropy. One man who had opposed the repudiation of the Anglo-Portuguese treaty was the former Foreign Secretary, Sir Charles Dilke. In the summer of 1896 Dilke wrote bitterly that 'the visible form of the declamations made at Brussels and Berlin is to be discovered in the ivory-stealing, the village-burning, the flogging, and the shooting, which are going on in the heart of Africa now'. And he recalled the words of General Gordon: 'I am sick of these people; it is they, and not the blacks, who need civilization.' Dilke's article appeared in the July issue of *Cosmopolis,* a magazine sponsored by Conrad's publisher; Conrad was in Brittany that summer, but he could have been sent the magazine. Later in the same month he wrote his first tale of ivory-stealing, 'An Outpost of Progress', and this was published the next year in *Cosmopolis.*

The following spring Dilke returned to the attack, this time in the House of Commons. A new horror had been added to the accusations of Congo atrocities; in their campaign against the

Arabs in the Eastern Congo, the State officers, who were regarded in Brussels as crusaders against slavery, were alleged to be making use of cannibal troops who ate the dead after an engagement. Dilke's authority was a book by S. L. Hinde, *The Fall of the Congo Arabs.* There are enough notable parallels between Hinde's observations and Marlow's to convince me that Conrad read Hinde's book. He could have found it in the London Library, from which he was borrowing copiously at this period. Hinde's impassioned protest about chain-gangs could have stirred unhappy memories of 1890. But cannibal troops dated only from the campaign against the Arabs, which began two years after Conrad left the Congo. Ford, in his exasperatingly fanciful account of Conrad's talk about his Congo experiences, suggests that this new motif was superimposed on Conrad's recollections:

> We [i.e. Conrad] had belonged to the Humanitarian Party. The Humanitarian Party did not approve of feeding our black troops on black prisoners: the Conservatives did. So the Conservatives had poisoned us or something the equivalent. And had put our quasi-corpse in charge of native bearers to take us, dead or alive, down to Boma on the coast.

So in 'Heart of Darkness' itself the crew's headman intimates to Marlow that he and his companions are ready to dispose of any prisoners who may be taken in a clash with Kurtz's followers; their expectations are disappointed when Marlow tips overboard the body of the helmsman. Given the morbid fascination that cannibalism held for all Europeans in nineteenth-century Africa, Conrad probably was told in 1890 that the crew of the *Roi des Belges* came from a cannibal tribe; but the notion of actually *supplying* them with their preferred food could only have come from the agitation rife in the late nineties.

In the Commons debate Curzon replied to Dilke with words that read like an obituary on Kurtz: 'It does seem that in the heart of Africa passions are roused and deeds are done such as are dissimilar to what we find in the other parts of the world, and in these remote and wild territories away from any contact with civilization men are converted into other than the human beings we know.' Such a melancholy dismissal of the affair by an Under-Secretary of State indicated that no action was to follow. But though nothing was done at an official level in 1897, the controversy continued in the correspondence columns of *The Times,* receiving new vigour when the accusations of the Swedish missionary Sjöblom, already widely spread on the Continent, reached the English press.

Conrad was less likely to pay heed to missionaries' tales than to those of English traders who had worked in the Congo State at the time of his own employment there. In September 1896 several papers carried a Reuter interview with one of these, Alfred Parminter; and a year later a diary kept in 1895 of the last few months of E. J. Glave's life appeared in *The Century Magazine* under the title 'Cruelty in the Congo Free State'. Both men had been pioneers in outposts established by Stanley in the eighties, and both stressed the rapid deterioration in the Africans' lot that had taken place in the nineties as the State gained a monopoly of the ivory and rubber trades. From the gruesome facts related by both, it again became clear that Leopold's one-time anti-slavery crusade had turned into a virtual slave-trading organization. Sometimes, according to Glave, the State employed Arabs to 'raid villages, take slaves, and give them back for ivory'. At other times the Arabs were dispatched to 'pacify' rebellious communities and bring the children back to be reared for the State army; the 'rebels' themselves were killed in these raids and their skulls brought in as trophies. The Belgian officer in charge of Stanley Falls, a Captain Rom, had edged his flowerbed with twenty-one such skulls.

It would be a mistake to suppose that these disclosures, however horrifying, occupied very much of the British public's attention in 1897. During the summer months, when Conrad's story about selling men for ivory was appearing in *Cosmopolis,* the misdeeds of Leopold were forgotten in the Diamond Jubilee of Queen Victoria. This was the heyday of imperialism in Britain. Throughout the year the press cheered on the Royal Niger Company in its advance into the domains of the Northern Nigerian emirs; and in 1898 there followed the even greater excitement of the West African Frontier Force's bid to get control of the territory north of Lagos in the teeth of French rivalry—a bit of brinkmanship which ended in the nineteenth century's last share-out in Africa, the Anglo-French Niger Treaty. *Blackwood's Magazine* for March 1899 starts with the second instalment of 'Heart of Darkness' and ends with 'The Struggle for Borgu'. And at the time Conrad was writing his story, Britain and France came close to war over another flag-planting episode, this time at Fashoda on the White Nile. Ford and Conrad used to drive the seven miles separating their houses in Kent in order to discuss the crisis.

'An Outpost of Progress' had, however, been noticed by one reader who saw little to choose between Belgian ambitions on the Congo and British ambitions on the Niger. Through his appreciation of the story R. B. Cunninghame-Graham, the pioneer socialist, got to know Conrad and eventually became his closest friend. The two men probably had only one patch of political ground in common: a detestation of latter-day imperialism in the crude assertiveness represented by Curzon's speech about dying nations. Shortly after the speech had been delivered, Cunninghame-Graham sent Conrad a copy of his anti-imperialist article entitled 'Bloody Niggers', and though Conrad demurred at its ferocity it may well have turned his thoughts in the direction of a fuller indictment of colonial exploitation than he had attempted in 'An Outpost of Progress'. Cunninghame-Graham was also trying his hand at exposure in a fictional form, and in October 1898 *The Saturday Review* published a sketch in which he aimed to show that the white merchant in the tropics 'exterminates the people whom he came to benefit, to bless, to rescue from their savagery'.

Some years later, when Conrad wrote to Cunninghame-Graham about Roger Casement's campaign, it was with the recommendation, 'He could tell you things! Things I've tried to forget; things I never did know. He has had as many years of Africa as I had months—almost.' The first wave of British anti-Congo agitation, which ran from 1895 through 1897, brought back for Conrad many things he might have preferred not to remember, and it added many things he had not known in 1890. The result is that in 'Heart of Darkness' everything is included: the savage and uncontrolled penal measures; the rapacity of the traders, symbolized by Kurtz's 'unsound methods'; the callous disregard for the survival of 'free' labour (the crew on the steamboat, legitimately paid in brass rods, have to exist on the same diet of pure cassava that killed Stanley's porters); and much else beside. Kurtz's ivory is 'fossil', and without a knowledge of the accusations rife at the time we may miss the force of this statement. 'Fossil' ivory was inevitably stolen from its original owner, since either he or his plunderer had buried it to escape detection; the unsentimental traveller Mary Kingsley, for whom ivory was 'everywhere an evil thing before which the quest for gold sinks into a parlour game', goes so far as to say that fossil ivory was usually the fruits of murder as well.

In one respect, Conrad goes beyond the details which could only have come to him from the agitation of 1895 to 1897, such as the liquidation risked by unwanted traders, the provisioning of cannibal followers, and Captain Rom's garden decorations, to anticipate what was to be the most important discovery leading on to the later campaign of E. D. Morel. Morel was to demonstrate from the Congo State's trading figures, which were indicative of small imports (largely firearms) and vast rubber and ivory exports, that more looting than legitimate trading was going on in the State. Kurtz, in Conrad's tale, has turned back into the wilderness without any trade goods at all, since he can get all the ivory he wants simply by allowing his adherents to raid the district: a trading method which, as Marlow says, is 'no method at all', but straight theft and slaughter.

3

Conrad's most forthright indictment of the colonialists' wanton disruption of African life was made in the first instalment of 'Heart of Darkness', which appeared in *Blackwood's Magazine* for February 1899. Cunninghame-Graham seems to have written an enthusiastic letter to Conrad, who replied in a tone of warning:

> You bless me indeed. Mind you don't curse me by and bye for the very same thing. There are two more instalments in which the idea is so wrapped up in secondary notions that You—even You!—may miss it. . . . So far the note struck chimes in with your convictions—mais après? There is an après. But I think that if you look a little into the episodes you will find in them the right intention though I fear nothing that is practically effective.

It was not that Cunninghame-Graham had got hold of the wrong end of the stick, but that he had not yet realized the stick had two pointed ends. 'Heart of Darkness' has a double theme, and Kurtz, when he appears, a double significance. On the one hand, he is the greatest exploiter of them all, the archpriest of the devil rapacity. He first appears in the book like the figure of Appetite in some morality drama, a universal wolf: 'I saw him open his mouth wide—it gave him a weirdly voracious aspect, as though he had wanted to swallow all the air, all the earth, all the men before him.' (p. 134) The ultimate in ruthless exploitation is represented by the heads on the post round Kurtz's house. But the manuscript of the tale reveals that Conrad cut down the allusions to Kurtz's cruelty and bloodthirstiness in order to stress the 'après'. For there is another aspect of Kurtz's life in the bush which affects Marlow more than the heads: 'After all, that was only a savage sight, while I seemed at one bound to have been transported into some lightless region of subtle horrors, where pure, uncomplicated savagery was a positive relief.' (p. 132)

Kurtz, the alleged lightbearer, is a physical, mental, and moral wreck. The obverse to the harm done by the white man to Africa was the harm that his 'moral isolation' (the term is Conrad's) in Africa did to the white man. The former aspect of the tale was what attracted the idealistic reformer Cunninghame-Graham, whereas for Conrad's more conservative friends such as William Blackwood it was a tale about 'the process of decivilization'. A review by the colonial administrator Hugh Clifford captures, by its triple insistence, a Victorian *frisson*: for Clifford 'Heart of Darkness' is about 'the demoralisation of the white man. . . . The de-nationalisation of the European, the "going Fantee" of civilised man'. This may have been the aspect of colonization which ranked first in Conrad's actual experience of the Congo, especially in his dealing with the Delcommunes. It is certainly the leading idea of the short story which Conrad described as the lightest part of the loot he carried off from Central Africa. 'An Outpost of Progress' rose from his recollection (he told Garnett) of 'all the bitterness of those days'.

The names of the short story's two main characters certainly derive from those days. A Keyaerts was one of the 'pilgrims' of the upstream voyage Conrad made to Stanley Falls, and a Carlier got the command of the Katanga Expedition steamboat which had been promised to Conrad. In the story, Carlier and Kayerts are two idle and unsuccessful traders on, significantly, the Kasai—the river the expedition was to ascend. A band of marauders from a Coast tribe arrives at the station, and raids the district for ivory; the station's African clerk quietly sells them the station labourers in exchange for the tusks, and the two white men slide into an uneasy complicity in the transaction. There is no one to judge their behaviour—except that each knows he is judged by the other. Inevitably they quarrel; Kayerts shoots Carlier and then, as the approaching steamer's whistle brings the threat of society's judgement on his act, hangs himself.

The hard, bright light of Conrad's narrative manner in 'An Outpost of Progress' imparts a documentary quality to this tale. And in fact the indolence of Kayerts and Carlier corresponds exactly to that of various traders set up in river stations in the eighties by Stanley, and described with vivid indignation in his book on the founding of the Congo State. Moreover, Conrad told G. Jean-Aubry that the tale was founded on a recent incident. By this he probably meant the traders' connivance at slave-dealing, rather than their violent end, which could scarcely have gone unrecorded. Such connivance was plausible, well documented, and—given the presence of European ivory-traders in Africa at all—virtually inevitable. Ivory, a metaphor for whiteness in Europe, proved in Africa to be the pitch that defiled. It needed carriers, very seldom voluntary, for its transport; it attracted Arabs in such strength that the Congo State had at first to turn a blind eye to Arab slave-raiding; and when the State finally made war on the Arabs, as rivals in ivory-trading rather than as slavers, it could only raise the troops it needed by press-gang methods. We have already seen that such troops were frequently cannibals. 'I should have been horrified at the idea in Europe!' wrote a young Belgian in the campaign, 'but it seems quite natural to me here.' The same point is driven home in an explicit authorial voice in 'An Outpost of Progress'. Lacking the restraints of society, Kayerts and Carlier behave in a quite natural way, acquiescing in the behaviour that is accepted in their environment. Their initial horror at the slave-deal had simply repeated the clichés they had heard in Europe:

> They believed their words. Everyone shows a respectful deference to certain sounds that he and his fellows can make. But about feelings people really know nothing. We talk with indignation or enthusiasm; we talk about oppression, cruelty, crime, devotion, self-sacrifice, virtue, and we know nothing real beyond the words. Nobody knows what suffering or sacrifice mean—except, perhaps the victims of the mysterious purpose of these illusions.

Kayerts and Carlier are hollow men; and Conrad at this epoch suspected all men of being hollow. No one had sufficient inner strength to sustain him in the wilderness once he was cut off from his own tribal sanctions. In thanking Cunninghame-Graham for a copy of his article 'Bloody Niggers', Conrad asks

> Et puis—pourquoi prêchez Vous au convertis? Mais je deviens stupide. Il n'y a pas des convertis aux idées de l'honneur, de la justice, de la pitié, de la liberté. Il n'y a que des gens qui sans savoir, sans comprendre, sans sentir s'extasient sur les mots, les repètent, les crient, s'imaginent y croire—sans croire à autre chose qu'au gain, à l'avantage personel, à la vanité satisfaite. Et les mots s'envolent; et il ne reste rien, entendez-vous? Absolument rien, oh homme de foi! Rien.

This suggests that on the eve of writing 'Heart of Darkness' Conrad concurred in the anti-imperialist feelings of Cunninghame-Graham and others partly out of a shared indignation at 'masquerading philanthropy', as he called it in his letter to Garnett, and partly from a disillusionment that bordered on nihilism. As a novelist, he rightly conceived that his role lay not so much in protesting at what men did as in probing what they were. And the probe revealed hollowness everywhere, the hollowness typified in 'Heart of Darkness' by the would-be Assistant Manager, 'this papier-maché Mephistopheles' who rouses in Marlow the thought 'that if I tried I could poke my forefinger through him and would find nothing inside but a little loose dirt'. (p. 81) It is a key image, connecting with a number of other hollownesses: the biblical whited sepulchre that is the city of Brussels; the 'boiler wallowing in the grass' at Matadi; the firebucket with a hole in it; the Manager's lack of entrails; the steamboat, resonant as a biscuit tin, that carries the lightbearers into darkest Africa; above all, the ivory cranium of Kurtz, the 'hollow sham', for whom there remain only words without referents, a voice which 'survived his strength to hide in the magnificent folds of eloquence the barren darkness of his heart'. (p. 147)

This theme of the hollow men bears out Conrad's remark to Blackwood, during the course of writing the longer tale, that it was a story much as 'An Outpost of Progress' was. But, he goes on, it 'takes in more—is a little wider—is less concentrated upon individuals'. This expansion takes three forms. First, instead of taking a recording angel's viewpoint by hovering omnisciently above the trading-post, we make a long journey towards it in the company of Marlow, and on the way experience with him much that prepares us for the 'decivilization' at the heart of darkness. Secondly, Kurtz's decivilization has taken a much more dramatic form than that of Kayerts and Carlier, whose going native was simply what Joyce Cary calls 'going plant'. Kurtz has become the divine king of the tribe who collect his ivory, and is the object of rites which, it is implied, involve human sacrifice and cannibalism. Lastly, after Kurtz's death, Marlow carries back to Europe a haunting memory of him, which he deliberately withholds from the woman Kurtz had intended to marry.

As a result of these elaborations, 'Heart of Darkness' is incomparably the richer tale. Yet it remains for almost every critic a flawed masterpiece. Graham Greene once sat down on the banks of the Congo to re-read 'Heart of Darkness' for the first time in thirty years. He noted that it was 'still a fine story, but its faults show now. The language too inflated for the situation. Kurtz never comes really alive. It is as if Conrad had taken an episode in his own life and tried to lend it, for the sake of "literature", a greater significance than it will hold.'

Kurtz's significance, I have suggested, is a double one: as exploiter and as degenerate. These are in fact two aspects of the same theme; away from the restraints of his own culture, the white man gives rein to his basic appetites and consequently brings misery to those he intended to enlighten. Colonial enterprise in the tropics might thus be held to be a disaster for mankind, both black and white. This is a large and complex theme, but in the hands of as good a writer as Conrad it was not an uncontrollable one. Yet in 'Heart of Darkness' it does seem at times to get out of control; and if we look more closely at the three aspects of the story which empower it to 'take in more' than 'An Outpost of Progress', namely the use of Marlow as narrator, Kurtz's atavism, and the scene with Kurtz's Intended, we may be able to discover the root cause of so many critics' dissatisfaction.

4

'Heart of Darkness' is a story told on a boat by a man called Marlow to a group of four professional men, amateur yachtsmen, one of whom passes it on to us. This gives us two narrators' voices between Conrad and ourselves. The first of these, the recorder of the tale, has the air of a typical reader of *Blackwood's,* a magazine read, Conrad once said, in every 'single club and messroom and man-of-war in the British Seas and Dominions'. His notions of Empire are romantic; he is unaware of the contradictions implicit in his lyrical account of the knights-errant of imperialism: 'Hunters for gold or pursuers of fame, they had all gone out on that stream, bearing the sword, and often the torch, messengers of the might within the land, bearers of a spark from the sacred fire.' (p.47) For him the City is wrapped in gloom but the eastern, seaward reaches of the Thames are bathed in an enticing light. It is a measure of the impact made by Marlow's narrative that, when at the end of the tale the recorder of it again looks down the estuary, he looks into the heart of an immense darkness.

This opening voice is certainly not Conrad's. About Marlow's voice we are at first less certain, but as the tale proceeds we are made to feel, albeit beneath the level of conscious recognition, that Marlow too is 'placed' within the frame of the picture. At first the indications of this are very unobtrusive; the last thing Conrad wants to do is to confuse his tale by intruding a counter-personality to Marlow's. One such indication occurs as Marlow begins to compare Roman and British imperialism, a comparison which Cunninghame-Graham had made rather clumsily in 'Bloody Niggers':

> The conquest of the earth, which mostly means the taking it away from those who have a different complexion or slightly flatter noses than ourselves, is not a pretty thing when you look into it too much. What redeems it is the idea only. An idea at the back of it; not a sentimental pretence, but an idea; and an unselfish belief in the idea— something you can set up and bow down before, and offer a sacrifice to. . . .(pp.50-51)

This carries momentary conviction, just as does the contrast drawn in *Lord Jim* between the sentimental pretence of heroic behaviour and the positive ideas of the seaman's code. But it has to be remembered that in that novel also the opposition of idea and pretence is Marlow's own, and so within the narratorial framework. Moreover, in the 'Heart of Darkness' passage, the opposition is undermined, not supported, by the notion of bowing down to an idol. We are to meet other idols in the tale, so that the metaphor establishes its own sinister resonance, a veritable

Marabar-cave 'boum' that is to vibrate to the last page of the story.

Much later, during the account of his navigation up the Congo, Marlow reflects on his response to the drumming he hears from riverside villages. The noise, to borrow Mary Kingsley's phrase, calls up all his Neolithic man. But, insists Marlow, the white man on the steamboat (which is itself the microcosm of a different social order)

> must meet that truth with his own true stuff—with his own inborn strength. Principles won't do. Acquisitions, clothes, pretty rags—rags that would fly off at the first good shake. No; you want a deliberate belief. An appeal to me in this fiendish row— is there? Very well; I hear; I admit, but I have a voice too, and for good or evil mine is the speech that cannot be silenced. (p. 97)

We wait to hear Marlow's voice speak out, wait for the deliberate belief that can stand up to the call of the wilderness. But Marlow has his head down among the leaky steampipes, or he is peering at the reach immediately ahead for snags; 'I had to watch the steering and circumvent those snags, and get the tin pot along by hook or by crook. There was surface-truth enough in these things to save a wiser man.' (p. 97) Marlow takes short views and does the task in hand. It is an admirable rule of life, but it tells us nothing about the deliberate belief that he claims to be the inborn strength of civilized man. We begin to suspect that Marlow makes a cult of efficiency without questioning the causes that efficiency serves.

In fact doubts have been stirred up at earlier points in the story, from the moment that Marlow looked at the multi-coloured map of Africa and reflected that some real work was going on in the red bits. The map displayed the European share-out of the continent in which it was unlikely that the red bits, however good their administration, had been taken over with any higher motives than governed the acquisition of the blue and purple ones. We feel a similar uneasiness about Marlow's praises of the Accountant who, in his starched elegance, 'had verily accomplished something'. (p. 68) It is true that Marlow's tone is here one of irony at his own expense; he does not conceal the Accountant's indifference to the trader dying in the corner of his office. But while Marlow feels distaste for the man's inhumanity, we are rather made to wonder, with Conrad, at the Accountant's inability to see in the dying trader a picture of his own likely end. And the apple-pie-order book-keeping which Marlow so much admires is only, as E.D. Morel was to demonstrate, the record of loot. There is similar short-sightedness in Marlow's pleasure over the manual of navigation which he picks up just before reaching the Inner Station. The 'honest concern for the right way of going to work' (p. 99) represented by *An Inquiry into some Points of Seamanship* must often have served dubious ends—no doubt fine seamanship was shown in the Middle Passage. In the same way Marlow's professional integrity is now being put to the service of an expedition aimed at seizing the ivory of a man whom his employers have deliberately left to rot in the bush.

Nowhere in the book is the contrast between Marlow's point of view and the view induced in us by the author more tangible than in Marlow's responses to the Harlequin. In patchwork clothing reminiscent of the multi-coloured map in the Brussels office, the Russian seaman-turned-trader embodies the hopes of countless young Europeans who became involved in African trade and exploration. For Marlow, this endows him with the glamour of youth, of 'the absolutely pure, uncalculating, unpractical spirit of adventure'. (p. 126) But even the romantic Marlow does not envy him his allegiance to Kurtz. In this aspect of the Harlequin's behaviour we are made to sense the menace of innocence; he resembles Graham Greene's eager young American who is as dangerous as a dumb leper who has lost his bell. If there is a national prejudice in Greene's remark, there is a similar one in Conrad's presentation of the Harlequin, whose refusal to see Kurtz for what he is when the evidence of Kurtz's demoralization is all around him represents, to the Polish Conrad, a Russian proclivity towards what has since been named double-think.

As the narrative proceeds Marlow becomes increasingly self-aware and even self-critical, so that it is not always possible to distinguish between the irony with which Conrad endows him and Conrad's irony at his expense. But right to the end it remains true, as Marlow himself tells us, that we see more in the story than Marlow could at the time: we see him. When Marlow throws his new pair of shoes into the river, the gesture implies more than his revulsion and guilt at having the helmsman's lifeblood on his feet. He is casting off the trappings of civilization in order to join Kurtz, just as King Lear flings off his clothes in order to commune with 'that same learned Theban', the bedlam beggar: 'I flung one shoe overboard, and became aware that that was exactly what I had been looking forward to—a talk with Kurtz.' (p. 113) Even when Marlow has seen Kurtz for the wreck he is, he puts upon his dying words an interpretation which is not necessarily or even probably that which Conrad himself wishes us to place upon 'The horror! the horror!' For Marlow, 'it was an affirmation, a moral victory paid for by innumerable defeats, by abominable terrors, by abominable satisfactions. But it was a victory!' (p. 151) A moral victory of the kind Marlow envisages would need to affirm the absolute good that Kurtz has rejected: 'Why, this is hell, nor am I out of it.' But what if the vision is not of moral truth, but of vacancy? The one interpretation gives Kurtz all he asks: justice. The other denies the existence of justice itself.

Conrad once told Edward Garnett that he was 'a perfect animal' until he went to the Congo in 1890. Something of what he meant is conveyed in a letter to Cunninghame-Graham:

> To be part of the animal kingdom under the conditions of this earth is very well— but as soon as you know of your slavery the pain, the anger, the strife—the tragedy begins. We can't return to nature, since we can't change our place in it. Our refuge is in stupidity, in drunkenness of all kinds, in lies, in beliefs, in murder, thieving, reforming—in negation, in contempt—each man according to the prompting of his particular devil.

At the time he wrote 'Heart of Darkness' Conrad's own refuge appears to have been in negation, but he chose as his narrator a man whose particular devil insisted only on prompt attention to the work in hand. This idol is a Victorian taskmaster, but Conrad plainly envies Marlow the refuge of his particular idolatry; there is nothing destructive or belittling in the irony that separates him from his *alter ego.* Rather Marlow is the kind of Englishman that Conrad believed he might have been if he had been born in England. At times in his career, Conrad takes on the personality of his creation. It was Marlow, rather than Conrad, who explained to William Blackwood that 'Heart of Darkness' was about 'the criminality of inefficiency and pure selfishness when tackling the civilizing work in Africa'; who told a Polish cousin that liberty 'can only be found under the English flag all over the world'; and who was to draw in the essay 'Well Done' exactly Marlow's distinction between the taste for adventure and the saving grace of fidelity—that turns out in the end to be fidelity not to a creed, a cause, or even a country, but to a ship.

Conrad grew up under a repressive colonial regime; he saw in Africa the misery caused by European exploitation; and in the late nineties, he responded warmly to anti-Congo agitation and even to Cunninghame-Graham's sweeping rejection of all colonial ventures. 'Heart of Darkness' grew out of all this disgust and disillusionment. At the same time Conrad, a naturalized Englishman, clung to the belief that things were somehow different in the red bits of the map. and created Marlow as the embodiment of this belief. And Marlow's vitality implies that he is much more than the projection of Conrad's affection for his adopted country. As the perspective of imperial history lengthens, it is possible to see that there existed in the closing years of the last century, alongside the noisy jingoism, a serious and even stoical concept of trusteeship, of the white man's burden. It had perhaps begun with Dilke's *Greater Britain* which Conrad read, and in the next century it was to produce a whole philosophy of government in Lugard's doctrine of Indirect Rule. Hobson's exposure of the financial interests behind colonialism could not touch it, because its fidelity, like Marlow's, was to surface truth, to 'what is nearest to hand and heart in the short moment of each human effort', as Conrad put it in 'Well Done'. Conrad himself had seen too deeply into the colonial process to be able to share this outlook, but his portrayal of Marlow in 'Heart of Darkness' shows how much he admired it. He even goes a stage farther in the tale, to explain, if not to excuse, why the burden sometimes proved intolerable. He makes Kurtz the victim, not just of solitude, but also of savagery.

5

On his first mention in Conrad's manuscript, Kurtz is called Klein. Conrad's first biographer, G. Jean-Aubry, was so sure that 'in *Heart of Darkness* the adventures which the author lends to Marlow, his mouthpiece, are no other than those of which he himself was at the same time witness and victim' that he identifies Kurtz completely with the trader from Stanley Falls, Georges Klein, who died on the downstream voyage of the *Roi des Belges* in September 1890. Norman Sherry has, however, shown that the real Klein could scarcely have attained Kurtz's reputation during his short and obscure career on the river. Sherry has his own candidate for the role of Kurtz in another trader called Arthur Hodister, a well-known representative of 'the party of virtue', and one regarded, like Conrad himself, as a protégé of the S.A.B.'s powerful chairman, Thys. But Kurtz has other possible godfathers—if the term is not too incongruous. The talk about Stanley's rearguard, for example, was as much about their demoralization as about their ill-treatment of their followers. Stories of demented behaviour circulated not only about Barttelot (whom Jerry Allen considers the actual model for Kurtz), but also about J.S. Jameson, who seems to have been the intellectual of the party. Like Kurtz and like the founder of the station in 'An Outpost of Progress', Jameson was an artist; one of the accusations against him was that he cold-bloodedly sketched cannibal feasts. His published diary was to dispel these rumours, but they were the kind of talk that Conrad heard in the Congo in 1890; as he noted in his own diary, the chief feature of the social life there was 'people speaking ill of each other'. Stanley captures this rumour-charged atmosphere when he writes in *In Darkest Africa* that

> quantities of human bones are said to be discovered by some reconnoitring party, human limbs are said to be found in cooking pots, sketches by an amateur artist are reported to have been made of whole families indulging in cannibal repasts: it is more than hinted at that Englishmen are implicated in raids, murder and cannibalism, that they have been making targets of native fugitives while swimming in the Aruwimi, all for the mere sake of infusing terror, alarm and grief among quiet English people, and to plague our friends at home.

Kurtz's high-flown rhetoric and his *folie de grandeur* are recognizable traits of Henry Stanley himself: 'He desired to have kings meet him at railway stations on his return from some ghastly Nowhere.' (p.148) And while Charles Stokes's guilelessness and enterprise contribute to the portrait of the Harlequin, there were other aspects of his life in Africa more suggestive of Kurtz: he amassed a vast hoard of ivory, he had an African wife, and he was made the object of passionate attachment by Africans living in what they thought of as Stokes's kingdom. A journalist travelling in the eighties through what was to become Tanganyika was everywhere told that 'the country belonged to Stokes. Stokes was their Sultan.' Another white chief who showed a Kurtz-like reluctance to leave his kingdom was of course Emin Pasha; and behind all these figures looms that of Leopold II himself, supplying Conrad with his most striking instance of the gap between philanthropic fancy and buccaneering fact.

'All Europe went to the making of Kurtz' (p.117), we are told, and elsewhere Conrad states:'J'ai pris grand soin de donner une origine cosmopolite à Kurtz.' As a symbol of European intrusion into Africa Kurtz may well have his origin, not in this or that Congo trader, but in a figure who already carried such a significance in a story Conrad would have read in 1898. This was 'Le Vieux du Zambèse', by Pierre Mille, which appeared in the trilingual journal *Cosmopolis* a month or so before 'Heart of Darkness' took shape in Conrad's imagination. Mille's career was to be an interesting parallel to Conrad's own. He was to write a fiery indictment of *L'Enfer du Congo Léopoldien,* and to develop into the leading French novelist to make use of colonial themes and settings. The *Cosmopolis* story is however little more than an anecdote. Among the passengers on a ship returning to Africa is an old Marseillais who has previously 'gone native' in the heart of the continent. He is very ill and at first taciturn; but when the narrator and his friends go ashore with him at Aden he begins to talk compulsively, like a broken piece of machinery clattering to a halt:

> Il parla—avec des vanteries de nègre, avec des câlineries mélancoliques d'Arabe muselman, avec d'incompréhensibles fureurs contre des gens et des choses que nous ignorions, et dont il citait les noms comme si l'Univers les connaissait, avec des phrases de respect mystique pour des barbares maîtres de terres dont j'ai oublié les noms, avec des silences brusquement défiants entrecoupés de crises d'atroce douleur. Souvent nous ne le comprenions plus et lui-même ne se comprenait pas; il se cherchait.
>
> —Il ne voit pas la trame de ses jours, disait Gallice.
>
> C'était vrai. Cet homme qui avait tant vécu ne pouvait pas concentrer sa vie, ne l'apercevait qu'en une série de tableaux mal liés, tels des rêves qui se succêdent en vertu d'assonances fausses, d'associations désraisonnables et dont le souvenir même s'efface. Il avait passé des marchés de porteurs avec Stanley, vendu des esclaves à Tipo-Tib, vu mourir deux cents hommes de soif dans le désert de Kalahari, cherché de l'or dans le Rand.

As the ship moves south from Aden, the old man of the Zambesi begins to fail, and one day a dramatic announcement is made of his death. The story ends lamely, and one is forced to guess at, rather than to perceive, Mille's intention. But it could have served to bring back the recollection of Klein's death and so to afford Conrad a clue to a far more significant story, in which the probably inoffensive Klein is transformed into the arch-exploiter Kurtz. Kurtz dies, like the old man of the Zambesi, on a European vessel away from his native wife and followers, but his death is given meaning by his last great effort to see 'la trame de ses jours'.

If Kurtz is a symbol, rather than a recollection, we can define with some precision the point in the story where Conrad, in his own phrase, pushed experience a little beyond 'the actual facts of the case'. The Congo steamboat captain Otto Lütken declared in 1930 that 'Heart of Darkness' bore all the marks of personal experience up to the beginning of the river voyage, but that the upstream journey did not. Jessie Conrad was able to assure Lütken that Conrad did in fact go to Stanley Falls. But the comment remains valid. Kurtz belongs to the part of the narrative that pushes beyond the facts of the case, and many readers feel that in one particular, Kurtz's 'unspeakable rites', Conrad pushed altogether too hard.

Mille's old man of the Zambesi has sombre things to recall—bestiality in mining compounds and the like—but there is no suggestion in the French story of the character's own involvement, whereas Kurtz has 'literally' taken a high seat among the devils of the land. There is a very simple failure in verisimilitude here. Many African peoples of the time venerated the superior strength of their alien rulers, whether they were Arabs, Europeans like Emin Pasha, or other Africans, but they did not seek to involve them in their religious practices. Moreover, indigenous African religions offer scant opportunities for escape from social restraints, and no African religion that has been put on record could accurately be described as devil worship.

It would of course be insensitive to let the rather smug cultural relativism of our own age distort our reading of 'Heart of Darkness'. Nor is Conrad himself wholly without relativism; he shows an awareness of the restraints of 'primitive' society, and implies that it is Kurtz, rather than his tribe, who seeks gratification in the ceremonies. The real trouble however about this part of the tale is not that it lacks veracity, or offends our late twentieth-century sensibility, but that Conrad's own inability to realize it imaginatively results in some disastrously bad writing. We make the journey to the Inner Station only to be enveloped in an adjectival fog. The deterioration can be measured by setting the description of the grove of death, already cited, alongside two later passages. First, the death of the helmsman:

> We two whites stood over him, and his lustrous and enquiring glance enveloped us both. I declare it looked as though he would presently put to us some question in an understandable language; but he died without uttering a sound, without moving a limb, without twitching a muscle. Only in the very last moment, as though in response to some sign we could not see, to some whisper we could not hear, he frowned heavily, and that frown gave to his black death-mask an inconceivably sombre, brooding, and menacing expression. The lustrous and enquiring glance faded swiftly into vacant glassiness. (pp. 112–13)

From a powerful start as we grasp the question implicit in the helmsman's 'lustrous and enquiring glance', this declines swiftly into triple phrases and epithets which rob the prose of its live, spoken quality (something that also happens to Marlow's Patusan narrative in *Lord Jim*), then into gratuitous mystification ('some whisper we could not hear'), and into repetitions which merely reiterate, without any of the cumulative force of the repeated 'slowly' in the earlier passage. There is here the beginning of an insecurity which has become calamitous by the time we encounter Kurtz's African mistress:

> She was savage and superb, wild-eyed and magnificent; there was something ominous and stately in her deliberate progress. And in the hush that had fallen suddenly upon the whole sorrowful land, the immense wilderness, the colossal body of the fecund and mysterious life seemed to look at her, pensive, as though it had been looking at the image of its own tenebrous and passionate soul.
>
> She came abreast of the steamer, stood still, and faced us. Her long shadow fell to the water's edge. Her face had a tragic and fierce aspect of wild sorrow and of dumb pain mingled with the fear of some struggling, half-shaped resolve. She stood looking at us without a stir, and like the wilderness itself, with an air of brooding over an inscrutable purpose. (pp.135-6)

Conrad fires verbiage at this 'wild and gorgeous apparition' with the abandon of the pilgrims firing into the bush, and with as negligible effect. Like the witchdoctors, she is a figure out of Rider

Haggard, a writer Conrad thought 'too horrible for words'.

Equally reminiscent of Rider Haggard is the situation which arises from the woman's 'half-shaped resolve', which is presumably to sacrifice, quite literally, the Harlequin as a way of retaining Kurtz—a fate that Marlow in his turn narrowly avoids. The Harlequin tells Marlow,

> She got in one day and kicked up a row about those miserable rags I picked up at the store room to mend my clothes with. I wasn't decent. At least it must have been that for she talked like a fury to Kurtz for an hour, pointing at me now and then.
>
> (p. 136-7)

This small scene is important, because it establishes that the nameless horrors are not Marlow's delusions but have an objective place in the story. So we cannot, with a knowledgeable allusion to the 'deceived narrator', explain away Conrad's more portentous prose as being 'in character' or exonerate him from a ninetyish zest for chilling our spines. We 'know' more, at this point in the story, than Marlow does, and a good deal more than the Harlequin: and what we 'know' is that human sacrifices are performed before Kurtz. That is, we are meant to believe in the unspeakable rites. Yet while Conrad wants us to believe in these horrors, he seems unable to realize them satisfactorily; and we find ourselves asking, with some exasperation, why they have to be thrust upon our notice.

An answer is implicit in the passage I have quoted about the African woman. She and the wilderness are one. The call of the wild comes from the Africans themselves, and tribal life is presented in this part of the story as an *agent* of demoralization. A similar power resides in the 'wild and passionate uproar' that Marlow hears from the riverside villages. He stays on board and is never put to the test, but Kurtz has been isolated from his own race. Such scientific relativism as Conrad picked up from reading Mary Kingsley was insufficient to withstand the cultural Darwinism, the deep dread of 'savagery', that informs nearly all late nineteenth-century writing on Africa. And this notion of savagery contributes a counter-argument to the book's leading idea that, through isolation from his own kind, the white man in the tropics becomes degenerate and spreads misery around him. Rather, the late Victorians believed, the white man was subject to appalling temptations, to a continual downward pull of savagery; he tends, wrote Benjamin Kidd in 1898, 'to sink slowly to the level around him'. Yet his presence was justified because savagery had to be overcome. These are conflicting views of colonialism which cannot consort happily in the same story.

Kurtz's decivilization is probably made by Conrad to take the highly unlikely form of his becoming the object of human sacrifice, as a result of recent events concerning a particular divine king in West Africa. Less than two years before Conrad wrote his tale, a group of English officials attempted to visit the King of Benin, whom they hoped to persuade both to resume trade with Europeans and to desist from the practice of human sacrifice. But they were ambushed and killed on the way. Retribution was quickly arranged, and a naval expedition captured the city in February 1897. It was met by the most gruesome sights ever encountered in African exploration. The city was strewn with sacrificial victims, and every report used the same phrase: Benin 'reeked with blood'.

The affair caused a considerable stir in England. Here, at the height of the wave of imperialist sentiment caused by the approaching Jubilee, was an event which seemed to demonstrate the need for the white man to assume the burden of colonial rule. As one member of the expedition put it: 'We have heard the Little Englander wail of interfering with the prerogatives of native royalty. There are, however, some prerogatives of native royalty that make interference necessary.' And as the file of raiders came across the first bodies on the narrow track, one English sailor spoke up with the very voice of Marlow: 'It is just about time someone did visit this place.' This is the aspect of colonialism that Conrad has in mind when he makes Marlow speak of the earth as a place where we must

> breathe dead hippo, so to speak, and not be contaminated. And there, don't you see? your strength comes in, the faith in your ability for the digging of unostentatious holes to bury the stuff in—your power of devotion not to yourself, but to an obscure, back-breaking business. (p.117)

There was of course another side even to the Benin raid. We now know that the frenetic sacrifices were prompted by the advent of the raiding party. Like Kurtz's followers, the Bini were afraid that their Oba would be taken from them. Nor were the motives behind the raid unmixed. Various public figures encouraged the undertaking on the grounds that Benin was rich in rubber. And the expedition brought back to the British Museum the greatest haul of cultural loot ever to leave tropical Africa. So too in the novel, Marlow's words about digging holes have another aspect: the only holes actually dug are—apart from the muddy hole in which Kurtz is deposited—the one that might have been connected with the philanthropic desire of giving the Matadi convicts something to do, and the holes in which the tribesmen try to conceal their ivory from Kurtz's marauding followers. But all this is fleeting irony compared with the persistent and contaminating smell of dead hippo. Kurtz is in part presented to us as the victim of the barbarism embodied in an African tribe and its religion. It is a theme which not only works against the theme of Kurtz's innate proclivities, but gives rise to the least realized and least convincing episodes in the tale.

6

Marlow's return journey to the coast appears to have figured large in the version of the story which Conrad told to Garnett, and probably to Ford as well, in the autumn of 1898. But in 'Heart of Darkness' as it finally took shape on paper this journey is passed over very rapidly, to leave room for the final episode of Marlow's return to Brussels, his visit to Kurtz's Intended, and the lie he tells her about Kurtz's last words. It is difficult not to regret the change. Kurtz's Good Angel is as stagey a figure as his Bad Angel. Yet Conrad attached great importance to this ending which, he told Blackwood, 'locks in—as it were—the whole 30000 words of narrative description into one suggestive view of a whole phase of life, and makes of that story something on quite another plane than an anecdote of a man who went mad in the Centre of Africa'. The term 'Intended', a little jarring to modern ears, carried powerful overtones for Conrad. Early in 1898, in reviewing a book in which Hugh Clifford had showed himself troubled as to what the recording angel might think of white imperialism, he had written: 'The intentions will, no doubt, count for something, though, of course, every nation's conquests are paved with good intentions.' The intentions of Leopold II and his fellow-philanthropists seemed to Conrad to have paved a green hell in the Congo, and he makes 'intentions' a keyword of 'Heart of Darkness'. The Intended is the guardian of all Kurtz meant his life to be. Discovering this, Marlow deliberately conceals from her the truth of what Kurtz's life has been.

A clue to the significance this concealment had for Conrad is offered by *The Inheritors,* the novel he and Ford began to write together at the time 'Heart of Darkness' was still on Conrad's desk. It is anything but a successful work, and in later years both novelists were anxious to disown it, yet the long letter Conrad wrote in reply to an unfavourable review in *The New York Times* shows his involvement to have been considerable; and in 1905 he wrote to Edward Sanderson: 'I am not ashamed to stand up for the book. . . . I haven't written it all myself but I worked very hard at it all the same.' Conrad certainly wrote the last pages, which contain a clear statement of the theme of *Lord Jim*, on which he was by that time engaged.

The Inheritors is, as Ford described it, 'a political work, rather allegorically backing Mr. Balfour'. It is also science fiction about the colonization of the earth by inhabitants of a fourth dimension, pure egoists 'with no ideals, prejudices, or remorse'. Some of the fourth dimensionists set out to 'smash' the Duc de Mersch and his supporters in the *système groenlandais* including the British Foreign Secretary called, rather confusingly, Churchill. This they achieve by ensuring that the novelist Callan witnesses the full rapacity of the undertaking and then exposes it in the English newspaper which has hitherto been de Mersch's warm supporter. The journalist Etchingham-Granger, who tells the story, is left to put to bed the edition containing Callan's article, which the editor has not seen. He realizes that publication of the article will totally discredit not only the monstrous de Mersch but also Churchill, who represents the best in the English political tradition. It will also result in the ruin of many who have invested in what they honestly believe to be a work of philanthropy. But because Etchingham-Granger is in love with the *femme fatale* among the fourth dimensionists he allows the article to stand—and is left at the end of the book in a state of Lord Jim-like remorse.

Most of these dramatis personae can be identified. The aristocratic Etchingham-Granger is of course Cunninghame-Graham, to whom Conrad often delivered fourth dimensionist lectures in letter form without making any impression on his quixotic idealism. Churchill is Arthur Balfour; Callan, Hall Caine, who was like Conrad a Heinemann author. But the real interest of *The Inheritors* for us is not that the work is a *roman à clef,* or science fiction, or political allegory, but that it hinges upon the ethics of exposure.

There are two exposures in the book, one in French by Radet, and one in English by Callan. Radet is a near-reversal for Conrad's continental-sounding second name, Teodor, and when we find him in altercation with an official of the *système* (Camille Delcommune, needless to say) he is a self-caricature of Conrad in 1891: 'a cadaverous, weatherworn, passion-worn individual, badger-grey, and worked up into a grotesquely attitudinized fury of injured self-esteem'. And his writings about the colonial enterprise have just the same powerful effect on Etchingham-Granger that 'Heart of Darkness' had on Cunninghame-Graham:

> I was reading about an inland valley, a broad, shadowy grey thing; immensely broad, immensely shadowy, winding away between immense half-invisible mountains into the silence of an unknown country. A little band of men, microscopic figures in that immensity, in those mists, crept slowly up it. A man among them was speaking; I seemed to hear his voice, low, monotonous, overpowered by the wan light and the silence and the vastness.

As he continues to read about 'that dun band that had cast remorse behind; that had no return, no future, that spread desolation desolately', the narrator seems to hear the slow words of the man who instigated all this, the Duc de Mersch, otherwise the Duc de Hainault, Leopold II:

> 'We have protected the natives, have kept their higher interests ever present in our minds. And through it all we have never forgotten the mission entrusted to us by Europe—to remove the evil of darkness from the earth—to root out barbarism with its nameless horrors, whose existence had been a blot on our consciences. Men of good will and self-sacrifice are doing it now—are laying down their precious lives to root out . . . to root out. . . .'
>
> Of course they *were* rooting them out.

The second exposure is Callan's article, described by the narrator towards the end of the story. The description has the ring of Conrad's own prose, and this is perhaps why he quotes from it in his letter to *The New York Times:*

> There were revolting details of cruelty to the miserable, helpless and defenceless; there were greed and self-seeking, stripped naked; but most revolting to see without a mask was that

> falsehood which had been hiding under the words that for ages had spurred men to noble deeds, to self-sacrifice, to heroism. What was appalling was the sudden perception that all the traditional ideas of honour, glory, conscience, had been committed to the upholding of a gigantic and atrocious fraud. The falsehood had spread stealthily, had eaten into the very heart of creeds and convictions that we lean upon in our passage between the past and the future. The old order had to live or perish with a lie.

No question is made of Radet's right to publish the truth about Greenland. But Etchingham-Granger is appalled at the thought of the effect that Callan's disclosures will have on the careers of Churchill and others. So when he lets the article go to press he acts not from altruism but from egotism, as is revealed to him in the final scene with the 'heroine'; a scene that is ablaze with light in deliberate contrast to the darkness that envelopes Marlow and the Intended whom he tries to protect with his altruistic lie.

Why are there two exposures? A tempting answer to make is that Conrad himself twice tried to expose the scandal of the Congo State; Ford claimed to have seen, in the form of letters to a French-language newspaper, articles which Conrad wrote, presumably, soon after his return from the Congo. But the existence of these letters, which I discuss in an appendix, is by no means certain. The other answer is that the two episodes represent the two minds in which Conrad found himself about colonization: the Polish mind which saw it as mere conquest and rapine masquerading in the guise of philanthropy, and the English mind clinging to the faith that some work of real benefit could be done. In 'Heart of Darkness' the English mind speaks through Marlow, who withholds the truth from Kurtz's Intended because he realizes that we are sustained by our fidelities, whatever the intrinsic worth—or worthlessness—of their objects. Conrad's intentions in the episode are clear enough. Yet once again, as in the pages dealing with the unspeakable rites, the complexity of Conrad's feeling imparts a feverish adjectival insistence which contrasts unhappily with the sinewy writing of the story's first part. Though the association with Hall Caine was made as a joke (Ford called his cat Hall Caine) there are places in the last episode of 'Heart of Darkness' where Conrad's style slides dangerously close to that of such a bestseller of the nineties.

7

Conrad then was responsible for three stories about the Congo. The first, 'An Outpost of Progress', is a clear, hard picture of the harm done to black and white alike by the colonial intrusion. The last, a novel for which Conrad supplied most of the ideas and some of the writing, has for subject the harm done by such exposure when it is undertaken for questionable motives. Between these comes 'Heart of Darkness', an intensely personal and autobiographical tale, in which the drive to draw upon both first-hand experience and recent agitation in order to enlarge upon the protest of 'An Outpost of Progress' is shot through with doubts. Ought so many good and trusting people to be shown that at the heart of an idealistic undertaking lay only 'a little, loose dirt'? The tribal loyalty which was Conrad's own true stuff cried out against it. The men he admired and typified in Marlow were committed to what Conrad wanted to believe and sometimes believed was a better sort of colonial activity: the obscure, backbreaking tasks of trusteeship that began, in Kipling's phrase, with clearing the land of evil. If people like these—and even Kurtz, with his English education, was 'one of us'—became demoralized in solitude, it was not enough to explain away their demoralization with 'l'homme est un animal méchant'; there must be a demoralizing power at work, the savagery of an inferior race. So Stanley, when he heard the stories about his rearguard—stories that must have pained Conrad in the Congo where he too was considered to be English—wondered if there were not 'a supernatural or malignant influence or agency at work to thwart every honest intention'. These stories caused great distress to the families of the men concerned, especially to Barttelot's Intended and Jameson's wife; the latter set out for Zanzibar in her anxiety to dispel the rumours. They had too a wider significance. They were a threat to the established order of late Victorian society, to the world represented by the four men who listen to Marlow's story. 'Try to be civil, Marlow,' one of them growls. Marlow has tried; he has exercised the restraint praised throughout the story, and so refused to rob Kurtz's Intended of her 'great and saving illusion'.

These are some of the cross-currents in a very complex tale. Its complexity is in part of its time, as one set of responses to the fact of imperialism gave way to another. It also derives from the cultural predicament of its author, once the son of a Polish freedom fighter, now a retired British master mariner. At times this complexity of attitudes brings the writing to the brink of disaster. The author's navigation is more like that of 'The Secret Sharer' than it is like Marlow's careful avoidance of snags. Yet we all relish a writer who takes risks. Because the colonial theme was one that in 1899 came home to men's businesses and bosoms it could no longer be treated with the De Maupassant-like coolness that Conrad has assumed in 'An Outpost of Progress'. A mesh of intellectual attitudes now gives the tale an extraordinary depth of focus; a turmoil of feelings gives it the intense, lived-through quality which has communicated its excitement to most subsequent novelists concerned with the colonial experience.

IDOLS OF THE DEN

ACHEBE'S Arrow of God

1

Several generations, each of them possessing its own insights into the friction of cultures in a colonial situation, have passed since *Blackwood's*, the empire-builders' magazine, published 'Heart of Darkness'. Readers of this generation must sometimes find themselves playing with the idea of re-writing Conrad's story from the viewpoint of one of Kurtz's adherents: some elderly head of a Bakongo family, perhaps, for whom a religious rite, speakable or unspeakable, was not an orgy and a bloodbath, but a duty responsibly performed for the glory of the gods and the alleviation of the tribe's estate. One reader of Conrad who actually has had the knowledge and initiative to do this is Chinua Achebe. Achebe's first novel, *Things Fall Apart,* set in Eastern Nigeria at the turn of the century, opened to English readers one of the complex and ordered rural societies that lay behind Marlow's momentary glimpses 'of rush walls, of peaked grass-roofs, of hands clapping, of feet stamping, of bodies swaying' in the great equatorial forests that extend from the Congo to the lower reaches of the Niger. Like every novelist of the colonial experience, Achebe is strongly influenced by Conrad. But he was stung into writing his first novel by the praise lavished on Joyce Cary's *Mister Johnson* as a faithful portrayal of Nigerian life, and his second novel of traditional Ibo life, *Arrow of God,* is set near to the Joyce Cary epoch: its events cover the greater part of 1921.

To speak of a 'novel of traditional Ibo life' implies a limitation which Achebe himself, in talking about his work, appears modestly prepared to accept as the duty of a writer in a new nation. 'The fundamental theme must first be disposed of,' he writes. 'This theme—put quite simply—is that African people did not hear of culture for the first time from Europeans; that their societies were not mindless but frequently had a philosophy of great depth and value and beauty, that they had poetry and; above all, they had dignity.' And in the same year, which was also the year *Arrow of God* appeared, Achebe admitted to a literary conference: 'I would be quite satisfied if my novels (especially the ones I set in the past) did no more than teach my readers that their past—with all its imperfections—was not one long night of savagery from which the first Europeans acting on God's behalf delivered them.' We may well feel that declarations such as these understate Achebe's real intentions as a novelist, and that in the end we shall do better to trust the tale, not the artist; but so clear a pointer by the novelist cannot be ignored, and first and foremost *Arrow of God*—his richest book to date—presents itself as the documentation of a way of life which is confirmed in all its details by historians and anthropologists.

Umuaro, the village-group or clan where most of the action is set, is a community in the normative and approbationary sense of the word. For Ibos, according to one of their own anthropologists, 'human interdependence is the greatest of all values' and *Arrow of God* displays this social cohesion at the lineage, village, and clan levels. The narrative centres upon the homestead of the Chief Priest, Ezeulu, and his extended family, in which marriage and parenthood are never private concerns: a son marries, and his bride is regarded by Ezeulu's two surviving wives and all his children as 'their new wife'. As the extended family coheres around the *obi* and its shrine, the village coheres around its marketplace and the market's protective deity. In these humming market crowds, there are few nameless faces. Names proliferate in a way that at first bewilders the English reader, until he realizes that many of them are there, like the names of off-stage figures in Shakespeare, to give a sense of the thickness of life, of a world in which everybody knows everybody else. Even an involuntary 'Nigerianism', rare in Achebe whose departures from standard English are deliberate and deft, can reveal, like the occasional Gallicism or Polish turn of phrase in Conrad's writing, social attitudes that differ radically from English ones. 'We have not come here to abuse ourselves!' someone shouts at an age group meeting—itself another aspect of Ibo social interdependence. (p. 104) The English 'abuse one another' is an individualizing form of the reflexive which would not express the protest the speaker is making.

Larger still than the individual marketplaces is the great *ilo,* the setting for those festivals which bring together not only the living members of the six villages but also those who belong to the world of spirits: the ancestors who may reappear in a masquerade, the gods represented in figures born on their custodians' heads. The New Yam Feast, a harvest offering to the clan's tutelary god Ulu, is the greatest of these festivals: 'it was the only assembly in Umuaro in which a man might look to his right and find his neighbour and look to his left and see a god'.(p.254) The failure of this great cumulative festival to take place in the year of the novel marks the collapse of the old tribal unity; the centre cannot hold.

Six miles from Umuaro is Okperi, seat of the British administration. Here, on 'Gorment Heel', is a non-community of five Englishmen, divided one from the other by class and by the intricate protocol of official life; if Wright the road-builder and a social outsider—the Public Works Department was not *pukka*—continues to play around with native women, Captain Winterbottom will go so far as barring him from the Club. Achebe has remarked that his people accepted the missionaries 'with humour', and Ibos have always regarded the British administration with a good deal of ironic amusement—a sane and confident response to colonial intrusion which puzzles black readers elsewhere, whose ancestors experienced more embittering culture-contacts. But there is more than amusement in the juxtaposition of the scene in which Ezeulu receives a visit from his age group friend Akuebue and that in which A.D.O. Clarke entertains Captain Winterbottom with 'the long, arduous ritual of alcohol, food, coffee, and more alcohol'.(p.125) In the easy banter between Ezeulu, Akuebue, and Ezeulu's son Edogo, who brings in a calabash of palm wine for the two older men, we feel a sense of community painfully lacking when Clarke's steward, emerging in crackling white from the kitchen, is reproved for proffering to Winterbottom scraggy chicken from the right and not the left. Government Hill officials live in an artificial group without women—Clarke is rather envious of Wright's sex life—and without children: Winterbottom too feels envy, as he watches his servants' pickin dancing in the year's first rain. For the white men, there is no such joy to be had from the climate; the rain presents itself in the image of a riot, the cool evening wind is 'treacherous'. They do not belong, and their alienation sharpens our awareness of the solidarity, the social cohesion of African life.

The community of Umuaro has continuity as well as cohesion. It is, like all Ibo communities, an acephalic society in which custom and tradition—'rules rather than rulers'—perform the functions elsewhere vested in overlords. Through the involvement of members of Ezeulu's household in various rites of passage such as marriage and second burial, Achebe gives us a feeling of the continuity of custom; the continuity of tradition is ensured by the principle that a man always tells the truth to his son. The white men at Okperi pride themselves on their clocks and calendars; 'they've no idea of time,' says Winterbottom, though half an hour later he is remembering with pride that a whole age group has been named from his destruction of Umuaro's firearms. Yet their lives are without the continuity seen in the lives of their Ibo neighbours; they are at the mercy of every change of policy emanating from Enugu and Lagos.

This cohesion and continuity of Ibo life have to be strong to take the stress of the energy and competitiveness, the urge to 'get up' which is encouraged by the Ibo view that 'the world is a marketplace and it is subject to bargain'. For all the collectivism of his society, the Ibo child is brought up to strive for individual achievement. 'Learning the Igbo way', writes V. C. Uchendu, 'involves constant adjustment to competitive situations. The domestic group, the play group, the age grade, and the wider Igbo society are extremely competitive, each with its own rules.' In the novel there are rivalries within the compound, such as those between Ezeulu's wives, or between his sons; rivalries between the age groups conscripted for road-building; rivalries between villages competing for farmland or for trade; even rivalries between the gods, such as B.I.Chukwukere has discussed elsewhere:

> A village-group possesses a guardian deity in the same way that each village, family and individual has one. Therefore one would assume that Igbo religion postulates a pantheon of gods. The paradox of this phenomenon, however, is that there is no hierarchical ordering of the pantheon in the 'action sphere' of Igbo peoples' relationship with these gods and other spiritual beings. Here the semblance of religious unity implicit in the fact of a common village-group guardian deity forcefully, as it were, gives way to an atomistic 'organisation' of gods, each manipulating its relationship with Igbo mortal beings in order to secure more power and influence in the very same way that the

latter themselves manipulate their own social relationships for material and spiritual benefits.

In this process of manipulation, this market bargaining, a god may abandon a group or a group abandon a god; the evidence of the missionary G. T. Basden that a god could be rejected or even destroyed is confirmed by several Ibo writers and there is even a saying: 'If a god becomes perky, we will show him what wood he is carved from.' In *Arrow of God* this fate befalls the deity of Aninta when he fails his people: 'Did they not carry him to the boundary between them and their neighbours and set fire on him?' (p.33)

There has perhaps been in recent anthropological writing a tendency to overstress the competitive aspect of Ibo social and religious life. D. I. Nwoga attempts to right the balance when he insists that 'the achievements of individuals were after all measured against established societal norms. The freedom of the individual was circumscribed by the demands of social cohesion and progress . . . . If one must . . . seek a religious counterpart of the Igbo mentality, it has to be seen as consonant with a situation of social stability rather than aggressive individualism.' An individual such as John Nwodika, in *Arrow of God,* who takes employment with Winterbottom so that eventually he will be able to set himself up in trade, also seeks ways for his whole clan of Umuaro to 'get up'. And within the group a continual process of adjustment is at work; the headstrong behaviour of individuals like Ezeulu and his son Obika is tested against the live-and-let-live ethos of the community encapsulated in the proverbs of Akuebue and other elders. It is a world that is perpetually astir. The checks and balances through which it preserves its equilibrium are a far more delicate mechanism than that of the clocks ticking on Government Hill. Any sudden interference can dislocate this finely-balanced society, so unchanging and yet so subject to change; so cohesive, yet so diverse.

2

So far we have followed Achebe's own signpost and taken a first distant view of *Arrow of God* as the presentation of a particular society—one alleged by European invaders to be 'primitive', but shown by the novelist to have philosophy, poetry, dignity. This social concern, which Achebe shares with most other African novelists, has been held by some European critics to imply that the established criteria of fiction have no relevance to the African novel; that Achebe's fictional world does not, as it were, turn, in the way that the European novel turns, on the poles of the author's world-view and his individualization of character. But African writers have themselves been quick to challenge this. When the success of Achebe's first novel, in 1958, tempted publishers into printing a good deal of fictionalized anthropology, a fellow Ibo, Nkem Nwankwo, wrote a hilarious novel—published in the same year as *Arrow of God*—about a likeable character lacking in every Ibo virtue and bored to death by the wisdom of the tribe. Clearly the Nigerian, like the English reader, expects more from his fiction than sociological analysis. And if we trust ourselves primarily to *Arrow of God* itself we shall find that all the seeming 'anthropology', a few minor details apart, relates directly to the tragedy of Ezeulu, in which Achebe's own criticism of life and his sensitivity to complexities of character come together in a story of great force and beauty.

Thus we may pick up a clue that will lead into the heart of the book from a small instance of picturesque but seemingly irrelevant local colour: a children's song. The children who are everywhere in the book—as they are in an Ibo village—afford Achebe the means of half-concealing and half-revealing his authorial intentions. The revelation has not been enough for some readers, who have found only anthropological detail in the children's games; and this may be the reason why, in the second (1974) edition, Achebe has cut most of the singing game which the children in Ezeulu's compound are playing on the eve of the feast of Pumpkin Leaves. 'Nwaka Dimkpolo' winds and unwinds like 'The House that Jack Built'. It starts with a series of demands for retribution, beginning from the fall of the *ukwa* (breadfruit) on Nwaka Dimkpolo:

> Who will punish this Ukwa for me?
> *E-e Nwaka Dimkpolo*
> Matchet will cut up this Ukwa for me
> *E-e Nwaka Dimkpolo*
> Who will punish this Matchet for me?

E-e Nwaka Dimkpolo
Blacksmith will hammer this Matchet. . . .

—and so on, till we get to the Earth; but since nothing can be done to the Earth, the song begins to unwind:

What did Earth do?
Earth swallowed Water
What did Water do?
Water put out Fire. . . . (pp. 79–80)

What was retribution now appears as the psychological process of compensation, also known as taking it out on someone else. This chain reaction recurs continually in the events of the story. As usual the Europeans, drawn in broader strokes than Achebe uses for his own people, supply a simple and entertaining example. Hurt by what is virtually a reprimand in a memorandum from the Senior District Officer (three years his junior and promoted over his head) Captain Winterbottom strides from his desk to the window and shouts 'Shut up there!' to the prisoners cutting the grass. Since they have no inferiors to whom to pass on the hurt, the worst returns to laughter; they remove themselves to a distance and start a new song:

When I cut grass and you cut
What's your right to call me names? (p. 67)

As often happens, Winterbottom's action mirrors a similar act of Ezeulu; in the previous chapter Ezeulu, enraged with his Christianized son but unable to reach him, 'takes out' his rage on Edogo. Edogo has, like the prisoners, a way of sublimating his resentment; he carves fearsome masks that express all his pent-up aggression. Oduche, the son who has been offered as sacrifice to white power, is less fortunate, and has to act as whipping boy at several points in the novel. At some point, that is, the chain reaction can go no farther:

Who will punish this Earth for me? . . .

'No, no, no,' Nkechi broke in.
'What can happen to Earth, silly girl?' asked Nwafo.
'I said it on purpose to test Nkechi,' said Obiageli.
'It is a lie, as old as you are you can't even tell a simple story.

> 'If it pains you, come and jump on my back, ant-hill nose.'
> 'Mother, if Obiageli abuses me again I shall beat her.'
> 'Touch her if you dare and I shall cure you of your madness this night.' (p.80)

There is an echoing reminder here of a children's squabble that flickered across a tense earlier scene in the novel. A deputation from Umuaro has arrived at the house of the town-crier in Okperi, with whom they are involved in a land dispute:

> A little girl came in from the inner compound calling her father.
> 'Go away, Ogbanje,' he said. 'Don't you see I have strangers?'
> 'Nweke slapped me.'
> 'I shall whip him later. Go and tell him I shall whip him.' (p.26)

This incident seems at the time quite irrelevant to the grim events that follow. A brawl breaks out, and one of the deputation, enraged at being called impotent, seizes and splits the *ikenga* of an Okperi man. A man's *ikenga* is the carved embodiment of his strength, his life force, and it is split only when he dies. The messenger's act is thus an abomination, a crime against the earth and the community; and abominations have no defence. Ibo law provides for continual processes of adjustment by which injuries to pride or person may be healed or at least balanced, as the children's squabbles remind us they are balanced in family life. But nothing other than disaster can overtake the man who directs his psychological hurt, his sense of being impaired, against the community itself and the objects that symbolize its continuity and vitality. This is the tragedy of Ezeulu. In his determination to make the community suffer for the humiliation it has inflicted upon him, he strikes at its very existence, the life-rhythms of the farming year. It is an assault on basic reality, and has to fail. What can happen to Earth?

At the time of the deputation to Okperi, five years prior to the main events of the novel, Ezeulu refuses his support to the subsequent conflict on the grounds that the land in dispute belongs to Okperi and that the splitting of the *ikenga* by the Umuaro messenger was an abomination. His strong god Ulu, called into existence generations before to empower the clan to resist the slave-raiders, will not fight an unjust war. In this stand Ezeulu is doing what is expected of a Chief Priest; according to the anthropologist M. S. O. Olisa, he should 'lead the society in uprightness, boldness (especially in declaring actions abominable), and in being absolutely impartial in all disputes between groups of individuals'. Out of this regard of his god for the truth, Ezeulu, once the war has been stopped by Winterbottom, gives evidence that the land is Okperi's. Resentment over this lingers in Umuaro. Inevitably, friction arises between Ezeulu and other men of title who are envious of his power—or, put another way, between Ulu and the guardian deities of the other villages in the group—and this friction is intensified when Ezeulu's son Oduche, whom he has been persuaded by Winterbottom to send to the new mission school, shuts up in a box the python which is sacred to one of these village derities. Ezeulu is held to be the white man's tool. Then a chance to show his solidarity with Umuaro against the white man comes when Ezeulu is summoned to Okperi, where Winterbottom plans to appoint him warrant chief over Umuaro. He refuses; a priest does not leave his village and his god. But the community is not behind him in this refusal. Confused by fear of the new power in the land, they insist that he should go to Okperi at the invitation of his white friend.

At Okperi, Ezeulu is detained by the white administrators, who are offended by the slight his refusal has cast upon their own tribal god, the British Empire; deeply resentful, he seeks a means of compensation for this humiliation that he has suffered at the hands of Umuaro. His opportunity comes three months after his release, at harvest time. One of Ezeulu's priestly duties has been to keep count of the months to the yam harvest. But in the guard room at Okperi he has failed to see two new moons in succession. Now he refuses to proclaim the New Yam Festival which would initiate the harvest. In this he believes he is acting as the agent of Ulu. But whether his refusal is the action of an avenging deity or a resentful man, it is a crime against the earth that feeds man. And the earth compels. Even before the sudden death of his son Obika, which seems to Ezeulu to show Ulu's desertion of him and which causes his mind finally to break, the reality-principle has driven the people to find a way to avoid starvation: the first fruits of harvest can safely be transferred to the new god of Christianity. But this harvest *in nomine Filii,* though it preserves the lives of the community, puts what may prove an intolerable strain upon its cohesion and continuity. 'In his extremity,' the novel concludes, 'many an Umuaro man had sent his son with a yam or two to offer to the new religion and to bring back the promised immunity. Thereafter any yam that was harvested in the man's fields was harvested in the name of the son.'

The measure of Ezeulu's downfall is the contrast between the lonely, demented figure at the end of the book, whose people have carried their tribute to a strange god, and the Chief Priest who only a few months previously summons the whole of Umuaro to the Feast of Pumpkin Leaves. On that occasion he is an awesome figure, his body painted so that he is half black and half white to symbolize his role as intermediary between the world of men and the world of spirits. The prelude to the rite is Ezeulu's re-enactment of the priesting of the first Ezeulu, the descent of the creative spirit upon the man strong enough to carry such live energy. 'I carried my *Alusi* and, with all the people behind me, set out on the journey. A man sang with the flute on my right and another replied on my left. From behind the heavy tread of all the people gave me strength.' (p. 88) When the divine power has been renewed in him by this recitation, he begins his god-possessed encirclement of the marketplace, while the women shower upon him the leaves that represent the sins and abominations of the past year. And the people are still behind him as he vanishes into his shrine to bury some of the leaves deep in the earth; village by village, the women circle the marketplace, crushing and stamping the past evils into the dust.

Here, as in many other places in the novel, Achebe succeeds triumphantly in making us share the religious emotions of Umuaro, even though we do not fully understand all that is happening. Indeed it is essential to our imaginative participation that we should not fully understand, any more than a Sicilian villager could be said 'fully' to understand the Mass. Yet for all this participation, we are never in any doubt that for Achebe himself all gods reside, in Blake's phrase, in the human breast. The recognition that Ulu has no objective reality, neither transcendent nor immanent, underlies the muted irony with which Achebe has Ezeulu ponder his physical and mental exhaustion the morning after the ceremony: 'the exhaustion he felt after the festival had nothing to do with advancing age. . . . It was part of the sacrifice. For who could trample the sins and abominations of all Umuaro into the dust and not bleed in the feet? Not even a priest as powerful as Ezeulu could hope to do that.'(p.107-8) Once again a point made with finesse about Ezeulu is made more crudely about his English counterpart, Winterbottom, who can also mistake inner emotions for external powers. In a zestful recollection of 'Heart of Darkness', Achebe has Winterbottom lie awake listening to distant drums and imagining unspeakable rites. 'Then one night he was terrified when it suddenly occurred to him that no matter where he lay awake at night in Nigeria the beating of the drums came with the same constancy and from the same elusive distance. Could it be that the throbbing came from his own heat-stricken brain?' (p. 36)

Achebe's ironic treatment of Ulu and other deities is something much more complicated than the simple suspension of disbelief which operates in the novels of Elechi Amadi, his strongest rival among Nigerian writers of traditional life. Whereas Amadi adopts the viewpoint of a credulous villager throughout, Achebe, even while he makes us participate in such a point of view, overrides it with a profound Conradian scepticism about the transcendent reality of any of the powers that move men to action. As an authorial stance, this is dangerously self-aware, and it is not surprising that it leads Achebe in his first novel into an occasional archness in his treatment of traditional religion. But in *Arrow of God* the ironic assumption of belief in Ulu's objective existence, in opposition to the author's and the reader's realization that he is a figment of Ezeulu's mind, is wholly successful. Perhaps this is because this tension reflects, first, the ambivalent attitude of the Ibo community towards its own gods, and secondly, a certain ambiguity in the story about the nature of Ulu.

This ambivalence and ambiguity are both revealed by the rivalry between Ezeulu and Ezedemili, the priest of Idemili. Ezedemili claims that his god has existed from the beginning of things; his name means Pillar of Water and he is thus a nature god holding up the raincloud in the sky—an account confirmed by earlier investigators of North Iboland. But Ulu, of whom we hear nothing outside the novel, was called into being by a powerful sacrifice at the time of the Abam raids, and partakes less of the character of a force of nature than of the personal spirit known as the *chi*. Ezeulu himself associates Ulu and the *chi*, though perhaps in a metaphoric way, when he reminds Umuaro, bent on war with Okperi, that 'Umuaro is today challenging its *chi*. Is there any man or woman in

Umuaro who does not know Ulu, the deity that destroys a man when his life is sweetest to him?'(p.32) Thus Ulu is linked, not with the objective environment, the unchallengeable forces of nature, but with the personal portion of the world power. If in the proverbial saying 'a man does not challenge his *chi'*, this power is presented as dominant over its carrier, it is in another saying presented as amenable to its carrier's manipulation. 'Let us not listen', jeers Ezeulu's rival Nwaka, 'to anyone trying to frighten us with the name of Ulu. If a man says yes, his *chi* also says yes.' (p.33) Clearly Ulu is an anthropomorphous god, who has had a beginning and will one day have an end, like the lesser gods of Umuaro which are brought out head-high at the New Yam Festival: 'Perhaps this year one or two more would disappear, following the men who made them in their own image and departed long ago.' (p.254) Ulu is what his custodian makes him; and what he makes him depends on what kind of man Ezeulu himself is.

The complexity of Ezeulu's character is suggested, with remarkable economy of means, in the opening chapter. He is watching the sky for the fourth new moon of the farming year; it will be his signal to eat another yam out of the store of thirteen that enables him to keep count of the months to harvest. He watches anxiously, because the life of the community depends upon his time-keeping and 'he must not take a risk'. Responsibility is the theme of many of Ezeulu's proverbs. Twice, during the quarrel with Okperi, he reminds Umuaro that a she-goat does not suffer parturition on the tether while there is an adult in the house. The same proverb is later spoken about Ezeulu when, in a spirit of responsibility towards the whole community, he answers Winterbottom's summons. But we last meet it used *against* Ezeulu by one of the anxious elders who beg him, at the crisis of the story, not to refuse to proclaim the New Yam Festival. And the ruthless exercise of power that this refusal represents is incipient on the first page of the novel, in the enjoyment Ezeulu experiences in making young men wince at his handshake. These two contrary drives of his nature, his will to dominate his community and his will to serve its needs, are shown in equipoise in the reflections which follow as he looks at the nature of his power. 'If he should refuse to name the day there would be no festival—no planting and no reaping. But could he refuse? No Chief Priest had ever refused. So it could not be done. . . . But . . . what kind of power was it if everyone knew it would never be used?' (p. 4)

Thus from the outset Ezeulu experiences in his own nature that tension between communal responsibility and individual ambition which *Arrow of God*, in confirmation of all the anthropologists tell us, shows to be the temper of Ibo village life. And just as the delicate equilibrium of such a community can be upset by the intervention of an alien power, so can the balance of Ezeulu's mind. These forces of disruption, which we must now examine, cause Ezeulu to remake his deity as an idol of the den: 'for everyone', writes Bacon, 'has his own individual den or cavern which intercepts and corrupts the light of nature.' And in the end the community has to withstand his megalomania for the sake of its survival—much as the fellow-villagers of the anthropologist V. C. Uchendu resisted the rainmaker who attempted to abuse his power by causing too great a drought—'and he was forced to abandon his profession altogether'.

3

The first force of disruption was military. Since the Ibos had no powerful chiefs, British penetration of Iboland at the turn of the century could not follow the usual imperial pattern of treaty-making with local rulers. Sir Claude Macdonald, first Consul-General to the Oil Rivers Protectorate, in fact hoped to achieve such 'peaceful penetration' and asked an astonished Foreign Office to send him five hundred treaty forms. But Macdonald left in 1895, and for the next decade Iboland was subjected to a series of patrols and punitive raids which the Aborigines Protection Society with some justification described as 'nigger hunting'. The Ibo historian J. C. Anene has described a typical raid such as is recalled in the traditions of practically every village group east of the Niger. The patrol would be preceded by a summons to the community to send its chief men to meet the white man at the nearest government-controlled town. Such a summons was often ignored, 'because the chiefs were looked upon as the representatives of the ancestral god and were so valuable to their communities that they were not normally allowed to travel outside their villages'. The area would be hastily evacuated, and messages would go to and fro between the fugitives and the military. When the white man ran out of patience he would achieve submission by burning a village or two to the ground and destroying its crops—which the people found 'was not the kind of war they had been used to'. It is fair to add that the most renowned of these military expeditions, that against Aro-chuku in 1902, was undertaken in part—albeit a minor part—to defend other Ibo areas from harassment by the Abam mercenaries who were in the pay of the Aro-chuku oracle. Even so, *Arrow of God* makes the specific point that a community such as Umuaro had been able to deal with the Abam in its own way.

In the novel, the age of military expeditions already seems remote to Clarke, the young A.D.O., when he reads *The Pacification of the Primitive Tribes of the Lower Niger* by George Allen—the District Commissioner who helped things to fall apart in Achebe's first novel. But it is still a living memory to the senior Christian in Umuaro, Moses Unachukwu:

> I have travelled in Olu and I have travelled in Igbo, and I can tell you that there is no escape from the white man. He has come. When Suffering knocks at your door and you say there is no seat left for him, he tells you not to worry because he has brought his own stool. The white man is like that. Before any of you here was old enough to tie a cloth between the legs I saw with my own eyes what the white man did to Abame. Then I knew there was no escape. As daylight chases away darkness so will the white man drive away all our customs. I know that as I say it now it passes by your ears, but it will happen. The white man has power which comes from the true God and it burns like fire . . . . The white man, the new religion, the soldiers, the new road—they are all part of the same thing. (pp. 104-5)

Moses' response to the new power he witnessed as a young boy is a typical Ibo one. He decides to learn to manipulate it for the benefit of himself and his group. At his baptism he takes the name of Moses because he intends to lead his people into the promised land. He travels to the great river of European commerce, learns the strangers' language, and gains a skill in carpentry which is highly appreciated by a nation of woodworkers.

After 1906 the show of military might in Eastern Nigeria was a good deal less formidable than it had been at the opening of the century. It seldom went beyond such action as that of Winterbottom when he breaks the guns of Umuaro and Okperi after putting a stop to their land-war. This intervention, and

Winterbottom's subsequent award of the disputed land to Okperi, is, in Ezeulu's eyes, a show of strength in vindication of Ulu; but Winterbottom naturally sees it as the victory of his own tribal god, British imperial power. He too has fought his tribal war, against the Germans in the Cameroons; and in civil life he retains his title of Captain with a pride comparable to Ezeulu's in his title of Chief Priest. Such retention of a title is of course a well-known sign of insecurity. Winterbottom's confidence has been impaired by his wife's desertion (Ezeulu too feels his polygamous family do not support him as they should) and by the challenge of younger members of his tribe proclaiming the power of their new deity, which is called Indirect Rule—so disastrously imposed on Iboland in the nineteen-twenties in place of the old authoritative paternalism exercised by Winterbottom's generation.

Like many of the earliest colonial administrators, Winterbottom has a romantic, 'missionary' belief in the civilizing mission; the storm-bent palm trees present themselves as fleeing giants to his Quixotic gaze. He bears much resemblance to G. T. Basden, who was the pioneer missionary among Achebe's own people; for the very voice of Winterbottom, paternal and knowing, we have only to go to Basden's 1921 study of Ibo life, while his later *Niger Ibos* has for frontispiece what is virtually a photograph of Ezeulu: the priest who is half man and half spirit, the spirit half being painted white, confronts with dignity the white photographer Basden whose black shadow falls across the foreground. In *Arrow of God* the relationship between Ezeulu and Winterbottom conveys just this same feeling of negative and positive, of attraction and repulsion. Winterbottom knows a great deal about the Ibos but he is totally unable to put himself into their place. He marvels over their love of titles, their tendency to turn themselves into little tyrants over their people—'it seems to be a trait in the character of the negro'—and (as he sips his third or can it be his fourth brandy-and-ginger?) the quantity of palm wine they are able to drink. And because of this lack of the real knowledge that comes through imaginative insight, he misinterprets Ezeulu's testimony against his own people as an acknowledgement of British might.

Acknowledgement of a kind is there, but it is of a nature that has always confused Ibo-English relations. For an Ibo man, once the new strength abroad in his land had been recognized, 'the task was not merely to control the British influences, but to capture it'. Like

Moses, Ezeulu realizes that the new force could be used to the benefit of the community towards whom his responsibility is so strong. Thus he agrees to send his son Oduche to be educated by the Christian mission in Umuaro. And in this way he becomes implicated in a further show of white power, this time by African Christians. Among the Ibos to harm a python, a creature sacred to Idemili, was an abomination—a crime against the community. The first generation of Christians therefore on occasion killed a python in order that their impunity might demonstrate the strength of their god *vis-à-vis* other deities. It is significant that the catechist who urges the Umuara Christians to such a show of strength is an outsider from the Niger Delta, with the 'assimilated' name of Goodcountry. Moses has the sense of responsibility strenuously to oppose the proposal, but Goodcountry's star pupil, Ezeulu's son Oduche, offers chapter and verse in support of python-slaying, and carries the day. Publicly humiliated, Moses stalks from the meeting with a challenge to Oduche to kill a python himself, and the hurt rhetorical question: 'Do I look like something you can put in your bag and walk away?' This vernacular image is made concrete when Oduche, not daring actually to kill a python, shuts one up in his box in the hope that it will die. The box was made by Moses with the skill in carpentry he acquired at the Onitsha mission. The python's struggles reproduce the resentment that Moses, as one of the first, technically-trained converts, experiences when his authority is questioned by the new generation of Christians with 'book-learning'; on a larger scale they reproduce the frustration that the society as a whole suffers when its guns are broken by the new administrators and its gods blasphemed against by the new religion.

Moreover, the python is a scapegoat. As such it is imaginatively associated with Ezeulu, who in the course of the novel is demoted by Umuaro from the role of intermediary between god and man, carrying their failings by virtue of his strength of character, to the scapegoat whom they drive out, loading their sins upon him. The process is not without its parallels in Western literature, while 'Wole Soyinka's play *The Strong Breed* furnishes a striking parallel in Nigeria. There too the roles of sin-bearer and scapegoat provide the work's dramatic tension: the son who tries to assume his father's role in carrying away the community's abominations in an exhausting purification rite finds that times have changed, and that the society of his own generation, anxious and asunder, can only disburden itself of its distress by hounding him to death. In a similar manner Ezeulu's position changes, from that of the priest burying the year's evils while his people stamp behind him, to that of the sacrificial victim driven out by those hungry to compensate for their own humiliation in seeing him humiliated.

As if to emphasize this contrast, the Feast of Pumpkin Leaves at which Ezeulu, although already threatened by mounting hostility engendered by the python episode, is still able to exercise his traditional powers, is quickly followed by a series of events that force him into the plight of the python in the box. They begin with yet another show of white power, this time one that is notably squalid: Obika, Ezeulu's favourite son, conscripted with his age group to work on the white man's road, falls foul of the P.W.D. man Wright and is flogged by him. Because the group of young workers is distressed but unable to retaliate, its frustration erupts in internal quarrels: 'it was so much easier to deal with an old quarrel than with a new, unprecedented incident'.(p.102) Among them the only voice of reason is that of a character, Nweke Ukpaka, who makes this brief appearance as Achebe's *raisonneur*. The world, Ezeulu says, is like a Mask dancing; to see it well you do not stand in one place. The same is true of Achebe's fictional world, but, like Conrad, he always gives us a passing glimpse, through a minor character, of his own view. 'The white man', according to Nweke Ukpaka,

> is like a hot soup and we must take him slowly-slowly from the edges of the bowl. . . . I know that the white man does not wish Umuaro well. That is why we must hold our *ofo* by him and give him no cause to say that we did this or failed to do that. For if we give him cause he will rejoice. Why? Because the very house he has been seeking ways of pulling down has caught fire of its own will. For this reason we shall go on working on his road; and when we finish we shall ask him if he has more work for us. But when dealing with a man who thinks you a fool it is good sometimes to remind him that you know what he knows but have chosen to appear foolish for the sake of peace. This white man thinks we are foolish; so we shall ask him one question . . . why we are not paid for working on his road. I have heard that throughout Olu and Igbo, whenever people do this kind of work the white man pays them. Why should our own be different?(pp.105–6)

Nweke's advice is intrinsically Ibo; the new power can be manipulated by verbal skill, by asking the right questions. Ezeulu is ready to act in this way in his son's defence: to go to Winterbottom and ask him why, if his son was not the aggressor, Wright should have beaten him. Such an encounter could have done nothing but good, since it would have confirmed for Winterbottom what he already suspects, that Wright is abusing his powers. But through his irascibility, Ezeulu fails to ask Obika if Wright struck the first blow; like many responsible fathers, he cannot believe his son to be other than irresponsible. And before the misunderstanding can be sorted out, while all Umuaro is feeling frustrated and hurt, Winterbottom sends for Ezeulu.

Winterbottom too has his frustrations. His freedom of action is boxed in by directives from headquarters. In accordance with the fashionable policy of Indirect Rule, which worked well in Northern Nigeria where there were powerful traditional rulers, he has to start appointing warrant chiefs. His choice lights on Ezeulu; for once it seems that a man of real status in Ibo society has been chosen. On top of these irritations, the D.O. is in the first morose stage of an attack of malaria, so that when Ezeulu initially responds with a firm refusal his message finds Winterbottom as debilitated and touchy as Ezeulu was, on the morrow of the Feast, when he heard of the flogging. In consequence, Winterbottom fails to go to Umuaro and ask Ezeulu why he has refused; had he done so, the two strong men would literally have met each other halfway with their questions. Instead he issues a warrant for Ezeulu's arrest—and is borne off, delirious, to hospital.

Affairs at Okperi are left in the hands of Clarke, a character born rather to be led than to lead, who bears a marked family likeness to Joyce Cary's Rudbeck in *Mister Johnson.* Achebe handles him with the insight of Ibo observers into the difference between the first and the second generation of British administrators. Clarke, like his superior officer, fails to ask the right question at the right time. In his touring of the district he has been instructed by Winterbottom to investigate the rumour that Wright has been flogging road-workers. But he has not yet acquired—though he will begin to do so before the end of the novel—Winterbottom's paternal concern for the people. Moreover, in the loneliness of this non-society, he is glad to accept Wright's hospitality and overtures of friendship, and these inhibit him from making enquiries about the road gangs. He rationalizes his failure to ask questions by constructing a theory that the way to get things done in colonial administration is to impose the demands of one's own culture, in the French way, rather than to enquire endlessly into the culture of the subject people. If he were less youthfully cocksure and more intelligently curious he might ask Ezeulu, to whom he finally offers the post of warrant chief on Winterbottom's behalf, the reason for his refusal. But his self-satisfaction at his benefactory powers is disagreeably frustrated by Ezeulu's behaviour, and he returns the Chief Priest to the guard room for the very reason—produced by Winterbottom himself—which had so often served as pretext for a show of strength in the days of the 'pacification': refusal to co-operate with the Administration.

4

The crisis of the novel, handled with a skill that will repay a close reading, comes in the sixteenth chapter with Ezeulu's return to Umuaro. He is free to go home because concern has been expressed by the Secretary for Native Affairs about the unsuitability of the warrant chiefs already appointed, and Political Officers have been told to refrain from further appointments. They are instructed—in one of Achebe's nimble parodies of officialese—'to handle the matter with tact so that the Administration did not confuse the minds of the natives or create the impression of indecision or lack of direction as such an impression would do untold harm'.(pp.222-3)* The harm of course is already done. Isolated for over a month at Okperi, cut off for the first time in his life from his own community, Ezeulu's mind twists with rage against the people of Umuaro who have shut him into this box of the white man. The first night in the guard room, he dreams a dream of frustration and persecution: the whole assembly of Umuaro elders turns on him because he cannot save them from the white man; they spit on him and call him the priest of a dead god.

Determined to make Umuaro pay for his humiliation, Ezeulu walks the six miles home in pouring rain which serves still further to

*There really was such a report, S. M. Grier's *Report on the Eastern Provinces by the Secretary for Native Affairs* (Lagos 1922).

feed his resentment: 'The rain was part of the suffering to which he had been exposed and for which he must exact the fullest redress.'(p.225) He is acting like the puff adder which will suffer every provocation, even letting itself be trodden upon, before it unerringly strikes. The image had already been used of Ezeulu during his detention at Okperi, where he was widely and admiringly held to be responsible for Winterbottom's critical illness. This evidence of his god's strength, together with his proud refusal to serve the Crown rather than Ulu, have together ensured that his credit at Umuaro stands higher than it has ever done before, and a great welcome awaits him. Villagers crowd into the family circle of Ezeulu's *obi*; and as they join in laughing at his grandson's insistence that he be carried by the priest's youngest daughter, Obiageli, a child scarcely bigger than himself, Ezeulu's resolution to challenge his community begins to weaken. Once again, the children in the story are made to serve an integral purpose. Obiageli's song, which we have already heard in the days before Ezeulu's exile when she was left alone to take care of the homestead, is a song of vigilance like 'The sheep's in the meadow, the cow's in the corn':

> Mother's goat is in the barn
> And the yams will not be safe.
> Father's goat is in the barn
> And the yams will all be eaten . . . .(p.230)

As she disappears, immensely proud of her burden, there revives in Ezeulu that pride in his own burden which once made him the trusted carrier of Ulu. And when Ofoka, a man who is neither friend nor enemy, comes to congratulate him on having gone out and wrestled alone with the white man, Ezeulu's pride in his responsibility brings back an ancestral memory of the priest's function:

> Yes, it was right that the Chief Priest should go ahead and confront danger before it reached his people. That was the responsibility of his priesthood. It had been like that from the first day when the six harassed villages got together and said to Ezeulu's ancestor: 'You will carry this deity for us.' At first he was afraid. What power had he in his body to carry such potent danger? But his people sang their support behind him and the flute man turned his head. So he went down on both knees and they put the deity on his head. He rose up and was transformed into a spirit. His people kept up their song behind him and he

> stepped forward on his first and decisive journey, compelling even the four days in the sky to give way to him.(p.233)

But though Ezeulu, at this memory, once again holds the power in his hands, he does not lift it to his own head. Instead he calls another of his children, Oduche, and urges him to seize the power which, during his stay in Okperi, he has seen reside in the written word. The solemnity of the commission is relieved by a flicker of that absurdity which plays round all culture-contacts:

> When I was in Okperi I saw a young white man who was able to write his book with the left hand. From his actions I could see that he had very little sense. But he had power; he could shout in my face; he could do what he liked. Why? Because he could write with his left hand. That is why I have called you. I want you to learn and master this man's knowledge so much that if you are suddenly woken up from sleep and asked what it is you will reply. You must learn it until you can write it with your left hand. That is all I want to tell you.(p.234)

So the unhappy Oduche, once the welcomes have died down, crouches over his Ibo primer by the light of a palm oil taper, while his younger brother and sister absorb an older and less alien tradition from their mother's story-telling.

The tale she tells so enchantingly is one of the most widely spread of African quest stories. A good child goes to the land of the spirits to seek his lost flute; he is truthful, polite, ungreedy, and obedient, and the spirits reward these social virtues with a pot which, when broken open, produces every good thing. Next day the boy's half-brother is commanded by his jealous mother to lose his flute and go on a similar quest. He shows himself to be untruthful, rude, greedy, and disobedient; and *his* pot, when broken, lets out all the ills that flesh is now heir to. In the novel's second edition Achebe gives only the opening of this story, but this is enough to ensure its recognition by the Ibo readers.

Ezeulu too has made a journey to the land of spirits, which in Ibo art have white faces. He too could bring back plenty or misery for his people. What is in the pot for them depends on whether the god he serves is a projection of those social instincts that bind and sustain the community, or a projection of his deeply egotistical resentment. Now, in this critical chapter's final paragraphs, Ezeulu is poised between reconciliation and revenge. But he is too weak from the trauma of his exile to be able to sustain the mental fight.

> 'Ta! Nwanu!' barked Ulu in his ear, as a spirit would in the ear of an impertinent human child. 'Who told you that this was your own fight?'
>
> Ezeulu trembled and said nothing.
>
> 'I say who told you that this was your own fight which you could arrange to suit you? You want to save your friends who brought you palm wine he-he-he-he!' laughed the deity the way spirits do—a dry, skeletal laugh.(p.240)

We have heard this laugh before, from Ezeulu himself, at several places in the story; its most telling occurrence is when Akuebue warns the Chief Priest that no one man can win judgement against a clan. The foreboding it then awakened in Akuebue is explained when we learn of the madness of Ezeulu's mother, whose maniacal laughter echoes through his dreams once he has thrown down his challenge to the community. This 'intervention' of Ulu is of course Ezeulu's surrender to the irrational, to the idols of the den; he abrogates all responsibility and luxuriates in the belief that he is no more than an arrow in the bow of his god. Resentment is exalted into retribution: vengeance is Ulu's.

Ezeulu's fatal decision—or Ulu's fatal decision—to postpone the New Yam Festival for a further two moons is presented with great narrative dexterity so that the reader's expectation is blended with his surprise. When Clarke, receiving the weekly Reuter's telegram, notices that it reports that Russian peasants, in revolt against the new regime, are refusing to grow crops, the English reader's mind may go to the most famous example of communal suicide on record, that of the Xosa cattle-slaying early in the century; while the Ibo reader will recall instances nearer home, such as the incident recorded by the anthropologist Margaret Green in 1937: because of the delays of indigenous justice in a case which had involved the removal of the sacred spear of the yam cult, the custodians of the cult were unable to proclaim the New Yam Festival. Like Ezeulu's refusal to proclaim the festival in *Arrow of God*, this crisis undermined the tradition of the community Margaret Green was living in; the British-controlled police had to be called in to avert bloodshed. Over and above his reminder of similar happenings on historical record, Achebe offers a fine clue of anticipations within the story itself, from Ezeulu's opening reflections—'If he should refuse to name the day there would be no festival—no planting and no reaping—' to his comment that the Christians' bell, with its message of 'leave your yam, leave your cocoyam and come to church' is singing 'the song of extermination' and so on to Moses' warning that if the road gang get themselves into trouble and end up cutting Captain Winterbottom's grass at Okperi they will miss the moon of planting.(pp.7, 52, 104)

As the hunger with which the Ibo farming year customarily ends is prolonged into famine, two elders of the village act a choric role by weighing up the meaning of Ezeulu's behaviour. We have grown to like Akuebue, but recognize he is a tradition-bound personality; Ofoka we know as a man who asks the right questions, and although Akuebue is given the last word, he is bewildered where Ofoka is incisive. It is Ofoka's interpretation we are more likely to accept, and eventually it is the one that Umuaro will accept.

> 'Sometimes I want to agree with those who say the man has caught his mother's madness,' said Ogbuefi Ofoka. 'When he came back from Okperi I went to his house and he talked like a sane man. I reminded him of his saying that a man must dance the dance prevailing in his time and told him we had come—too late—to accept its wisdom. But today he would rather see the six villages ruined than eat two yams.'
>
> 'I have had the same thoughts myself,' said Akuebue, who was visiting his in-law. 'I know Ezeulu better than most people. He is a proud man and the most stubborn person you know is only his messenger; but he would not falsify the decision of Ulu. If he did it Ulu would not spare him to begin with. So, I don't know.'
>
> 'I have not said that Ezeulu is telling a lie with the name of Ulu or that he is not. What we told him was to go and eat the yams and we would take the consequences. But he would not do it. Why? Because the six villages allowed the white man to take him away. That is the reason. He has been trying to see how he could punish Umuaro and now he has the chance. The house he has been planning to pull down has caught fire and saved him the labour.'
>
> . . . .
>
> 'I don't know.'
>
> 'Let me tell you one thing. A priest like Ezeulu leads a god to ruin himself. It has happened before.'
>
> 'Or perhaps a god like Ulu leads a priest to ruin himself.'(p.266)

It is clear from this that the more traditional element in the clan requires a sign from *ani mmo*, the abode of spirits, before they accept Ofoka's view that Ezeulu is trying to get his own back on Umuaro. The sign comes with the sudden death of Obika, presumably from heart failure, when he is masquerading as a night spirit at the second burial of an important villager. There is something particularly awe-inspiring about this death of a man at the time when he is possessed by a supernatural power (indeed 'Wole Soyinka in *The Road* builds a whole play round this theme) and our awe is the measure of Achebe's art in making us denizens of his Ibo village group. But also from our 'outsider's' view—and surely most Ibo readers are now outsiders in this sense—of Ezeulu as a megalomaniac rather than the instrument of a divine power, there is an awe-inspiring fitness in the catastrophe. Of the masquerading costume donned by night spirits such as Obika carries, Basden writes: 'A man must be physically strong to endure the heat, semi-suffocation and strain demanded of him when so disguised. He is indeed far from being a disembodied spirit; there is nothing ethereal about him.' In his surrender to the irrational, seen by him as the spiritual power of Ulu and the white power of the new regime that appears to work with Ulu, Ezeulu fails to realize that man cannot live by spirit alone. The physical realities of existence also demand our deference, and in running as a night spirit when debilitated by malnutrition and fever Obika challenges those realities. Like father, like son; the strong man who should be the carrier is transformed into the scapegoat when his father's sins are visited upon him.

Ezeulu reproaches his god in a lament rich in proverbial images. Why has Ulu not looked after his own? 'When was it ever heard that a child was scalded by the piece of yam its own mother put in its palm? What man would send his son with a potsherd to bring fire from a neighbour's hut and then unleash rain on him? Who ever sent his son up the palm to gather nuts and then took an axe and felled the tree?' (p.286) The proverbs, echoing similar ones spoken earlier in the novel, strike home with ironic force. Ezeulu himself has failed to look after his own. He has ceased to serve an Ulu who personifies the clan's collective strength and wellbeing, and has gone a-whoring after strange gods in the recesses of a mind that now loses its last hold upon reality.

5

Between Ezeulu's return from Okperi and the catastrophe of the story another festival takes place, a minor village affair called Akwu Nro. On a casual reading it might be dismissed as an 'anthropological' episode. In fact it is firmly structural. Occurring between Ezeulu's defiance of the British and his defiance of his own clan, it is the eye of the storm. It affords us, in its honouring of the dead, a last glimpse of the clan united by its traditional reverences. Yet the rivalries that give Ibo life its tension still obtain: the crowd's acclaim goes to Obika for his vigorous ejection of an ill-wisher and for his skilful performance of the sacrifice rather than to his brother Edogo who has carved the ceremonial Mask.

Edogo moves through the crowd, studying his handiwork from different positions, satisfying himself that the weakness he suspected in its features—'a certain fineness which belonged not to an Agaba but to a Maiden Spirit'—no longer shows now the mask is in action. Many are praising the carver, but to Edogo's disappointment no one compares the mask with the famous Agaba of Umuagu: 'He had not after all set out to excel the greatest carver in Umuaro but he had hoped that someone would link their two names.' (p. 251) This anxiety of Edogo's is in character. It is also the self-questioning of the artist in any medium. In just this way a modern Edogo might hunt for understanding comment through the notices of his new book. So it is possible to see in this passage Achebe's half-satirical and half-appealing awareness of his concern for his own art. I have placed the Agaba of Achebe beside the Agaba of Conrad: has it a comparable 'fierceness'?

It is not a word one easily associates with Achebe. The terms that come most readily to mind in an attempt to evaluate his quality as a novelist are such epithets as 'deft' and 'dextrous'. He is a highly skilled craftsman, acutely aware, among other things, of the importance that must be given to tone, or voice, in a novel written in a language different from that of its setting. This carefulness led Achebe in his first novel, *Things Fall Apart,* to adopt for his third-person narrative the viewpoint of a moderate and responsible member of the tribe who has lived through the book's events as they unroll at the end of the last century. The effect of this, it has often been said, is to give the book a classical gravity, simplicity, and decorum. Yet a reader who compares the book's total effect with the turbulent vitality of Ibo rural life as he has observed it—and it cannot have changed profoundly—might be forgiven for finding that effect at times more Ossianic than Homeric. In his second novel, *No Longer at Ease,* Achebe again tells a story as it might strike a contemporary. But now the viewpoint has become very close indeed to the outlook of the hero, a young, well-educated civil servant caught up in the moral confusions of Lagos in the nineteen-fifties. In this tragedy the sufferings of the protagonist have to be endured alone and unnoticed. And the voice that recounts them is correspondingly muted, without passion or resonance, like the voice of a studio news-reader. Only briefly at the end does it vibrate with the overtones of a communal Stoicism: 'the most terrible sight in the world cannot put out the eye'. But for the most part Achebe, like his hero Obi, 'talks "is" and "was" '; and just as Obi's countrymen complain that they expected more of the man they paid to educate in England, readers of *No Longer at Ease* on its publication were troubled lest they should be forced in the end to group Achebe with those South African novelists trounced by Roy Campbell:

> You praise the firm restraint with which they write—
> I'm with you there, of course.
> They use the snaffle and the curb all right,
> But where's the bloody horse?

Fortunately four years later *Arrow of God* showed the horse to be alive and kicking, and Achebe very much in the saddle. Here was a taut, nervous prose, a real stylistic advance on the rather static archaisms of *Things Fall Apart* and the nerveless English colloquialisms of *No Longer at Ease.* It reflects a society in which words still have inherent power and have not yet become arbitrary labels. Edogo and his wife do not voice their fear that their child is a spirit child who will return by death to the spirit world, because 'utterance had power to change fear into a living truth'. (p. 117) Such a conviction shapes the formal speeches made in the clan's debates. The communal energy of proverbs and the challenge of rhetorical questions build up the conflict of attitudes and of personalities into the stylistic equivalent of that thrust and counter-thrust of social forces which anthropologists have shown to be the temper of traditional Ibo life. An apt example is offered in a conversation between Ezeulu and Akuebue, whose real affection for one another does not prevent contentions that, like many Ibo arguments, are 'dangerous-looking scenes' for the bystander. Ezeulu is speaking:

> 'Do not make me laugh,' he said. 'If someone came to you and said that Ezeulu sent his son to a strange religion so as to please another man· what would you tell him? I say don't make me laugh. Shall I tell you why I sent my son? Then listen. A disease that has never been seen before cannot be cured with everyday herbs. When we want to make a charm we look for the animal whose blood can match its power; if a chicken cannot do it we look for a goat or a ram; if that is not sufficient we send for a bull. But sometimes even a bull does not suffice, then we must look for a human. Do you think it is the sound of the death-cry gurgling through blood that we want to hear? No, my friend, we do it because we have reached the very end of things and we know that neither a cock nor a goat nor even a bull will do. And our fathers have told us that it may even happen to an unfortunate generation that they are pushed beyond the end of things, and their back is broken and hung over a fire. When this happens they may sacrifice their own blood. This is what our sages meant when they said that a man who has nowhere else to put his hand for support puts it on his own knee. That was why our ancestors when they were pushed beyond the end of things by the warriors of Abam sacrificed not a stranger but one of themselves and made the great medicine which they called Ulu. (pp. 164–5)

Power has been carved into the lineaments of this prose. It is transparently simple, yet it bears out Blake's dictum about the wide and impassable gulf between simplicity and insipidity. A crackling impetus is given to Ezeulu's speech by cumulative repetitions, by the rising intonation of questions, by emphatic connective inversions ('This is what' . . . 'That was why'), by ferocious images and the gnomic force of proverbs. And if we are to attempt to discover why Achebe's writing achieves such vigour in *Arrow of God,* it may help us to look closely at the substance as well as at the style of what Ezeulu is here saying.

Arrow of God appeared four years after Nigeria's Independence. The interim was a time of mounting resentment and apprehension for the Ibo. British partiality for the North appeared to them to have been built into the Independence constitution. They looked to the results of a new census to right the balance; but the results, which indicated that the East and West together now outnumbered the North, were declared void on the grounds that the returns must have been false. Ibo men who left their overcrowded and overcultivated farmlands in order to work in the North found themselves discriminated against and sometimes in physical danger. The impossible task of sifting the truth from the falsehood in all the accusations and counter-accusations of the time must be left to the historians. For us as readers of Achebe the important fact is that he wrote his third novel at a time when the Ibo people believed themselves to be shut up in a box: even that they were hung over a fire. It would not be long before their frustration would be pushed beyond the edge of things and they would sacrifice their own sons in the Civil War of 1967–9. I am not of course claiming that Achebe, who performed a sufficiently remarkable feat of prophecy in his next novel by describing the first military *coup* some months before it took place, is foretelling the Civil War in Ezeulu's eloquence. But I would suggest that *Arrow of God,* like some other outstanding political novels, derives much of its vitality from the fact that it was written at a time of sharpened political awareness. If the arrow flies fast and true it is because the bow of the writer's sensibility has been tightly drawn.

Ezeulu is not, however, Achebe's spokesman. He is his tragic hero, and as such is in a position where circumstances may impel but cannot compel his moral choice. In the end he chooses to risk the destruction of his people. A no less tragic choice was made, possibly for no better motives, by the Ibo political leaders in 1967; and if European readers of *Arrow of God* are painfully aware as they read of the disaster incipient in the delayed planting, this is in part because the near-starvation of people in the Ibo heartland in 1969 brought fully home to them the total dependence of an agricultural people on the due observance of seedtime and harvest. Achebe himself is in some degree a victim of the war; he has written little since it ended, and as yet nothing of comparable distinction with his first four novels. But there is time yet. If *Arrow of God* is a story of frustration and of the suicidal defiance which is an individual way of escape from that frustration, it is also a story of resilience. A blind and desperate act of vengeance offends against the community and against the earth that nourishes it, but both renew themselves; the question 'What can happen to Earth?' asserts an acceptance of forces that are far more powerful than the idols of the den.

THE BIRTH OF KRISHNA

FORSTER'S A Passage to India

1

We will plunge *in medias res.* The central episode of *A Passage to India* is the case of Rex v. Aziz which is presided over by Mr Das, Assistant Magistrate at Chandrapore. Mr Das refuses to listen to speculations about the evidence that might have been given by the elder of the two ladies who visited the Marabar Caves in Dr Aziz's company:

> 'An extraneous element is being introduced into the case,' said the Magistrate. 'I must repeat that as a witness Mrs. Moore does not exist. Neither you, Mr. Amritrao, nor Mr. McBryde, you, have any right to surmise what that lady would have said. She is not here, and consequently she can say nothing.' (p. 235)

In writing this scene, Forster worried a good deal lest he should not get the legal details of the trial right. What matters, however, is that he has got Mr Das right. When the magistrate insists that neither side may quote the absent Mrs Moore in evidence he states what any Indian magistrate might have said with equal emphasis shortly after World War I, for he is affirming a principle of justice which the Turtons and the Burtons had recently put into jeopardy.

Alarmed by a wave of what it considered 'revolutionary' crimes, the Raj sought a way of perpetuating beyond the 1918 Armistice the special powers, involving much curtailment of civil rights, which it had exercised during the War. To this end the notorious Rowlatt Acts were passed early in 1919. The second of these allowed courts (I quote the summary of B. G. Horniman) 'to accept in evidence, in certain circumstances, recorded statements of persons dead or missing or otherwise incapable of giving evidence without [their] having been subject to the test of cross-examination'. In the storm of protest aroused by this and other provisions of the Act (never, in the event, enforced) Indians repeatedly invoked the rational principles of earlier British rule against the prejudices of the newer imperialism. It was the same kind of confrontation as had taken place in the eighteen-eighties, when the Ilbert Act, allowing Indians to try cases involving Europeans, aroused bitter resentment among the English in India; and this too is echoed in the novel when the ladies of Chandrapore send a telegram to the Lieutenant-Governor's wife protesting against the charge of indecent assault on Miss Quested being heard by Mr Das. Ronny Heaslop, whatever his feelings as Miss Quested's husband-to-be, cannot quite approve of this move, because as Chief Magistrate he likes to think that his old Das is all right. So, in a rather different sense from Ronny's, he is; and never more so than when he rejects the distortion of the judicial process implicit in the second Rowlatt Act. Nervous but courageous, he stands up for the values of the old pre-Mutiny Raj, in which Forster's Clapham Sect forebears had played some part, against the overbearing sahibs and even more overbearing memsahibs with their special chairs.

Yet in another sense, Mr Das is all wrong in maintaining that Mrs Moore does not exist. It may be doubly true that she is no longer present: she has left India and as we subsequently discover she has died at sea. But absence, Professor Godbole has recently insisted, implies presence: 'absence is not non-existence, and we are therefore entitled to repeat, "Come, come, come, come"'. (p.186) When Mahmoud Ali's hysteria causes Mrs Moore's name to 'burst on the court like a whirlwind', the crowd outside takes up the 'invocation' with a rhythmic chant of *Esmiss Esmoor.* They are calling upon her to come. Then the chanting suddenly stops, 'as if the prayer had been heard and the relics exhibited'. (p. 235) In the silence after the whirlwind the still small voice of truth speaks through Adela as the delusion of her prepared 'information' yields to her memory of the picnic *sub specie aeternitatis.* She withdraws the charge and Aziz is saved. Mrs Moore has given her evidence.

There is no shying away from this being, if not an actual miracle, at least an intrusion of the numinous. Yet it is the invention of an agnostic novelist. This indeed may be the very reason why we are so ready to accept the implications of the scene, however much we may jib at, say, Greene's miracle in *The End of the Affair.* In *A Passage to India* the writer himself appears reluctant to believe that anything has occurred that cannot be explained in psychological terms. The episode offers us, by implication, other reasons for Adela behaving as she does. First the lowly but god-like figure of the man pulling the punkah brings to her attention the otherness of existences outside the narrow cavern of her own sufferings. Then her lifelong respect for the truth is encouraged by the honest and rather likeable McBryde. 'Smoothly the voice in the distance proceeded, leading along the paths of truth, and the airs from the punkah behind her wafted her on . . . .' (p. 237) In such ways Adela's own feelings for the true and the beautiful operate alongside the goodness of Mrs Moore. But together goodness, truth, and beauty combine into something, not Adela herself, making for righteousness; Fielding's observation that she is going to have 'a nervous breakdown' is, and is meant to be, notably inadequate.

For two reasons Mr Das's emphatic denial of the existence of Mrs Moore offers a good point of departure for a reading of *A Passage to India.* By its linkage of the topical with the metaphysical, the incident strikingly illustrates the point made by Lowes Dickinson, in a letter to Forster soon after the novel was published, that its surface is in touch with its depths: 'whereas in your other books your kind of double vision squints—this world, and a world or worlds behind—here it all comes together'. This 'double vision' gives a powerful depth of focus to scene after scene of the book. Yet Mr Das's remarks also show that this linkage is not unity but tension worth exploring both as a leading theme of the novel and also, as far as we can re-discover it, the shaping experience behind it. A miracle is needed to save Aziz; the rectitude, intelligence, and moral courage of Mr Das do not suffice against the terrible persistence of Adela's echo. If Forster reaches so unexpectedly after the superhuman it is because events in India between, on the one hand, his first visit to the country and the book's conception and, on the other, his second visit and the book's completion, convinced him that in that place and at that time the liberal virtues had been rendered powerless.

2

Life for Edwardian intellectuals was amazingly free of what Leonard Woolf called the horrible urgency of politics. One event alone, according to Woolf, captured their imagination.

> Over the body and fate of one obscure, Jewish captain in the French army, a kind of cosmic conflict went on year after year, between the establishment of Church, Army and State on the one side and the small band of intellectuals who fought for truth, reason and justice on the other.

Forster's most political novel was also to centre upon a trial in which a man narrowly escapes being wrongfully convicted as the result of racial prejudice. But its setting was not France, but India; and what was going on in Britain's overseas possessions was of no more concern to the average, well-educated member of the English middle classes in the first quarter of this century than Peter Walsh's life out East was of concern to Clarissa Dalloway. Nothing demonstrates this unconcern more strikingly than the deafening silence with which English intellectuals, in 1919 and 1920, greeted what Forster called the public infamy of Amritsar.

Events in India at the time require perhaps a brief recapitulation. The constitutional reforms initiated by the Montagu Declaration of August 1917 had done little to meet popular political demands, which had been strengthened by resentment at wartime hardships as well as by the encouragement of the Russian Revolution and of American pronouncements on self-determination. The Rowlatt Acts were designed to check this unrest. To meet this new move of the Raj, Gandhi, who had suspended his political activity for the duration of the war, devised *satyagraha* or civil disobedience. A *hartal* organized for 6 April 1919 passed off for the most part without violence. But when Gandhi was prevented from entering the Punjab, riots broke out in several towns of the province. In Amritsar, where the *hartal* had been uneventful, the arrest of two Gandhist doctors on the 10th gave rise to serious rioting in which five European men were killed. General Dyer took over control of the town, which remained quiet for the next two days. Then on the 13th a large crowd gathered in the public space known as the Jallianwala Bagh. Dyer arrived with a column mainly of Gurkhas whom he ordered to open fire. When they withdrew they left 379 men and boys dead or dying, and an uncalculated number of wounded.

For those who believed that Dyer's action put an end to an incipient revolt in the Punjab, this was the Amritsar Affair. Others, appalled by the facts that many people in the square had not heard the proclamation against assemblies (some had merely come into town for a religious festival), that no warning to disperse was given, that escape from the square was almost impossible, and that the firing continued for ten minutes, called it the Amritsar Massacre. The Hunter Committee which was appointed six months later to enquire into the Punjab disorders censured Dyer's action, and its censure was upheld by the Secretary of State for India. But Dyer had his impassioned defenders in the Commons, and the Lords passed a motion deploring the censure. Public sympathy for Dyer ran high; a consolatory fund was opened and quickly reached £28,000.

Forster's Wilcoxes no doubt contributed generously; but what were the Schlegels doing? Official censorship has been blamed for their silence. Certainly before the Hunter Committee report in May 1920 few details of the 'rising' in the Punjab reached English newspapers. Yet *The Times* of 19 April 1919 carried a report that 'At Amritsar, on April 13, the mob defied the proclamation forbidding public meetings. Firing ensued, and 200 casualties occurred.' And the day's leading article also referred to the shootings. Even though the figure of those killed was short of the facts, it was a good deal in excess of, say, the number killed on a comparable occasion forty years later at Sharpeville. One has to conclude that in 1919 even the most sensitive and scrupulous readers of *The Times* paid scant attention to what was being done in their name in the Punjab.

Forster however was an honourable exception to this indifference. The knowledge and interest he had acquired in his student days were deepened when he visited India in 1912–13, not in the course of duty but just for the pleasure of it. In describing this visit as 'wonderful' he was not using a slang intensifier. His Indian experiences were the biggest revelation of his life, and he transmuted them into a book which has enlightenment for its theme. Not that all the revelations were agreeable. The arrogance of Anglo-India was brought home to him before his ship had even reached the Suez Canal—more particularly in the personality of a table-companion who was Mrs Turton and Mrs McBryde rolled into one: 'Never forget that you're superior to every native in India except the Rajas, and they're on an equality.' Out of such encounters, Forster built the Civil Station of Chandrapore with a vivacity that caused one Anglo-Indian reader who 'hated the book' to exclaim: 'But hang it all! It's an *exact* picture of provincial life, in an up-country station, before the war.' A better revelation, the 'wonderful' aspect of Forster's pre-war visit, was the Indian gift for genuine personal relationships represented above all by 'Saeed', who gave Forster hospitality at Aurangabad, and took him to the Ellora Caves. The 'capacity for friendship triumphing over suspicion and forgetfulness' that Saeed displayed is celebrated in the opening chapters of *A Passage to India* as vividly as the exclusiveness of Anglo-India is satirized.

Forster however made the mistake of trying to transmute experience into fiction too quickly. His statement in an interview: 'I began it in 1912, and then came the war' suggests the writing of the novel was interrupted, but in his introduction to *Maurice* P. N. Furbank indicates that it was for a time abandoned:

> India made a profound impression on him; it gave him a new viewpoint and—as he thought—shook him for ever out of his insular and suburban preöccupations. . . . He began an Indian novel on his return, but soon got into difficulties and could not see his way through it. Privately he accused himself of feebleness, and began to wonder if anyone so idle had the right to pass judgments on those who worked for their living.

From 1915 to 1919 Forster did work, though not for his living, with the international Red Cross in Alexandria, an experience that gave him further insights into a colonial situation. There was plenty to rouse his amused asperity. Of a book by the Inspector-General for Prisons he wrote:

> He seems to have achieved a great deal. Not only did he start the Turf Club at Cairo and the Sporting Club at Alexandria, but he built a Reformatory that radiated in spokes from a central observation point so that the inmates remained under supervision even in the lavatory. Few men have done so much, and no one except Coles Pasha has done it for the fellahin.

Behind the irony is a concern that arose from Forster's official inspections of hospitals where the fellahin 'recruited' for the Egyptian Labour Corps died in great numbers and great squalor. Twice in 1919 he wrote letters to British newspapers on their behalf. In such ways, his awareness of Imperial politics persisted, and in 1920 it bore fruit in his share of a Fabian pamphlet, *The*

Government of Egypt, 'with notes on Egypt by E. M. Forster'.

Forster observed towards the end of his Egyptian sojourn a cooling-off and even a hostility in attitudes towards the British, which he attributed to the wartime exaction of forced labour. He was to observe a far worse deterioration in the relations between Indians and British as a consequence of the Amritsar disaster. News of the massacre reached him earlier than it did most people, by way of a letter from his friend Malcolm Darling, who must also have told him more about the affair when he came home on leave in 1920. Darling, a liberal-minded administrator, was actually in the Punjab at the time, and was made wretched by the violence of both sides. He thought Home Rule, the ultimate objective of the Montagu reforms, a terrifying prospect, but he also made himself unpopular at the Club by criticizing Dyer's action. It is not surprising that in the novel Fielding, who is half in and half out of white officialdom, is given a name that portmanteaus 'Darling' and 'Forster'. For Forster's reactions to the massacre were strong and deep, so that *A Passage to India* abounds in echoes of the Punjab troubles.

The Chandrapore affair, like the Amritsar one, takes place at the hottest time of year, when the disturbances to be expected at a current religious festival have rendered the European community edgy. Trouble starts with the arrest of a local doctor, as it had begun in Amritsar with the arrest of two doctors. Before Aziz's trial, the Sweepers—Gandhi's Untouchables—go on strike; from the Civil Station, a *hartal* and a strike were indistinguishable, and assuming this viewpoint Forster at one stage wrote: 'Sweepers were acquiring racial solidarity. Something was behind the people, some new and insolent force.' Fielding's support for Aziz earns for him the sort of disapproval lavished by real Anglo-Indians of the time upon Gandhi's close associate B. G. Horniman, who wrote the first independent account of the Amritsar massacre, which Forster could have read in 1921. Horniman was editor of the *Bombay Chronicle,* and in the manuscript of the novel Fielding, faced with the prospect of unemployment, considers journalism as a possible means to his staying on in India.

Most interesting of all the parallels is that between Adela Quested's situation in the book and that of Marcella Sherwood in real life. (Again, names are significant. Adela acquired her unusual first name at a late stage in the book's composition.) Miss Sherwood was a missionary teacher at Amritsar and so, like Adela, only on the fringe of Anglo-Indian society. In the disturbances of 10 April she was set upon by the mob and left for dead. The excessive collapse of Adela Quested, so surprising for a tough and 'advanced' young woman, is the rather awkward result of Forster's need to create a situation such as Miss Sherwood's that might give rise to a hysterical desire for revenge on the part of the white community. Their emotions fanned by rumours that Adela's life is in the balance, members of the Chandrapore Club regret (to quote again from the MSS) 'the good old days . . . when an Englishman who was wronged could go out and shoot right and left until his honour felt satisfied and no questions be asked afterwards'. General Dyer's extreme emotional response to the attack on Miss Sherwood, and the influence that his apprehensions about white women and children had on his behaviour in the Jallianwala Bagh, came out clearly at the enquiry. His infamous 'crawling order' enforced in the street where Miss Sherwood was attacked finds an echo in Mrs Turton's outburst: 'Why, they ought to crawl from here to the caves on their hands and knees whenever an Englishwoman's in sight . . . .' And English popular reaction at home after Dyer's disgrace was very much in tune with Major Callendar's insistence that 'there's not such a thing as cruelty after a thing like this'. (p. 225)

The one person who seems to have retained a sane view of the incident was Miss Sherwood herself. In spite of the fact that she had been subjected to very real injury, she behaved with the generosity and regard for the truth that mark Adela's conduct once the echo has been exorcized. She refused the compensation offered her by the Government of India. In December 1919 she wrote a letter to *The Times* in which she pointed out that she owed her survival to her rescue by parents of her Indian pupils. She also put right some misreporting of an attack on a hospital similar to the one Forster makes the culminating point of the riot in *A Passage to India*. 'A mob went to the Zenana Mission Hospital also with intent to burn it, but was harangued by Hindu and Mahomedan neighbours, and desisted.' This incident becomes the clowning of Dr Panna Lal and the speech-making of the Nawab outside the Minto Hospital; in themselves an indication of the serio-comic handling of civic disorders in the novel. 'The Marabar Caves had been a terrible strain on the local administration; they altered a good many lives and wrecked several careers, but they did not break up a continent or even dislocate a district.' (p.247) The troops, to the disappointment of the very stupid subaltern, are never called in, and Dr Aziz does not suffer the fate so many suffered in the Punjab, transportation to the Andaman Islands. In the manuscripts, there is one victim of the riot—'a punkah wallah'—but Forster wisely dropped this idea; the irony was too neat, and even one 'real' casualty would have robbed the Chandrapore affair of its triviality.

Trivial as it is in itself, the Chandrapore affair has intangible but deeply serious consequences. Even before the end of the Caves section, the Indians have closed ranks in a Muslim-Hindu entente and their attitude to the British has hardened. The Nawab Bahadur gives up his Imperial title. Hamidullah, whose agreeable good sense in the first part of the book suggests that he was modelled on Forster's friend Sayed Ross Masood, now turns on Ronny and Adela with savage contempt. Aziz, though 'without natural affection for the land of his birth' (p. 279), becomes a nationalist, and plans to leave British India. These are exactly the ways Indian intellectuals reacted to the massacre and its aftermath. Dyer's exoneration at the hands of the Lords caused Rabindranath Tagore to write home to India: 'The unashamed condonation of butchery expressed in their speeches and echoed in their newspapers is ugly in its frightfulness. . . . The late events have conclusively proved that our true salvation lies in our own hands.' He himself returned the insignia of knighthood to the Palace. Jawaharlal Nehru, who had hitherto kept aloof from Congress, found himself shortly after the massacre in a railway carriage with a group of British officers who were jubilant over Dyer's action. From that day, he threw in his lot with Congress. And the years following Amritsar were the time of closest Hindu-Muslim co-operation inside the Congress Party.

On his return to the sub-continent, Forster was quick to remark such changes and to record them in the articles which he wrote as Indian Correspondent for *The Nation and Athenaeum*. The English, he noticed on this second visit, were a good deal more polite than they had been before the war. But this improvement in their manners came too late to prevent the withdrawal of the educated Indians into their own social institutions. There emerges from these articles a new sense of the *irrelevance* of the English in

India. As Forster puts it in the novel: 'when the Indian does ignore his rulers, he becomes genuinely unaware of their existence'. (p. 241) The visit of the Prince of Wales, Forster says, should never have taken place when people had other things to think about. The boycott of the Prince's visit to Calcutta had been rehearsed with an efficiency that showed Indians could do very well without the British. The Raj, for its part, was showing an exaggerated deference to the wishes of the Indian Princes, but the real centre of Indian political life—from which Forster derived no great hopes—now lay elsewhere.

In the last section of the novel, this hardening of attitudes is represented in the changes that have come over Aziz and Fielding and over their relationship. Aziz finds it difficult to be civil, let alone friendly, towards the English and to avoid them he has withdrawn into a Native State as court physician. Fielding is exasperated by this professional suicide but he has to accept ruefully the 'otherness', the everlasting muddle—as it seems to him—of India, just as Forster had to resign himself to the muddle of Dewas State Senior when he was its ruler's private secretary in 1921. Though at the end of the book Fielding and Aziz are friends again, their ways have to part; and the harmony of their last ride, when Fielding tells Aziz about his marriage, much in the way that Aziz first sealed their friendship by talking to Fielding about his wife, ends with the spirited cadenza of a political slanging-match. Not until the British quit India will Fielding and Aziz be able tranquilly to enjoy their friendship. In 1921 this prospect was long indeed.

The development of the story in *A Passage to India* is thus in many ways the development, or rather the deterioration, of the relationship between rulers and ruled in the sub-continent between 1912 and 1922: perhaps the most formative decade in Indian history. In his pre-war visit Forster realized how fragile were the few arches of good race relations raised against the oppressive Indian sky. Things had been easier in the days of the Nabobs, of Macaulay, of the Arya Samaj; but since the eighteen-eighties officials like McBryde—the best of a bad bunch in the novel—had taken the Mutiny records for their Bible rather than the Bhagavad Gita. A real-life parallel occurs to the reader: Kipling's father had belonged to the old India; Kipling himself was absorbed willy nilly into the new, into the defiant possessiveness that culminated in the

Curzon era. From then on, the aggressive imperialism of the rulers and the increasingly aggressive nationalism of the ruled confronted each other monolithically. Amritsar virtually put an end to civilized communication. Although Forster in 1921 made a brief stay in British India, most of this second visit was spent in the Native States—in particular in the obscure principality which his friend Maurice Darling called 'the oddest corner of the world outside Alice in Wonderland'.

3

So far we have moved on the surface of Forster's story, that surface on which lie, in the novel's wonderful opening chapter, the amorphous, mud-coloured confusion of Chandrapore and the neat, soulless grid of its Civil Station, the East and West that seem never to meet. But the same opening chapter brings before us also the promise of depths: the depth of the sky's vault from which a common blessing can be poured out on to city and station alike, the depth of the primeval rocks that thrust skywards the menacing 'fists and fingers' of the Marabar Hills, containing the extraordinary caves. D. H. Lawrence complained that Forster did not go down to the root to meet India. In a sense he was right. Forster could not himself go the whole way down to the meeting-place of East and West which was for him not any primordial instinct but rather the sense of the numinous, of the 'other kingdom' which was common to the religious thought of East and West as they had once met in Alexandria. But *A Passage to India* acknowledges that while the humanists cannot communicate at this level, there are those who may be able to do so. 'My wife's after something,' says Fielding in that last ride he and Aziz take together. 'You and I and Miss Quested are, roughly speaking, not after anything. We jog on as decently as we can, you a little in front—a laudable little party. But my wife is not with us.' (p. 331)

Here for the last time our attention is being drawn to a contrast made throughout the novel between the seekers and those who are 'not after anything'. The achievements of the laudable little party in the Mosque section are overthrown in the long Caves movement; and there is present in both these sections an awareness of the strengths of the other group. This awareness dominates the Temple section, where the seekers are found to be in tune with India in a way that lies outside the experience and the powers of those who jog on as decently as they can.

'Miss Quested—what a name!' remarks Mrs Turton, so making quite sure on the novelist's behalf that we shall not miss its aptness. Yet it was not designed in the first place to fit Adela's over-cerebral curiosity. In *Howard's End* Miss Quested is among the clever guests who discomfort Mrs Wilcox at the Schlegels' luncheon party. *A Passage to India* gives Hampstead as her habitat. In manuscript pages which represent Forster's earliest conception of her, she is a caricature of the feminist of 1913: unresponsive to kindness, physically unattractive with a 'planky body and mottled face', and intellectually domineering. Even in the final version we recognize the justice of Aziz's reflection: 'This pose of "seeing India" which had seduced him to Miss Quested at Chandrapore was only a form of ruling India.' (p. 319) In the earliest version too Adela was even more obsessed than in the final text by that aspect of the Bloomsbury religion that J. M. Keynes was so glad to discard, 'the duty to know *exactly* what one means and feels'. 'Her friends in England had always threshed out a problem from every point of view until their hair flew about, and their cheeks were crimsoned.' This sounds like an evening at the Stracheys'. It is certainly no way to behave in India, where even Fielding's easy-going play of mind around politics and religion distresses his Indian friends. Between this pre-war conception of Adela and the published book, Forster wrote *Maurice.* Whatever its shortcomings as a novel, the writing of this book effected a psychological release which enabled him to present Adela much more charitably when he returned to his Indian novel. So even in the opening chapters, in their final form, Adela is given credit for good sense and consideration and a total absence of race prejudice. The trouble is that her cool head does not go with a warm heart.

Aziz, by contrast, has a warm heart, as his immediate and generous responses to every civility or kindness show. But his head is anything but cool. Imprudence follows imprudence. His confidences to Mrs Moore narrowly escape reaching the ears of Major Callendar; he cannot resist making an enemy for life of Dr Panna Lal; his impulsive invitation to the Marabar Caves outing would have nearly ruined him financially, even if all had gone as he wished. So it is the function of Fielding, who has been blessed by nature and endowed by experience with a cool head and a warm heart, to bring together Aziz at his best and Adela at her best. Inevitably this gives him the strong backing of his author. Fielding is the most laudable member of this little party. He represents in part, we feel, Forster himself in 1913, freed by the revelations of his Indian experience from the limitations of Bloomsbury as well as those of Sawston, but still affectionately eager to share his revelations with chosen friends in the English world he has come from.

In the first part of *A Passage to India,* personality meets personality to build an arch above the formless confusion of an Indian city and in defiance of the *apartheid* implicit in the lay-out of Chandrapore's Civil Station. Hindus dislike the arch of European and Muslim architecture, we are told by Forster's friend J. R. Ackerley, because the arch never sleeps; but this tension in the arch gives the image its appeal for Forster, since it suggests a deliberate election or naming of the friend, and the response of the other to this initiative. Mrs Moore and Aziz make such an election of one another in the shadow of the mosque. Fielding and Aziz begin to build their relationship beneath the Moghul arches of Fielding's garden house. In each case we have a sense of stressful form triumphing over the inertia of non-relationship; sharply definitive, black upon white, the ninety-nine attributes of God stand out upon the mosque's arcade. Such energy and definition are missing when Ronny and Adela become engaged. Nor is any bridge successfully built at Fielding's tea party, for it partakes a little too much of that good intention of bringing the races together as abstractions which made the Collector's Bridge Party such a fiasco. What little harmony is accomplished is soon wrecked by Ronny's intrusion (' "Well it's nothing I've said," said Ronny reassuringly. "I never even spoke to him." ') Still, the same five well-intentioned people are to be brought together at the Marabar Caves. At the end of Part I we have great hopes of this new encounter, for we have already seen something of what the secret understanding of the heart can achieve in despite of the misunderstandings due to prejudice such as Ronny's amusement at Aziz's missing collar stud, or the suspicion of Aziz's friends that he has been poisoned at Fielding's house.

The picnic however—quite apart from its disastrous conclusion—builds no arch to unite the five beings for whom it was intended. Godbole never gets there. Fielding arrives late, only to be irritated by Adela's disappearance and irked by Mrs Moore's listlessness. The earth, formless, void, and scorched, does not bless the occasion, nor does the sky into which the sun rises without splendour. The ladies behave as they should and manage to appear gratified by yet another elephant, but Mrs Moore is unwell and Adela is uneasy; even before the catastrophe, Mrs Moore has succumbed to the terrible echo. And although Aziz is discharged at the end of the trial without a stain on his character, the Caves section of the book ends with the arches that were built in Part I broken and in ruins. Ambition and the herd instinct have separated Ronny from Adela, suspicion has turned Aziz against Fielding, Mrs Moore's departure and death have taken her away from Aziz.

Something incomprehensible to both the clear head and the generous heart has entered the experience of the main characters. If significant form dominates the first section of the book, the second is dominated by a negation of form: the confusing echo, and the puzzle of what did happen in the cave to terrify Adela. The manuscript shows that Forster was as puzzled as his readers. When he started the book, he knew only that 'something important' was to occur at the Marabar Caves. In his 1922–4 completion of the story he re-wrote the episode several times, and it is possible to find a rejected version in which Adela suffers actual assault and other rejected passages which imply that she is the victim of a hallucination. It is all a muddle. And muddle was the aspect of Indian life that Forster, like Fielding, could not assimilate. 'There was no place for anything and nothing was in its place,' he wrote in an article published in 1914. 'There was no time either. All the small change of the north rang false, and nothing remained certain but the dome of the sky and the disk of the sun.' It is a theme that often recurs in Forster's uncollected writings on India; and through the letters from Dewas in 1921 there runs a vein of pure distress at the interminable confusion of court life. A similar dislike of muddle makes Fielding and Adela discuss so seriously exactly what can have happened in the cave. They reach no answer, because if an answer exists it is beyond the reach of their 'spiritual tether'. 'Perhaps life is a mystery, not a muddle; they could not tell . . . . They had not the apparatus for judging.' (p. 274) Muddle or mystery, they are both dwarfed by the occurrence. Fielding, as he counts explanations one to four, moves back into the ranks of the Europeans who have ordered that the countless Marabar Caves shall be numbered in white paint: people who range their lives coldly on shelves, weigh their emotions like potatoes, and name a bird not to greet it but to docket it.

Fielding's goodwill, so effective in the first part of the book, is enfeebled and rendered helpless in the second. Although he does not desert his friend, he is not able to prevent the trial, since his own mishandling of the Anglo-Indians bars his access to Adela. It is as if Forster, in the early twenties, were looking back on himself as he had been at the time of his first visit to India, and regretting that he had lost a key he had then held. Friendship between Englishman and Muslim, the descendent of the Nabob and the descendent of the Moghul, could not withstand the racial antagonisms of those round them. Since Amritsar, personal relations were no longer enough:

> 'It is no good', he thought as he returned past the mosque, 'we all build upon sand; and the more modern the country gets, the worse'll be the crash. In the old eighteenth century, when cruelty and injustice rage, an invisible power repaired their ravages. Everything echoes now; there's no stopping the echo. The original sound may be harmless, but the echo is always evil.' This reflection about an echo lay at the verge of Fielding's mind. He could never develop it. It belonged to the universe that he had missed or rejected. And the mosque missed it too. Like himself, those shallow arcades provided but a limited asylum. 'There is no God but God' doesn't carry us far through the complexities of matter and spirit; it is only a game with words, really, a religious pun, not a religious truth. (pp. 286–7)

Response to the echo, then, is the test of the characters' ability to go down to the root and meet India. In one of the many rejected portions of manuscript in the Caves section, Fielding, idly thinking that there might be leopards about, climbs up to inspect a cave. He tests the echo by reciting poetry: first, the opening of *Paradise Lost,* then the first lines of Meredith's 'The Woods of Westermain'—'a poem that he had once admired even more than *Paradise Lost* because it was adventurous and sane, and sang of the triumphs as well as the fall of man'—and lastly Aziz's Persian quatrain about the secret understanding of the heart. The response of course is always 'Boum'. Finally—

> 'Go to Hell!' he shouted and scuttled out like an excitable schoolboy before the avalanche fell. He could hear it smashing onto the empty floor and thought 'Anyhow it missed me that time!' How intimate in comparison was the sky. 'Bad places,' he thought, looking round him at the distended throats. Into that which resembled a cobra's, he chucked a stone, and the same sound gushed out and seemed to mortify the air.

In the book, this is all reduced to 'Fielding ran up to see one cave. He wasn't impressed.' (p. 166) But the rather heavy portentousness of the incident in the manuscript helps us to understand the bafflement of the laudable little party in the face of something which, with some portentousness of our own, we shall have to call the mystery of evil. Adela's experience in the cave—in another manuscript passage it is described as the sensation of something black writhing round her—causes her to become all but absorbed into Anglo-India, whose puritanism is a debased and mindless version of the Miltonic concepts of good and evil. She has lost Ronny's field glasses, the Western scientific instrument that enabled her to see that the distant snake could in fact be nothing but a tree root. Now evil has taken a tangible form, and just as all the denizens of the Civil Station pontificate about the 'evil nature' of Indians, so Adela begins to think of Aziz not as a person but as a Satanic force, a 'principle of evil'.

The Meredith quotation—'Enter these enchanted woods/You who dare'—is personal to Fielding and fits well with his realization that no villain was needed in this particular situation and that Adela's horror can have been self-induced. In 'The Woods of Westermain', nature is paradisial, except for those who bring their own disharmony with them:

> . . . but bring you a note
> Wrangling, howso'er remote
> Discords out of discords spin
> Round and round derisive din.

Personal relations are for Forster oases of order, form, harmony, in a muddled universe, and Meredith's poem is eloquent about these:

> Here the ancient battle ends,
> Joining two astonished friends,
> Who the kiss can give and take
> With more warmth than in that world

Where the tiger claws the snake,
Snake her tiger clasps infurled,
And the issue of their fight
People lands in snarling plight.

Snakes and tigers of course abound in the novel, as if scattered by Forster in mischievous preparation for the symbol-chasers' drag-hunt. Fielding's good sense keeps the creatures in their place. The tiger he meets in the bazaar, from whence the Civil Station expects so much violence, is literally a paper one; the real cobra which he and Aziz meet on their last ride is 'doing nothing in particular' and they leave it room to do it in. Yet brutality does break out from the bazaar after Aziz's release: 'The earth and sky were insanely ugly, the spirit of evil again strode abroad.' (p. 245) Much as Fielding would like to believe that the Russell Viper which invades the college classrooms is doing nothing in particular, he has, by virtue of his official position as Principal, to acknowledge that it could have been brought in by human malice—just as Ronny's official position compels him to try and convict a Pathan for attempted rape. And because of this commonsense recognition that there are human agents for evil acts, Fielding is ready (to the rage of Hamidullah) to consider the possibility of objective evil lurking in a Marabar Cave in the shape of the guide or of a wandering Pathan.

Lastly, there is Aziz's attitude to evil, defined in his tender Persian quatrain. The love of friends is for him more than order, form, harmony; it is a refuge. He has to invent enemies—to see, in Shankara's famous simile, the serpent where there is only a rope—in order to reinforce his friendships. When he plays the protective host, first at the mosque and then at the caves, he conjures up leopards from the Marabar Hills and 'a black cobra, very venomous' in order to assert the strength of the arch he is building against a hostile world. 'Saeed and I got askew slightly,' Forster wote in 1913 after a visit to the Ellora Caves. 'He would guard and order me and invent imaginary perils of beast and reptile.' Aziz's warnings to Fielding about the malice of the police inspector and others arise from a similar protectiveness and possessiveness. The instinct is to exclude; and exclusiveness for a time wrecks the friendship of Aziz and Fielding. Fielding must not be kind to the 'treacherous hideous harridan' if he is to be allowed to remain intimate with Aziz. All invitations exclude somebody; or so think the rational trio, Aziz, Adela, and Fielding.

These characters, who belong to the black on white tradition of Europe and the Near East and who, whether they are Christian, Muslim, or Humanist, are all 'people of the book', live in a universe of moral and aesthetic discriminations. Election of the good implies a repudiation of the bad. Yet to shout 'Go to Hell' at the echo only redoubles it. The arrest of two Indian doctors at Amritsar led to five European deaths, and a brutal attack on Miss Sherwood; these in their turn led to nearly four hundred Indian deaths. So in *A Passage to India* the paper tigers of Mohurram generate a fear that gives scope to the callousness of Callendar, which unleashes a savagery in the crowd. There is 'no stopping the echo'; no stopping, that is, the attribution of evil to everything that we exclude from our own rigorous concept of the good.

4

Fielding's reflections about the echo occur at a stage in the novel's progress when he has brushed against but scarcely been affected by another concept of evil which is increasingly to dominate the work. Professor Godbole's insistence that 'when evil occurs, it expresses the whole of the universe. Similarly when good occurs' (p. 186) exasperates Fielding, because it seems to deny the reality of suffering, particularly the suffering of Adela and of Aziz. In the same way Lowes Dickinson, with whom Forster visited Hindu palaces and temples in 1912, recoiled before 'this refusal to recognise ultimate antagonisms, this "mush" '—much as he had rejected the Platonism of his youth because he felt it ignored the existence of pain. Yet at Chhatapur, Lowes Dickinson was able to attune the Maharajah's metaphysics, which merely embarrassed Forster, to his own knowledge of Platonism, and to speak with him so much 'as one seeker with another' that there, according to Forster's biography of Dickinson, India came near winning. Indeed Dickinson himself admits as much when he ends his expostulations about mush with the question: 'is this, after all, the truest and profoundest vision?' Helped by hearing this talk of the two seekers at Chhatapur, Forster went on himself to discuss religion with the mystically-inclined ruler of Dewas State Senior:

He believes that we—men, birds, everything—are part of

God . . . but when I asked why we had any of us ever been severed from God, he explained it by God becoming unconscious that we were parts of him . . . . Salvation, then, is the thrill which *we* feel when God again becomes conscious of us, and all our life we must train our perceptions so that we may be capable of feeling when the time comes.

I think I see what lies at the back of this—if you believe that the universe was God's *conscious* creation you are faced with the fact that he has consciously created suffering and sin, and this the Indian refuses to believe.

In the novel Godbole, once he has headed Fielding off his irrelevant talk of suffering and brought the discussion back to good and evil, defines evil in terms very close to those used by the Maharajah:

Good and evil are different as their names imply. But, in my own humble opinion, they are both of them aspects of my Lord. He is present in the one, absent in the other, and the difference between presence and absence is great, as great as my feeble mind can grasp. Yet absence implies presence, absence is not non-existence, and we are therefore entitled to repeat 'Come, come, come, come'. (p. 186)

In the reading that, a little before his second visit to India, Forster undertook for his popular account of Hellenic philosophy in *Alexandria: a Guide,* he was struck by the similarities between Eastern and Western mysticism. For the Neo-Platonists, the good was not something to be carved out of life by discrimination; the good was the transforming vision through which a world from which God appeared absent became suddenly filled with the divine presence. In the novel, such a transformation is the shared belief and shared experience of two characters who barely encounter one another, Mrs Moore and Professor Godbole. Godbole is a Brahman and a philosopher. Mrs Moore presumably knows little if anything of either Brahminical thought or the Neo-Platonism of Alexandria, but by birth and temperament she belongs, as her references to Grasmere suggest, to the tradition of English Romantic mysticism. Her current of feeling is represented by Wordsworth's sense of the supernatural in the unifying light that falls over a wide landscape, by Coleridge's mariner blessing the watersnakes by moonlight (much as she herself greets the wasp), by Blake's belief that everything that lives is holy. Her meeting with Aziz in Part I, though it is an election of kindred natures, also has a supernatural sanction: 'God is here.' (p. 22) Over the finite arch of the mosque is the wider arch of the moonlit sky, transfiguring the scene. But India, as the hot season approaches, affords few such visionary gleams; the friendship of Fielding and Aziz is sealed in Aziz's squalid bungalow, in intolerable heat, and Fielding is driven out by Beelzebub's flies from even this poor shrine.

No Grasmere sunrise, no bridal of the earth and sky, occurs on the way to the caves; 'it was as if virtue had failed in the celestial fount'. (p. 144) As the opening chapter has it, the sky settles everything, and the earth can do little by herself. Untouched by heavenly virtue, the landscape of the Marabar Caves is the 'unloving earth, without a throb to answer ours' of Whitman's poem from which Forster took his title. Here Adela and Mrs Moore are both overwhelmed by the caves' echo. For Adela, believing in personal relationships as the highest good and realizing, at the cave's mouth, that she is approaching the consummation of a loveless match with Ronny, it takes the form, whether hallucinatory or not, of a bodily assault. Mrs Moore has always trusted an ultra-personal relationship, the over-arching love of God giving meaning to the love of men; her experience in the caves is of a metaphysical darkness and emptiness, the meaninglessness of matter devoid of spirit.

This is a worse experience than Adela's. Yet Mrs Moore is still able to tell Adela, out of her dejection, 'There are different ways of evil and I prefer mine to yours.' (p. 214) Adela's is the Manichean way of excluding and condemning a part of existence as an irredeemable force of ill. Mrs Moore's way is a vision of life from which God appears so totally withdrawn that she can no longer conceive of his existence. She cannot, however, postulate active evil; she knows Aziz to be innocent, and her mere presence, emptied as it is of all vitality and grace, is enough to check Adela's echo. Though she cannot know it, her desolation is of the kind recognized in both Eastern and Western mysticism as the experience of chosen natures, a prelude to the experience of God. Absence implies presence. 'All those who worship what is not the true cause', states the Isa Upanishad, 'enter into blind darkness; those who delight in the true cause enter, as it were, into greater darkness.' In losing her belief that God will come in another song, Mrs Moore attains an oriental renunciation, just as the Emperor Babur, of whom Aziz has been talking before they enter the caves, renounced his own life in order to save his son's; elsewhere, Forster describes this sacrifice as the one Indian thing in the Muslim ruler's life.

Babur's prayer is answered, and virtue goes out of him into his son. Unobtrusively but persistently, Forster implies that such a transference occurs when the old, frail, and no longer useful Mrs Moore leaves India, to return as a sustaining presence at the trial. We have already seen how much Mrs Moore is alive at the point when Mr Das maintains she does not exist. Aziz and his friends rightly refuse to believe she is dead when they are told so by Fielding; and even the rational Fielding finds himself using her name to conjure Aziz into a further renunciation of the damages which are his due.

In such ways as these the novel opens before the reader the possibility that a sacramental view of life may be better able to overcome the escalation of evil than can the ethical decisiveness of more rational philosophies. 'Truth is not truth in that exacting land unless there go with it kindness and more kindness and kindness again, unless the Word that was with God also is God.' (pp. 254-5) But at Chandrapore, where the educated Indians (like Forster's pre-war Indian friends) are nearly all Muslims, Mrs Moore's affiliation with Eastern thought is not as clear as it needs to be. The presence of Hinduism, for three quarters of the book, has to be implied by the absence of Professor Godbole. He fails to get to the caves, whose echo he alone of the party could have understood and interpreted. Indeed he does begin to interpret it to Fielding, but Fielding is too worried to listen, and when he next turns to the Brahman for counsel—this time about the way his own somewhat boorish behaviour to Ronny has echoed the Anglo-Indians' anger—he finds Godbole has slipped away. At the time of Mrs Moore's transformation into Esmiss Esmoor no clear concept of the Hindu view of life has been put before the reader, and Forster showed his awareness of this in his discovery (recalled in a 1952 interview) that architecturally the book, at the end of the second section, needed a *lump*. Such a lump was to hand in 1921 in Forster's unique experience of the Gokul Ashtami ceremony which he made the opening of the Temple section.

At last we have caught Godbole. Or have we? We see, with a discriminating eye for their absurdity, the twinkling legs and the pince-nez pulled off his nose by the jasmine wreath. But these are not Godbole, any more than the festival's formless, tawdry confusion of sights and sounds is the Hindu religion. At the same time Godbole's thoughts are not Godbole either, for he chants in the presence of God and so moves in god-like power out of himself to invoke other forms of life: a wasp on a stone, and Mrs Moore:

> He was a Brahman, she Christian, but it made no difference, it made no difference whether she was a trick of his memory or a telepathic appeal. It was his duty, as it was his desire, to place himself in the position of the God and to love her, and to place himself in her position and to say to the God, 'Come, come, come, come.' This was all he could do. How inadequate! But each according to his own capacities, and he knew that his own were small. 'One old Englishwoman and one little, little wasp,' he thought, as he stepped out of the temple into the grey of a pouring wet morning. 'It does not seem much, still it is more than I am myself.' (pp. 302–3)

Here Forster also seems to step beyond the bounds of his own personality, beyond the blend of wonder and exasperation which gives his account of the festival such liveliness, to conceive of an experience which is ultra-personal and sacramental: an experience he had met with in the English Romantic tradition, in the Alexandrian Platonists, and in *bhakti* devotional writings of India, but which lay just beyond the reach of his Muslim friends and of himself. Just as at Dewas Forster was profoundly moved by the Birth of Krishna which brought him very close to his Hindu friends, so at Mau, in the presence of the god and of the Esmiss Esmoor called down by Godbole's devout concentration, Aziz and Fielding are restored to one another. Although the section of the novel is called 'Temple', it contains no religious edifice, only a shrine in a corridor; the sacramental reunion takes place, in accordance with the comprehensiveness of the Hindu faith, under a sky which is in full harmony with earth in the beautiful, renewing monsoon: 'The air was thick with religion and rain.' (p.310) In the palace shrine, the forces of evil are transformed to painted yellow tigers and a papier-mâché cobra. The rain dampens the aggressiveness of the bees that drive the English visitors out of the Muslim shrine. We recall the flies, the buzzing and besmirching feelings of racial hostility, that almost drove Fielding away from Aziz's bungalow in Part I; the evil rumours and suspicions that put an end to their friendship in Part II:

'Look at those flies on the ceiling. Why have you not drowned them?'
'Huzoor, they return.'
'Like all evil things.' (p. 290)

But now, in the ritual of the Birth, 'flies awoke and claimed their share of God's bounty'. (p. 302) Things are different at Mau. Fielding has returned, not, as Aziz feared, with Adela, but with Stella and Ralph Moore: shadowy and elusive presences who are yet as effectual as their mother had once been in healing the wounds inflicted by racial arrogance.

Nature has set the scene for a reunion and Mrs Moore has returned through her children. Yet at first Aziz, cut off from all that is happening at the altar, reacts as to a disturbance rather than a benediction. The calling of Mrs Moore's name at the trial rendered Mahmoud Ali hysterical. Now the maiden name of Fielding's wife wakens 'furies' in Aziz. This is Panic, the frantic resentment that flares up at the divine intrusion. It persists in Aziz's hostility towards Ralph at the Guest House, until his bitter remarks are drowned in the gunfire and ceremonial chanting that greet the release of a prisoner. So the chant round the courthouse at Aziz's trial was the prelude to his own release. Still half-resentful of his involuntary response to Mrs Moore's son—'You are an Oriental'—he resumes his former role of host by taking Ralph on the lake to see the conclusion of the Hindu ceremony. But this time, virtue does not fail in the celestial fount. Together they glimpse the wonder of the open shrine, and Aziz hears again, through the procession's invocation of Radha, bride of Krishna, 'the syllables of salvation that had sounded during his trial at Chandrapore'. (p. 327)

Mrs Moore's other child now appears, and precipitates the mock catastrophe that washes away the last bitterness left by the real catastrophe of the Marabar Caves. By a sudden movement towards Aziz at the moment the boats collide, Stella flings the whole party into the healing waters from which Aziz and Fielding emerge with their friendship restored. In the short stay at Mau that follows, Fielding and Stella find their union has been 'blessed'. 'There seemed a link between them at last—that link outside either participant that is necessary to every relationship.' (p. 331) Such is the effect of the Seekers on the laudable little party, that in the end Aziz is even able to write a kind letter to Adela: 'As I fell into our largest Mau tank under circumstances our other friends will relate, I thought how brave Miss Quested was, and decided to tell her so.' (pp. 330-1) There remains just one 'breathing'—to use the Wordsworthian term—from the unseen power:

> Something—not a sight, but a sound—flitted past him, and caused him to re-read his letter to Miss Quested. Hadn't he wanted to say something else to her? Taking out his pen, he added: 'For my own part, I shall henceforth connect you with the name that is very sacred in my mind, namely, Mrs. Moore.' (p. 333)

5

Every fresh reading of *A Passage to India* yields hitherto unobserved instances of Forster's fineness of perception and workmanship, the virtue the Augustans would have termed delicacy. Yet on finishing the book his thought was 'This is a failure'. An imputed failure, in the book's reception, must certainly have seemed possible. Forster knew that the supernatural elements in the novel were bound to cause Bloomsbury some embarrassments. 'Oh Lord,' Roger Fry complained, a little incongruously, 'I wish he weren't a mystic, or that he would keep his mysticism out of his books.' Against such responses Forster took his precautions. He hedged round the miraculous with a profusion of 'natural' explanations, as we have already seen in the instance of Adela's evidence. The shrine opens for Ralph, but Aziz knows it to be the *chhatri* of the Rajah's father; there are plenty of hyenas to collide with the Nawab's car, without the assistance of a ghost. Words like 'telepathy', 'nervous breakdown', 'hallucination' offer handholds for the sceptical reader.

Lightness of tone is another safeguard. Forster shows a Marvell-like skill in placing his flippancies where they will distract our scepticism, so that we are left without a defence against the miraculous and the oracular when they occur. Because Mr Turton has flung open the zinc doors of the station waiting room and manifested himself as a little tin god, we are ready to share Ralph's wonder at the canopied king floating in the darkness. Ronny Heaslop bawls 'Krishna!' into the night and, getting no reply, fines the peon eight annas for his non-appearance; here certainly absence is taken to imply presence. And the belief of the kitchen boy that if he cuts a snake in half it will become two snakes confirms the novel's demonstration that hatred and violence are not merely self-perpetuating but self-propagating as well.

Despite the recoil of some readers from Forster's 'mysticism', the book certainly did not fail in its reception. Yet today, when it has become a classic, critics who are unperturbed by its recognition of unseen powers often express misgivings about the last section. The cause would seem to lie in what Forster omits rather than what he commits. A list of equivalencies may help. First, the stages in Forster's own experience can be set alongside the movements of the novel. Mosque, Caves, Temple: a pre-war visit to India, distress at violence in Flanders, Russia, Ireland, Egypt, and above all in the Punjab as recounted by Malcolm Darling, and then a post-war sojourn in a Native State. To these we may add a series of 'philosophical' equivalents: personal relationships achieved in defiance of collective hatred; collective hatred overwhelming personal relationships; the divine dispelling the collective hatred, and hallowing personal relationships anew. But when we look for the *politique* to lay alongside the *mystique,* as we must do to confirm Dickinson's claim that Forster brings together 'this world and a world or worlds behind', the correspondences break down. The equivalent of the Mosque section is obviously the abrasive dealings between British and Indians in the subcontinent that paid homage to the recently-crowned George V. The Marabar Caves affair is correlative to the Amritsar affair. But the Birth of Krishna has no historical counterpart; it is an experience out of time, occurring in a small princely state that is itself marooned outside of history, on the edge of the Deccan. Before the festival day is out, the Sweepers' Band will have fallen apart into hungry and despised individuals.

There is a real structural flaw here. The tension between surface and depths of which I spoke earlier has culminated in a breaking-up of the surface. The King George V High School has become a granary. We miss Mr Das. It is difficult not to agree with Andrew Rutherford that Forster in his real-life admiration for the Maharajah of Dewas State Senior fails to balance 'the Maharajah's capacity for friendship against the injustice and suffering caused, presumably, by his maladministration'. Not only Marxist critics must feel at times in reading *A Passage to India* that the friendship between an Indian doctor and an English schoolmaster ought to be shown to have some bearing on the lives of the peons and punkah wallahs. 'That link outside either participant that is necessary to every relationship' is after all as much social as spiritual. One wishes both characters had been given a little more professional solidity, since their work can be assumed to have something to do with social change. In a pre-war section of the manuscript we are at least told that Aziz qualified as a doctor in Germany—but only, apparently, to explain his quoting Heine in the original.

If this lack of social substantiality is most felt in the Temple section, the reason may be that Dewas State Senior offered Forster a refuge from political developments that were distasteful to him and that he briefly parodies in Aziz's political slogans at the end. Forster hated imperial domineering but he had no quarrel with imperial domination, so that critics with the advantage of half a century's hindsight have taken him to task for a too easy acceptance of the British right to rule India. A sentence which is often seized upon—oddly, it represents a last-minute alteration—occurs when Mrs Moore ponders her son's lecture to her upon his work: 'One touch of regret—not the canny substitute, but the true regret from the heart—would have made him a different man, and the British Empire a different institution.' (p. 54) Mrs Moore has lived most of her life under the Queen Empress, and might be expected to see things differently from her creator. Yet Forster in his 1922 article 'Too Late' takes exactly Mrs Moore's line when he writes: 'Never in history did ill breeding contribute so much towards the dissolution of an Empire.'

Too late: in 1921–2 Forster sought the racial harmony, that was so hard of attainment in British India, in the eighteenth-century atmosphere of a small Native State. But could it be that he was too early? A little later he might have been able to discover a fusion of religious awareness with political action, for such a fusion was at the heart of Gandhi's fight for independence. If Forster had been able to stay in an ashram rather than in a decaying palace he would have found quite as much absurdity to furnish entertaining letters home; but he might also have discovered, in the Mahatma's doctrine of *ahimsa,* an essentially Indian way of overcoming the echo. Unfortunately, Gandhi in 1921 was still a bogey-man to Forster's Indian and Anglo-Indian friends alike, and Forster's own background and inclinations made it impossible for him to see at that time that the religious consciousness of the *bhakti* and the mystic could operate in the world of telegrams and anger, boycotts and lathi charges. Dewas State Senior in 1921 could not fully counterpoise the horror of Amritsar, and our realization of this gives a deeper meaning to the book's conclusion: not yet, not there. *A Passage to India* cannot be wholly detached from the ten years' experience that underlies it, any more than an Eastern rug can be free of the imperfection that recalls the maker's labours. A flaw in the pattern shows the weaver is less than Allah; in this way, Forster is an Oriental.

THE MARRIAGE OF KRISHNA

NARAYAN'S The Man-Eater of Malgudi

1

'It's the original violence which has started a cycle—violence which goes on in undying waves once started, either in retaliation or as an original starting-ground—the despair of Gandhi—.' These reflections which arise in the course of a small difference between husband and wife in one of R. K. Narayan's novels seem to belong to the world of the Marabar Caves rather than to the placid world of Malgudi. But then this South Indian novelist has been too easily stereotyped by many readers. It has been his misfortune that while his reputation has grown with healthy slowness over his long career as a novelist, his cult has more recently sprung up in an ivy-like fashion beside that reputation and now threatens to smother it in a luxuriant growth.

Several features of his work combine to make him a typical cult novelist. Like Jane Austen, who is similarly dogged by the Janeites, he offers his devotees a topographical security that grows from book to book. We know it all like the backs of our hands: the animated torpor of human and animal life around the fountain in Malgudi's Market Road, the well laid out respectability of the British and post-British 'Extensions', the maze of narrow streets humming with the activity of innumerable printing presses—from one of which, surely, must issue the small drab paperbacks that give us the freedom of this South Indian town. His books afford us too in lavish measure the delight offered by all cult novelists (Dickens being the most prolific example) of encounters with characters whose extraordinariness is, in the inescapable cliché, unforgettable: the Madras rake, for example, who dominates a few pages of *The Bachelor of Arts* before he disappears into the wrong brothel, leaving with us the reverberant phrase, 'Mother is a rare commodity'. The hero of *The Financial Expert,* hunting for red lotus by a lonely pool, sees something stir and shouts 'Who are you?' and the answer comes back: 'I'm Dr Pal, journalist, correspondent and author.' If we are Narayanites we here settle ourselves further into the book, well satisfied; this is what we came for.

Many of these characters are comic in a Shakespearean way: they are encapsulated in, and nourish themselves on, inexhaustible self-delusions. The buoyancy of the old landlord in *Mr Sampath*—a cantankerous miser who fancies himself a Holy Man—is proof against all attempts at deflation:

> He bared his teeth. 'How do you like them?'
> 'Most of them are missing,' Srinivas said.
> 'Never mind the missing ones, but they stayed long enough when they did. . . .'

Not only the characters but also the course of the various stories remind us repeatedly of Shakespearean comedy. The movement is from order to disorder and back again; the characters enter a world of 'distracting illusions and hysterics' which seems, like Forster's world of telegrams and anger, to be real enough at the time, but in retrospect is recognized as *maya,* a dream that hath no bottom. The Bachelor of Arts, desperate with longing for a girl whose horoscope renders her ineligible, drops out of society and wanders as another false Holy Man, until the reality of the village people's veneration awakens him to truth and restores him to his family—and a more suitable bride. The hero of *The Guide* reaches a similar false position after a whole career of confidence tricks. In his new role, he is as fatuous a *guru* as ever booked the Albert Hall: 'What can a crocodile do to you if your conscience is clear and your mind untroubled?' The question is answered when the local crocodile dies in the drought and is found to contain ten thousand rupees' worth of feminine jewellery. But the faith of the villagers compels the Guide, willy nilly, to fast that rain may fall; and we are given to understand that ultimately this is what he wills also, and that, as he becomes a leader in truth, sense is at last given to his nonsensical question. For Narayan shares with some characters of Shakespeare's last plays the belief that the divine powers will, in their own good time, set all to rights, and that in order to grasp this and break free from the nightmare of illusory evil, 'it is required', in the words of *The Winter's Tale,* 'you do awake your faith'. At the end of the autobiographical *The English Teacher,* the narrator's Hermione actually does return, without even a romance's pretence at plausibility, and long after the fire has consumed her body in a scene of unbearable verisimilitude.

Narayan is in short a happy novelist. In the eyes of his devotees the radiant quality of his imagination proceeds from an essentially Indian serenity and detachment; indeed the cult of the novelist is closely associated with the larger cult of oriental otherworldliness that draws Western youth in its hundreds along the overland route to India. The judicious reader, however, as distinct from the devotee, is likely to be less than happy in Narayan's happiness. Confronted by the magnitude of Indian distress, he may even wonder if Narayan does not outdo the complacency of his own characters. 'Never mind the missing ones.' Much is missing, in V. S. Naipaul's view, from Narayan's presentation of Indian life:

> He operates from deep within his society. Some years ago he told me in London that, whatever happened, India would go on. He said it casually; it was a conviction so deep it required no stressing. It is a negative attitude, part of that older India which was incapable of self-assessment. It has this result: the India of Narayan's novels is not the India the visitor sees. He tells an Indian truth. Too much that is overwhelming has been left out; too much has been taken for granted. There is a contradiction in Narayan, between his form, which implies concern, and his attitude, which denies it; and in this calm contradiction lies his magic, which some have called Tchekovian.

But here, V. S. Naipaul makes an antithesis which is open to question. It is hard to see where a writer's attitude can be discovered if it is not to be found in those elements which give his work its form: the tone of his writing and the ordering of his narrative. Narayan's technique as a story-teller is the source of that luminous quality which to his cult-followers is so comforting a sign of his serene fatalism, and to others so uncomfortable a sign of his social unawareness. My purpose here is to try, by a close reading of one of Narayan's best novels. *The Man-Eater of Malgudi*, to demonstrate that the luminosity manifest through the form of the book is in fact the light of genuine social concern. Non-attachment is not indifference; we cannot assume that the older India was incapable of self-assessment, or that the India that 'goes on' does not encompass the Young India that Gandhi exhorted to relentless self-criticism.

2

In saying to Naipaul that India would go on, Narayan meant, he has explained in a recent interview with V. Pandurañga Rao, that India would always remain a cultural unity 'through our sacred books'. And Ved Mehta's account of another interview reveals that in the rhythm of Narayan's working day—routine would be too arid a word—his writing forms a bridge between the hours he strolls through Mysore encountering friend and stranger and the time he spends reading and meditating upon the *puranas.* Of these storehouses of mythology, together with the Great Epic, and the *Ramayana* which he has recently Englished, Narayan writes:

> One read them all through one's life with a fresh understanding at each stage. Our minds are trained to accept without surprise characters of godly or demoniac proportions with actions and reactions set in limitless worlds and progressing through an incalculable time-scale. With the impact of modern literature we began to look at our gods, demons, sages and kings, not as some remote concoctions but as types and symbols, possessing psychological validity even when seen against the contemporary background.

In the hour or so between these two forms of activity, Narayan writes rapidly and revises very little. He is by his own admission 'an inattentive, quick writer', and though he disarmingly quotes in his defence Forster's comments on Eliza Fay—'slapdash people have equal literary rights, provided they write slapdash . . . . She wrote as well as she could, she wrote nothing that she herself was not'—the reader of Narayan has to learn not to be distracted by solecisms and inelegancies. He is inattentive to his medium, to the colouring and connotations of English words, because his attention is focused so unswervingly on the message, the scene before his inner eye. As V. Y. Kantak has well said, 'the flat monotony has the effect of reflecting inner space—the excitement, the rapid crossing of thoughts and feelings'. We are aware of the same kind of attentiveness in much Indian music, in which the performer (and incidentally Narayan is himself a skilful musician), as he improvises, has the air of receiving his music from unheard dictation. And although Narayan never wrestles with words, his method as a writer, far from being slapdash, is one of care and sensitivity.

> He picked up his pen; the sentence was shaping so very delicately; he felt he had to wait upon it carefully, tenderly, lest it should elude him once again: it was something like the very first moment when a face emerges on the printing paper in the developing tray—something tender and fluid, one had to be very careful if one were not to lose it for ever . . . . He poised his pen as if he were listening to some faint voice and taking dictation. He held his breath, for fear that he might lose the thread, and concentrated all his being on the sentence, when he heard a terrific clatter up the stairs. He gnashed his teeth. 'The demons are always waiting around to create a disturbance; they are terrified of any mental concentration.' The printer appeared in the doorway, his face beaming.

Srinivas, whom we here find at work as editor and sole writer of a pugnacious weekly called *The Banner,* is the hero of *Mr Sampath* (in the US, *The Printer of Malgudi*), the first novel to win Narayan acclaim outside India. Though it was published thirteen years before *The Man-Eater of Malgudi,* it is closely related to it; for a further Shakespearean trait in Narayan's work, and one which accompanies the method of composition that he here both describes and illustrates, is a tendency to return to a theme that he has not handled to his entire satisfaction in an earlier book.

Srinivas is a spiritual seeker, questing for a knowledge of the rhythm of life as it is represented in the sandalwood figure of Nataraja, Lord of the Dance:

> It had become a part of him, this little image. He often sat before it, contemplated its proportions, and addressed it thus: 'Oh, God, you are trampling a demon under your foot, and you show us a rhythm, though you appear to be still. I grasp the symbol but vaguely. You hold a flare in your hand. May a ray of that light illumine my mind!'

Throughout the first half of the novel, Srinivas is attempting to gain his equilibrium in the dance; although this is rather a solemn description of a number of very entertaining episodes in which he has to reconcile the claims of friends and family with his love of abstruse speculation. In these episodes, the role of the printer Sampath appears at first to be a helpful one. Srinivas, though he thunders against slum landlords in *The Banner,* scarcely notices that the dwelling to which he has brought his wife is as bad a slum as any; it is Sampath who organizes all the claimants to the rent into rendering the house habitable.

But from the moment that Srinivas thought of the demons and Sampath appeared, we have suspected that this impudent organization man who takes charge of all and sundry and forces them to dance to his own rhythm is, in the symbol that Srinivas cannot grasp without enlightenment, the demon that Nataraja must tread under his feet. In a highly disturbing and Dickensian episode, Sampath takes Srinivas to his house and entertains him by making his four small daughters dance to the harmonium while they sing about Krishna and the cowherds and about Shiva; the scene is a sad travesty of the two great dances of life and of death in Indian mythology. And the mixture of admiration and revulsion that Srinivas feels for Sampath when he sees him among his family characterizes their whole relationship, from the day that Sampath accompanies him to court to register the journal and vigorously tells lies on his behalf.

So it is a bad day for Srinivas when Sampath, who has never sent him a bill, goes out of business as a printer. Before long he has manipulated Srinivas and his artist friend, Ravi, into new careers in his fresh enterprise, a film studio: a world of distracting illusions and hysterics where celluloid and shadows replace solid metal type and the enlightening word. Here the god Shiva is a paunchy actor who has been playing the divine role in films for twenty years, and his consort Parvati is 'a little piece of georgette, powder and curves' who, significantly, has been employed because she is the exact likeness of the ideal (and so in Indian terms *real*) beauty envisaged by the romantic Ravi. Before long, 'Shiva' has walked out in a temper, and the irrepressible Sampath has stepped into his role. But the gods are not mocked, and the particular mythological subject, the Burning of Kama (Eros) by the fiery eye of Shiva, proves a dangerous choice. If Shiva in his manifestation as Nataraja dances the dance of creation, he is also the Destroyer who dances the dance of destruction: mad with desire for his false beauty, Ravi runs berserk and breaks up the studio.

When Srinivas, some days later, secures Ravi's release from the police, the police inspector asks him casually what happened to *The Banner*. The question has the effect of leading Srinivas back into the dance of life as, 'looking at the point of light in the inspector's belt-buckle, which caught a ray of light from the shop opposite', he puts behind him the chaos of false relationships that the film studio represented, and answers: 'If I had a press, I could start it tomorrow.' The inspector helps him find a new printer, one who keeps to his right steps and place in the scheme of things; and back in this real world Srinivas can continue to seek his own equilibrium between involvement and non-attachment. As for Sampath, he is left at the end with the film abandoned and his bounciness deflated. His role has been that of the demon Ravana, of whom Narayan has written elsewhere that 'he attempted to move Mount Kailas, where Shiva was consorting with his wife; Shiva answered his masterly impudence by steadying the swaying mountain, pressing it down with his toe, so that Ravana was caught under it and shouted for life, recognizing after all a superior force in Shiva.'

So in *Mr Sampath* Narayan bridges the two worlds of Malgudi and of Mount Kailas: the disturbance of Srinivas's quest for the good life by Mr Sampath, and the havoc wrought among the gods by the demons or *rakshasas.* It is a *tour de force,* but one leaving us a little too aware of the amount of force that has been used. Srinivas is over-explicit about his search for the underlying rhythm, there is something a trifle facile about the introduction of mythology through its preposterous handling in the Indian cinema, and the word 'symbol' occurs rather too often. Sampath conceals his non-existent staff behind a curtain which reminds the fascinated Srinivas of the holy of holies in the temple: 'There was a symbolism in it: it seemed to be expressive of life itself.' Such insistence suggests that vehicle and tenor do not exactly fit, and need constant adjustment by the author. In colour-printing terms, the registration is not quite right.

Mr Sampath, in particular, is not demonic enough. In spite of elaborate attempts to associate him with the tiger and the snake which, with the legendary demon, comprised the power of darkness subdued by the Lord of the Dance, Mr Sampath remains more of a man misled into a world of illusions than a creator of illusion himself. One reason for this is that he was modelled on the real-life printer of Narayan's journal, *Indian Thought.* To some degree Narayan has incorporated the more bumptious side of this personage into Mr Sampath, reserving his more likeable traits for Nataraj in *The Man-Eater of Malgudi.* But he is too gentle a writer to turn even a difficult acquaintance into a *rakshasa.* In consequence, Mr Sampath lacks definition as the modernizing disturber and oppressor of traditional Indian life, and has to be provided with such auxiliaries as Shilling, the British bank manager, and De Mello the Hollywood director. Thirteen years later, Narayan returns to his theme with a story that affords a much better objective correlative. Moreover, in this later novel, *The Man-Eater of Malgudi,* he gives his tale a social and political dimension which firmly connects the surface and the depths, the mundane and the mythological.

3

The first chapter of *The Man-Eater of Malgudi* admits us to the small and secure world of the printer Nataraj. Continuity in stability is the theme of the opening paragraphs: the Albert Mission School attended by Nataraj's son must have been there since the days of the Prince Consort; the kitchen fire has been aglow for generations; Deepavali recurs as reassuringly as the European Christmas; the press parlour has been furnished with substantial Victoriana 'resurrected from our family lumber room'. Nataraj's moderately prosperous, moderately busy life is shared between three places. First, there is the press on Market Street which comprises a parlour where his friends the poet and the journalist pass their ample free time, a printing shop in which most of the work is done by 'my well-wisher (I dare not call him staff) Sastri', and an empty attic upstairs. Secondly, there is the old family house in Kabir Street, just behind Market Road, occupied since the break-up of the large, clannish family only by Nataraj, his wife and small son. Third, and in some ways the most important, is the river at the end of Kabir Street, where every dawn Nataraj performs his ablutions with brahminical care. In going to and from the river, Nataraj has his 'well-defined encounters'; it is a term that may cover all the social transactions between Malgudi characters in the book's early chapters. Nataraj's negotiations with his customers, or the prolonged ritual of his bargaining with the old wastepaper merchant, are typical of the delicate social adjustments that everyone is adept at making in this stable and circumscribed community.

Now the personal and social orderliness of this world is disrupted by the intrusion of H. Vasu, M.A., Taxidermist. He starts by breaking an accepted taboo when he thrusts his head through the blue curtain of Nataraj's printing shop, and he goes on as he has begun by trampling on all the Malgudi proprieties. By the end of the second chapter he has installed himself and his taxidermical gear in Nataraj's attic. His next act is to snatch Nataraj away from his morning's work and rush him off in his jeep to the hill village from which he proposes to track the tiger he so much resembles.

It is on this drive to Mempi that the exact nature of Vasu's bullying aggression declares itself. For him people, in a way that is clean contrary to the Malgudi ethos, are means not ends. 'More people will have to die on the roads, if our nation is to develop any road sense at all!' he exclaims as villagers jump for their lives out of the jeep's path (p. 38); both the practice and the theory are startling innovations on an Indian country road, where men, beasts, and machines adjust to each other's claims in well-defined (if sometimes vituperative) encounters. And Vasu rides in an equally roughshod way over the proprieties of family life. Children, since they can be of no use to him, he ignores. As for marriage: 'You don't have to own a coffee estate because you like to have a cup of coffee now and then.' (p. 38) His rhetorical questions expose his determination to make humanity dance to his own tune. ' "You want to know about me?" he asked. I wonder what he would have done if I had said, "No, I prefer to go home and eat my food." ' And again: ' "Can you guess his age?" (I wanted to say that I could do so unerringly.)' We rejoice when Nataraj refuses to play this particular game. ' "You want to know what I'll do next?" "No, I'm not interested, I'm busy." ' (pp. 15–16, 31, 103) Vasu's questions demote people to ventriloquists' dolls and so help him to affirm that 'He was the lord of the universe, he had no use for other people's words.' (p. 37)

Above all, Vasu makes use of Nataraj, whose life he invades. One of his first acts is to introduce a forest ranger to him in the hope that, if Nataraj prints the forester's manuscript, the forester will provide the big game licence that Vasu covets. The forester however proves incorruptible. But Nataraj is fascinated by the bully, and while half his nature cries out in protest the other half is only too ready to be made use of. Narayan hints at deep-reaching causes for the resultant love-hate relationship which is so brilliantly and comically developed in the first half of the novel. Perhaps because his father was a withdrawn recluse and all the uncles of his childhood removed themselves overnight in the break-up of the extended family, Nataraj quickly develops a father-fixation on Vasu. He wants to be noticed, even if it means being bullied, and his regression is rapid. When, as the result of Vasu's snatching him away with no money on him, he finds himself anna-less and hungry in Mempi, he eyes a brown bun and appeals to Vasu 'pathetically like a child at a fair tugging at the sleeve of his elder'. Even when Vasu, still in occupation of the attic, has shown that he has no further use for Nataraj and has actually had a summons served upon him, Nataraj suffers wretchedly from this hostility: 'I stood like a child at the treadle, hoping that he would look at me and nod and that all would be well again. He was a terrible specimen of humanity, no doubt, but I wanted to be on talking terms with him.' (p. 94)

No less masochistic are Nataraj's fantasies of being kidnapped when he is carried off to Mempi; or his subsequent obsession, with which he terrifies both his wife and his son, that Vasu is going to kidnap the child. Narayan has a way of confronting his readers with the kind of regressive fantasy they are least ready to acknowledge as their own. But Nataraj's fears afford more than a shock of recognition. They represent his descent into a world of illusion, a kind of anti-creation lorded over by Vasu. The situation is perfectly plain to everybody else: Vasu's presence is intolerable, he is exploiting Nataraj's good nature, and he must be told to go. The Sanitary Inspector says so, when he comes about the appalling stink resulting from Vasu's taxidermy. The forester says so, when he comes to investigate Vasu's poaching activities. Sastri says so; as a pious Hindu, he is particularly affronted by the stuffed carcases on the staircase behind the press and by the prostitutes who go up and down the stairs, once Vasu's expeditions to the forest have been checked by the forester and he has 'turned his tracking instinct in another direction'. And the old man whose grandson's dog has been wilfully shot by Vasu also says that Vasu must go. It is indicative of Nataraj's demoralization that he is not even able to find a puppy to console the grandson. Nataraj has gone to pieces. He abandons himself to envious fantasies of Vasu's sexual prowess while all the real work of the press falls on Sastri's frail shoulders.

At this point Sastri, the 'orthodox-minded Sanskrit semi-scholar', whose name, as Edwin Gerow reminds us, means 'Doctor' or 'learned', introduces a new perspective into the half-told tale. To Sastri, seeing events in their eternal aspect, Vasu is a *rakshasa,* 'a demonic creature who possessed enormous strength, strange powers, and genius, but recognized no sort of restraints of man or God'. And he recalls various stories from the epics and *puranas* which, for an Indian reader, must certainly endow the story with an anagogical significance. Now we realize the timeliness of Sastri's departure from the press just before Vasu thrusts his face through the blue curtain; and that face, with its 'large powerful eyes under thick eyebrows, a large forehead and a shock of unkempt hair, like a black halo', takes on a striking resemblance to the faces of demons in Indian paintings. A previous Narayan hero, Sriram of *Waiting for the Mahatma*, was led astray from Gandhi's path of truth by just such a being, in the form of a terrorist working for that most illusory of independence movements, the Indian National Army. And both Vasu and Jagadish in *Waiting for the Mahatma* are typical demons in being 'strong-minded, intelligent, and capable of offering arguments to establish they are righteous'—to quote from Narayan's own account of the powers of darkness in *Gods, Demons, and Others.*

Vasu's occupation confirms his demonic nature. *Rakshasas* eat raw flesh and drink blood; and to Nataraj, who has been brought up quite literally never to hurt a fly, Vasu's indiscriminate slaughter of anything with wings or four legs is deeply repugnant. Moreover, the mythologists tell us that *rakshasas* animate dead bodies. In exercising his skill at making dead animals look as if they were still alive, Vasu is at the demiurge's task of producing an illusory cosmos: 'This man had set himself up as a rival to Nature.' (So Mr Sampath had proclaimed: 'We will make stars, if the ready-made ones are not available.') In *The Man-Eater of Malgudi,* Nataraj is particularly outraged when Vasu shoots and stuffs an eagle, because this is a bird sacred to Vishnu, Protector of all creatures; Garuda, the eagle of mythology, was put out of action by Mahista, one of the demons named by the learned Sastri. Another he names is Ravana, the mighty demon of the *Ramayana* whose defeat at the hands of Vishnu's avatar Rama is traditionally interpreted as the overcoming of darkness by light.

Vasu is indeed what Nataraj calls him towards the end of the story, a prince of darkness. Once we have grasped this we feel the force of the brahminical prayer to the rising sun for illumination, which Nataraj recites each morning at the river, and which furnishes a more natural and less obtrusive alignment of the hero on the side of truth than does Srinivas's prayer to Nataraja in *Mr Sampath.* In *The Man-Eater of Malgudi.* the hero is actually called after the Lord of the Dance. Vasu's name has a variety of meanings. It can suggest 'a ray of light' or even 'the sun', but its predominant meanings are 'wealth' and 'power.' Perhaps the phrase 'the power and the glory' can suggest the spell that Vasu casts over Nataraj, causing him in the first half of the novel to follow a false light and to move to a rhythm other than that of the dance of life. In consequence, he finds himself alienated from the harmonious relationships of an ordered society. Only Sastri continues to sustain that social activity of which the press is a pleasing symbol; he works away behind the blue curtain, no party to the chatter about Five Year Plans that goes on in the parlour.

Not that the Five Year Plan under discussion is irrelevant to Narayan's purpose. It belongs to that third dimension which gives this novel a substantiality lacking in *Mr Sampath*. Between the two novels, Narayan attempted, bravely if not wholly successfully, a novel about Gandhi and the independence movement. Its hero, having embarked on the way of *ahimsa,* loses his protective grandmother, the old hidebound Indian traditions (though Granny does not die—her toes begin to wriggle on the funeral pyre, and she fades away to Benares). But he is at last found worthy, after many trials, of the hand of Bharati, or Mother India. As this summary suggests, the political allegory rather edges out the comedy of human relationships on one side and on the other the romance of mythological events, both of which had come together so effectively in *Mr Sampath.* But *Waiting for the Mahatma* at least attuned Narayan's readers to the third dimension of *The Man-Eater of Malgudi,* of which V. Panduranga Rao writes: 'To us in India the novel is an allegory of the coming of modernity to India and more particularly to South India.'

Nehru's Five Year Plans for Indian industrialization undertook the formidable task of changing the age-old mode of existence of a subcontinent. The Man-Eater is convinced he is a necessary part of this awakening; the connection between Narayan's hilarious fable and the political world is made from time to time in a way that is no less firm for being funny. Vasu, thwarted of his big game, stuffs little animals, and Nataraj comments that he 'seemed to have turned his attention to small things in keeping with our

Government's zeal for small industries'. (p.216) There is no doubt, moreover, that Malgudi needs to be roused from its torpor—the Sanitary Inspector has cause to feel discouraged—and that Nataraj needs to be prodded out of his groove. Nataraj's comfortable existence is largely made up, as are many middle-class lives in India and elsewhere, of a pattern of what the anthropologists call avoidance relationships. It is a salutary experience for him to be rushed away in Vasu's jeep and dumped down, without a coin in his pocket or a button in his shirt, in Mempi village, where he must rely on alms to obtain tea and fly-smirched buns and a bus ride home:

> I sat there and no one noticed me: arms stretched right over my head for glasses of tea; sometimes brown tea trickled over the side of the glass tumbler and fell on my clothes . . . . I wanted to do and say anything I could to please this man, whom at normal times I'd have passed as just another man selling tea in unwashed tumblers. (pp.46,48)

Nataraj's fastidiousness is often a withdrawal from life. He shudders at the toddy-palm's smell of fermenting juices, destined for the 'low taverns' of the city, but he cannot get away from the tree because it overhangs the spot on the river which is most convenient for his ritual purification.

Yet while we recognize Nataraj's over-exclusiveness, we recognize too that Vasu's violent onslaught may not be the best or the only method of curing it. A much worse stench than the smell of toddy emanates from Vasu's workshop, and his insistence that this is the smell of progress impresses us no more than it does Nataraj: 'I was appalled at his notion of democracy as being a common acceptance of bad odours.' (p. 63) There were many like Nataraj in India in the fifties and sixties who recoiled before the programme of industrialization, not because they were obscurantists, but because they felt it to be a betrayal of the Gandhian ideal of development from the grass-roots level.

The Man-Eater of Malgudi appeared a year after the initiation of the Third Five Year Plan. An even more up-to-date allusion in the novel occurs at the beginning of the chapter in which Nataraj tries to head the old grandfather off the subject of the shot dog, but is defeated in this aim by Sastri's stern reminders of the facts of the case. ' "Now is the testing time for Nehru," the journalist was saying. "If the Chinese on our border are not rolled back—".' (p. 88) The Chinese invasion of 1962 was a profound shock to those who had put their trust in Nehru's decade-long policy of Peaceful Co-existence, which the journalist Sen is presumably criticizing when he talks about the government's 'drift'. Up to that time there was a widespread popular admiration for China's successful 'Westernization', similar to Nataraj's fascination with Vasu's purposefulness. Nataraj should be, but is not, warned by Vasu's story of how he—like China—turned against his own instructor in the art of self-defence. The forester argues vigorously but without effect to rescue Nataraj from the spell Vasu has cast over him. He has better success in curtailing Vasu's activities in the jungle. And the forester is only one of a number of lean men in khaki who represent the forces of law and order in the novel. Up in the hills to the north of Malgudi—as was happening in fact at the time, much further north and in much higher hills—a lot of men like him check the predator's career of destruction and plunder. The forester's collection of Golden Thoughts seems a good joke of a slightly Hurree Babu tinge: 'He had culled epigrammatic sentiments and moralizings from every source—*Bhagavad-Gita, Upanishads,* Shakespeare, Mahatma Gandhi, the Bible, Emerson, Lord Avebury and Confucius—and had translated them into Tamil.' (p. 33) Yet this *pot-pourri* of Eastern *dharma* and Western duty, if it scarcely deserves the name of an ideology, lends plenty of power to the forester's elbow.

But *The Man-Eater of Malgudi* is not an Indian *Animal Farm.* Its political allegory can change aim with Swiftian rapidity, and much that may be read as the story of Chinese Communist aggression may equally well serve as a satire upon Western neo-colonial activities in India. Vasu's jeep is the vehicle of an invading army, but it is also to be associated with another army of experts bringing Aid to India. And Vasu's taxidermy is the perfect equivalent for those tourist-orientated industries which are the bane of the Third World. As Nataraj overcomes his natural revulsion against Vasu's stuffing of shot animals, he begins to display an awe of industry for industry's sake. He has no idea where Vasu's markets are, is uncritical of the fact that his is a one-man concern, and echoes, with a rich fatuity, all the P.R.O. phrases: 'From this humble town of Malgudi, stuffed carcasses radiate to the four corners of the earth. . . .' (p. 67)

Whether neo-imperialism operates from East or West, it finds a ready tool in Nataraj, who as printer has always been ready to leave the big undertakings to the foreign expert—the original Heidelberg next door. The comedy of personal relationships is linked to the political satire in the way Vasu's assumption of superiority ('He was pleased to think that humanity could move only after securing a clearance certificate from him') (p. 134) dovetails with Nataraj's sense of inferiority, his 'colonial mentality'. Between them, the two characters act out the psychological processes of colonial rule as they have been analysed by Mannoni and others. Twice in earlier novels Narayan has touched upon the tensions of a dependency relationship: in Sriram's encounter with a pleasant English planter in *Waiting for the Mahatma,* and in Srinivas's encounter with an unpleasant English bank manager in *Mr Sampath.* Like these heroes, Nataraj, in his dealings with Vasu, fluctuates between shrillness and servility: exactly the behaviour that, before independence, the British criticized in their Indian subjects, without any recognition that it was a form of conduct that arose from the colonial situation itself. Nataraj even begins to show that most depressing by-product of the dependency relationship, a tendency to bully other people in compensation for being bullied.

For a novel which affords to one of its critics 'the somewhat unnerving spectacle of an obviously gifted novelist writing about nothing', *The Man-Eater of Malgudi* must appear to be yielding here a bumper crop of meanings—as many, in fact, as were coaxed out of Scripture by the Schoolmen. But equally elaborate exegesis is still the practice of Sanskrit scholars, and I believe that in Narayan's fiction the meanings are none the less present because they are so gracefully unobtrusive. Two things ensure this reticence: first, the narrative tone, 'style' in its widest sense, which is as pellucid as glass bubbled here and there with a mild jokiness, and so seems to disclaim all portentousness and even profundity. Secondly, the three meanings fit deftly together, without any awkward smudging or overlap, like the colours in the labels for soft-drink bottles that Nataraj and Sastri are endeavouring to print from the beginning to the end of the book. In a normally alert reading, we experience only the psychedelic gaiety of the finished printing: the hilarious tale of Nataraj's difficulties as he comes to be looked at askance as 'joint owner of the poaching and stuffing factory'. The three-colour effect is even more striking in the second half of the novel, as events develop, come to a crisis, and are resolved.

4

The second part of *The Man-Eater of Malgudi* begins with a visitor whom Nataraj, lost as he now is in a world of illusions, at first fails to recognize. Then he realizes he is Muthu from the tea-shop in Mempi, and overwhelms him with questions about his affairs and family: 'in order to cover my initial lapse I now tried to show off my knowledge of his problems'. (p. 113) This is reassuring. We are taking a step back towards the world of careful social adjustments. We are further reassured when Muthu refuses payment for the tea he gave Nataraj at Mempi. The relationship he has come to claim is not commercial but communal. He wants the educated man from the city to help solve a village problem: how to cure a sick elephant.

This cannot be referred to the original Heidelberg next door, and Nataraj has to make a move out of the state of mental and moral inertia to which he has been reduced by the presence of Vasu. His first move is one which, unlike the terrifying jeep ride with Vasu, demands what is for Nataraj considerable physical effort. He pedals a borrowed bicycle to the surgery of Dr Joshi, who has been trained and equipped by the World Quadruped Relief League, Calif. Here is the right kind of Aid, designed to help India's rural economy. Moreover it is given in a co-operative spirit; the local organizations have to provide the buildings for an animal hospital. But owing to a delay in the printing of invitations to the foundation ceremony ('I wonder where they got them printed,' Nataraj muses), none of this Indian support has materialized and the vet, who has yet to see a cow, sits idle and useless in his dusty compound next to the crematorium. True to the right principles of Aid in the teeth of all these discouragements, he does not assume total responsibility even for the temple elephant. It is up to Nataraj to go to Mempi and get the elephant back to Malgudi.

The elephant, whose name is Kumar, or Faith, is lying down and shows no inclination to move; moreover an element in the temple committee refuses to let it be moved. (We later discover this element to be in league with Vasu, who probably poisoned the elephant; the political allegory is very near the surface here.) Faced with 'an immobile elephant, an equally immobile doctor and a mentally immobile committee', Nataraj feels desperate: 'there seemed little to do except pray for the elephant'. (p. 124) He is right in this. In doing the little he can, he has performed his steps in the dance, his *dharma,* and the rest must be left to the Goddess of Good Fortune. The opposition is providentially called away and a mahout no less providentially arrives. The elephant rises and trots away towards Malgudi, and Muthu runs back to the temple to thank the Goddess. It was required that Nataraj should awake his Faith, so that life could get moving again.

This development does not please Vasu, who roars up in his jeep and attempts once again to take charge of Nataraj, though with considerably less success than heretofore. Having been foiled in his plan of shooting and looting tigers—or, in other words, in straight exploitation—he now strikes a favourite neo-colonialist attitude, and presents himself to Nataraj and his friends as a conservationist. For this we may read a patron, or rather a patronizer, of indigenous culture for his own dubious ends. In this new role he offers help in collecting money for the festival which is to take place at the Krishna temple to celebrate the completion of the poem about Krishna and Radha (in monosyllabic verse) which Nataraj and Sastri have been printing for their friend the poet. 'Offers' is perhaps not the word for Vasu's behaviour. He starts by handing his well-filled purse to Nataraj, claims it back some days later, takes over the subscription file with vague talk of astronomical sums, and fends off any requests for advance payments with 'keep your expenses down. Don't imagine you are millionaires'. (p. 151) Anyone who has ever been at the receiving end of a certain kind of Aid programme will follow this allegory without difficulty and with positive glee.

Vasu's fatherly interest in Festivals of the Arts is of course a cover-up for his real activities. He is still on Kumar's track, and Nataraj is horrified to discover that the Man-Eater intends to shoot the elephant during the procession that will follow the temple celebration:

> I can make ten thousand out of the parts of this elephant—the tusks, if my calculation is right, must weigh forty pounds, that's eight hundred rupees. I have already an order for the legs, mounted as umbrella stands, and each hair on its tail can be sold for twelve annas for rings and bangles; most women fancy them

> and it's not for us to question their taste. My first business will be to take out the hairs and keep them apart, while the blood is still hot; trunk, legs, even the nails—it's a perfect animal in that way. Every bit of it is valuable. I've already several inquiries from France and Germany and from Hong-Kong. (pp. 173-4)

Only an economic adviser or a demon from the *Ramayana* could conceive of an elephant dispersed into bangles and umbrella stands as a perfect animal.

To keep Vasu to his own part of the press building, an iron grille has been erected between the staircase and the printing shop, and a thickly-woven bamboo mat hung over it. It says much for Narayan's deftness that even this bold political allegory is far from blatant. Nataraj, still fascinated by the world of demonic illusions, cannot resist peeping through a hole in the iron and bamboo curtains, by means of which he can from time to time glimpse 'a lovely circular vision of a hyena's snout or the legs of some woman or the hefty feet of Vasu himself stumping upstairs'. (p.137) Through this iron grille, on the eve of the festival, the temple prostitute, Rangi, whispers the news of Vasu's plan to shoot the elephant. Is she the beautiful spy passing information of an impending invasion? The thought barely intrudes because we are so much enjoying the cross-purposes of the encounter at the psychological level. Nataraj is convinced that Rangi wants to seduce him, and he is only too ready to be seduced; but the key of the grille is in the parlour where Sastri and the poet, guardians of morality, are snatching an hour's sleep. Rangi, in any case, is not the glamour girl of Nataraj's fantasies: 'She sat down on the last step, took out of the folds at her waist a pouch and from it a betel-nut and leaf and two inches of tobacco, put them into her mouth and started chewing.' (p.159) She is concerned with Nataraj only as he is a possible means of saving the elephant, now living in the compound of the temple. She belongs to the real world of the gods and not the illusory world of the demons; to Nataraj's fevered gaze she appears a figure from temple sculptures, or even 'a goddess carved out of cinder'. And here we recall the third of the demons named by Sastri, Bhasmasura, who was overcome by Vishnu in his most surprising avatar as the beautiful dancing girl Mohini, equated by the commentators with Lust. The divine can manifest itself through many channels: sometimes through one whose *dharma* is to be a prostitute.

Nataraj has grown in initiative since the day he got the elephant on to its feet. He is up all night on the eve of the festival, completing the printing of the poem. On the day, he is here, there, and everywhere, organizing events with an energy that makes him a real lord of the dance, as his wife tartly indicates: 'now I have your breakfast on the fire, and I know how you will dance for it and make us dance who serve you, the moment you come out of the bathroom'. (p.167) But the better Nataraj's organization, the more surely he is playing into Vasu's hands. Not only does the destruction of Kumar appear inevitable, but also, since a stampede will have to be caused to justify the shooting, the deaths of a number of people in the vast and happy crowd. Nataraj enters the temple 'obsessed with plans' to save these lives.

The account of the temple ceremony is a compelling piece of writing: the Marriage of Krishna, avatar of Vishnu, described by Professor Godbole himself. Much the same confusion prevails as in Forster's novel. The Mayor, as he likes to be called, has to deliver his speech against the thunder of drums from the temple; children rush back and forth between the two ceremonies, screaming with joy and trying to snatch the fruit offerings from the feet of the gods. There is, one suspects, the same tawdriness that offended Forster in the dressed-up images and in Rangi's clumsy dancing before them, and probably little architectural merit in the temple built in the sixties of the last century. But the tawdriness and the confusion are not there for Nataraj, who is swept up, as never before in his 'circumscribed life', in the transfiguring happiness of the crowd—the happiness Forster also sensed in the Gokul Ashtami ceremony at Dewas State Senior and sought to express in *A Passage to India.* It does not really matter that the story of Krishna's marriage with Radha is chanted 'incoherently and cacophonously', for the recitation itself, as J. Gonda tells us, is of great liturgical power:

> The constant celebration of God's love for Radha, that is, for the prototype of the human soul, wrought by the post-Caitanya poets into a model of perfection, came to be, beside bhakti and the chanting of songs recounting God's deeds, a means of attaining salvation. Hearing the sacred history is indeed the best means of attaining God himself.

By these means—the sense of community, the eloquence of the

sacred writings—Nataraj is truly carried into the dance, into a reality in which Vasu is only 'an irrelevant thought'. At the recollection of how Vishnu saved the elephant Gajendra, all his anxiety is transmuted to faith in his cry to the God to save Kumar and those whose lives are in danger.

Like Adela's moment of illumination in Forster's novel, this seems to the bystanders a nervous collapse. And on one level of the story this is what it is. Nataraj is exhausted, and must be hurried home to rest and recover. The chapter that follows captures the detachment of convalescence, of lying at a distance from important events as the day passes and a fading light moves up the wall. Kumar's safety now rests with the God, and Nataraj, having acted his destined part or *dharma,* should be able to free himself from all concern with the outcome of his actions.

But this he cannot do. Anxiety grows afresh as the evening advances, and the friends who have made a last attempt to dissuade Vasu return dejected, having been met only with brutality. The hours before midnight are ruled by the demons, and the procession is to start at eleven. In the event, it starts three hours late; this may be a Forsterian muddle—or it may be that protective powers are looking after Kumar. They do not need any further action from Nataraj, who none the less finds himself compelled to creep into the attic, where he makes out the figure of Vasu at the window, his gun at the ready. His head full of film-struck fantasies, Nataraj picks up the gun as the procession approaches—only to drop it in terror and flee as Vasu's alarm clock goes off.

Nataraj is not needed to play the role of giant-killer because the giant has already killed himself:

> Then there was Bhasmasura [Sastri had said at the end of the first half of the book], who acquired a special boon that everything he touched should be scorched, while nothing could ever destroy him. He made humanity suffer. God Vishnu was incarnated as a dancer of great beauty, named Mohini, with whom the *asura* became infatuated. She promised to yield to him only if he imitated all the gestures and movements of her own dancing. At one point in the dance Mohini placed her palms on her head, and the demon followed this gesture in complete forgetfulness and was reduced to ashes that very second. (pp. 96-97)

Mohini-Rangi is the only witness of Vasu's end. He forces her to keep watch for him in the mosquito-ridden attic, fanning the insects from his face while he sleeps. Worn out by her temple dancing, she falls asleep also, to be wakened by a shout of exasperation from Vasu. He brings the whole strength of his palms down on his forehead—and ends the career of H. Vasu, taxidermist.

Does Narayan get away with it? There is of course good literary precedent for such spontaneous combustion, but to quote *Bleak House* scarcely justifies the device. It is however the measure of Narayan's ability to make us share his world-view that this outrageous dénouement seems not only very funny but also right and true. The 'facts' about Vasu's death are saved up for the very end of the book, and are revealed to us after a period of great confusion in which Vasu's diabolical influence seems to linger; Nataraj is shunned as a suspected murderer, and he himself, characteristically enough, begins to wonder if he did in fact kill Vasu. From this nightmarish situation, parodying the pseudo-realism of the European detective novel, we are freed when Sastri reveals the truth. Sastri slipped away at the point where police enquiries began, much as Professor Godbole slipped away during the Marabar Caves affair, because wisdom can have no dealings with the *maya* of evidence and witnesses. But he returns in his role of guardian to free Nataraj from his last lingering fantasies and to bring him back into the rhythm of existence by a determined effort to complete the printing of the soft drink labels. 'Yes, Sastri, I am at your service,' says Nataraj; the service of reality now, and not of illusion which has been dispelled because 'Every demon carries within him, unknown to himself, a tiny seed of self-destruction, and goes up in thin air at the most unexpected moment. Otherwise what is to happen to humanity?' (p. 242)

The social and political dimension of *The Man-Eater of Malgudi,* even more than the religious dimension, has the merit of making a Narayanite reading of the novel untenable. The 'total acceptance' of which V.S.Naipaul speaks is there as a religious acceptance of what life will demand; but there is no acceptance of dirt, corruption, procrastination, and social indifference. The Adjournment Lawyer, to whom Nataraj turns for advice in the confusion that arises over the tenancy of the attic, is a touchstone for our reading. 'This hopeless tangle is "solved" in the only Indian way possible, by the adjournment lawyer—that is, by postponing and postponing the crisis,' writes Edwin Gerow, in an essay that throws an understanding light on the tale's mythological aspects, but does not refer to its historical placing. But far from being an integral part of traditional society, the Adjournment Lawyer presents himself to Nataraj, returning from his morning purification, as another man-eater: 'When I saw him in the distance I cried to myself, "I am undone, Mr. Adjournment will get me now."' (p.5) And his advice not to mix accounts, though it enables him indefinitely to put off paying Nataraj's bills, is, as Nataraj discovered, 'rather a coarse lesson' to teach a society where one good turn deserves another.

Far from condoning the stagnation of traditional life, *The Man-Eater of Malgudi* offers a fable for the developing world. Traditional India, the novel makes plain, needs to be awakened out of its stagnation, but not by Vasu's methods nor with Vasu's intentions. Nothing but harm can come of imposing alien political philosophies and economic aims on India; what is required is growth from the grass roots. As in Julius Nyerere's fable of the centipede, all the legs need to move a little, and then the body politic will find that it is on the march.

There is no incompatibility between this appeal to 'get up and go' and the belief that the powers of social and moral disorder are self-destructive. 'Evil on itself shall back recoil/And mix no more with goodness': the seventeenth century could combine this Miltonic certainty with political radicalism. And the puritan ethic of a later generation blended surprisingly well with the Indian concept of *dharma*—which is one reason why Kipling, contrary to all Western expectation, has many Indian admirers. The educations of Gandhi and of the South Indian leader C. Rajagopalachari—like Narayan, a Tamil Brahman—were a mixture of the two traditions. Narayan himself grew up in a home 'crammed' with the works of Ruskin and Carlyle, and Ruskin's writings contributed almost as much as the Indian sacred books to Gandhi's formulation of the 'Victorian' virtues of industry, sobriety, punctuality, devotion to duty, which in the novel are embodied in the figure of Sastri.

But while Indian thought was receptive to the gospel of work, it in its turn, by virtue of its belief that men should perform right actions without seeking the fruit of action, took the strain out of puritan effort and the self-righteousness out of Victorian energy. The conviction that we need to care and not to care propels

Narayan's gentle mockery of his characters' anxieties as his novel approaches its crisis. And the resolution of that crisis, in a way that is once again Shakespearean, puts human endeavour in its proper perspective. A serene and enlightening wisdom in the end makes *The Man-Eater of Malgudi* not a mythological romance, nor a political satire—though it has aspects of both these—but the rarest of literary forms, a true comedy.

THE POSSESSED

GREENE'S The Comedians

1

> The tall black door in the narrow city street remained closed. I rang and knocked and rang again. I couldn't hear the bell ringing; to ring it again and again was simply an act of faith or despair, and later sitting in a hut in French Guinea, where I never meant to find myself, I remembered this first going astray, the buses passing at the corner and the pale autumn sun. (*Journey without Maps,* p. 1)

We have of course been here before, have stood with Charles Marlow in front of 'a narrow and deserted street in deep shadow, high houses, innumerable windows with venetian blinds, a dead silence . . . immense double doors. . .'. In calling this start to his Liberian adventure a going astray, Graham Greene in 1936 spoke more truth than he knew. He not only needed to shake off the influence of Conrad from the style and form of his books; he needed also to detach his responses to experience from their dependence upon the responses which he held—not quite accurately—Conrad to have made to his African experiences. They were responses still represented in the thirties by such works as Céline's *Voyage au Bout de la Nuit* and Kurt Heuser's *Reise ins der Innere,* while Laurens van der Post's *Venture to the Interior* was a belated exercise in the genre. Taken together with Greene's *Journey without Maps* these names and titles illustrate the multinational character of the European's quest for his own soul in the dark continent. It was a joke of the thirties to enquire if someone was going to a psycho-analyst or going to Africa. But Greene is perfectly solemn when he asserts, in *Journey without Maps,* that the heart of darkness was common to both: 'Mungo Park, Livingstone, Stanley, Rimbaud, Conrad represented only another method to Freud's, a more costly, less easy method calling for physical as well as mental strength.'

Psycho-analysis differs however from African travel in that it is costly only to the patient. When Greene, with that facility which is the chief stumbling-block to his admirers, writes that Africa will always be for him 'the Africa of the Victorian atlas, the blank unexplored continent the shape of the human heart', we think of Stanley's overstrained carriers and find ourselves asking 'Whose heart?' And Stanley, together with other nineteenth-century travellers including both Rimbaud and Conrad, had other excuses than psychological annexation, for being in Africa. Greene's foot trek across Liberia was a courageous undertaking at a time when yellow fever and malaria were still real dangers. Yet *Journey without Maps* makes astonishing reading today because, as Barbara Greene admits in her own account of their venture, this walk of three hundred and fifty miles through the Liberian bush had no justification and benefited no one; least of all the twenty-five carriers who bore the real brunt of the long and not very well timed marches and who had to find their own way back, with dangerously full pockets, from the coast to the interior.

A happy extrovert, 'exhilarated by the fun and novelty of everything', Barbara Greene responded to the carriers, and to the villagers, missionaries, and politicians encountered on the journey, with a warm, outgoing attentiveness that is nowhere to be found in Greene's book. Where his cousin sought novelty, Greene looked for the familiar, for the confirmation in the primitive villages of the interior of those early terrors and delights—the terrors preponderating—which psycho-analysis had already rendered to him at a dangerously early age. Thus Liberian masquerades are equated with the primal evil, the hell that lay about Greene in his infancy; they represent a stage farther back than the seediness of the Coast, which is made to correspond to the seedy, unreal cities of Greene's youth. The doubtful validity of these analogies need not concern us here. In Greene's portentous transference of private emotions to the unfamiliar what we miss is not so much the anthropologist's curiosity as the novelist's insight.

At times in reading this exasperating book it is hard to avoid the suspicion that Greene in writing it has burdened many a mud village with a significance that he did not at the time feel. Indeed at one point he confesses that what he experienced in the villages of the interior, along with the excitement of uncovering a primal memory, was the agonizing boredom of childhood, the feeling of apartness:

which came before one had learnt the fatal trick of transferring emotion, of flashing back enchantingly all day long one's own image, a period when other people were as distinct from oneself as this Liberian forest. I sometimes wonder whether, if one had stayed longer, if one had not been driven out again by one's tiredness and fear, one might have relearned the way to live without transference, with a lost objectivity.

The remark brings us the relief of hitting the trail again after long wanderings in the forest. For here, in a book which contains so much of the worst of Greene, is a pointer to his potential best. Greene's long career as a novelist has been a fight for a lost objectivity. And because this career also spans the years in which the European has gradually learnt to look at the tropics not as his possessions, his moral testing-ground, his child-surrogates, or any other kind of appendage to his own existence, but as a number of societies with identities of their own, it is not surprising that Greene attains this lost objectivity most securely in his novel of neo-colonialism, *The Comedians*. Inexplicably side-stepped by the critics, this is a book that can at least challenge comparison, as a study of political remote control by material interests, with *Nostromo*. Greene, that is, came much closer to Conrad in the sixties than he did thirty years previously when he tried to follow him through the door of darkness.

Africa was not, however, to restore his lost objectivity to Greene. He still falls far short of it in *The Heart of the Matter,* written after a prolonged spell of wartime duty in Freetown. Greene seeks in this novel to extend the metaphor of the heart. The police officer Scobie loves the Coast because human nature is there to be found without disguise: 'Here you could love human beings nearly as God loved them, knowing the worst.' The seedy colonial port is the setting for an *imitatio Christi,* an attempted sharing of the divine readiness to suffer with creation. 'If one knew, he wondered, the facts, would one have to feel pity even for the planets? if one reached what they called the heart of the matter?' The trouble is that Scobie, in his determination to love the unlovable, is anthropomorphically transferring to God his own error—itself a form, Conor Cruise O'Brien suggests, of superimposition—of seeing almost everyone round him as unlovely and pitiable. Scobie's wife is not undisguised when she appears to him, in the steamy siesta, like a joint under a meat-cover. All that is undisguised here is contempt:

> One is never quite sure whether the evident waves of hate are coming from Scobie or from some hidden source playing around him—perhaps the same source that emits in the narrative a constant hum of tender approbation for Scobie himself. The reader is invited to add contempt to the pity Scobie feels for Louise, and to experience, for Scobie himself, a more exalted kind of pity, tenderness bordering on admiration.

Greene has himself maintained that there is no blurring of viewpoints, that this scene between Scobie and his wife is the novel's first exposure of Scobie's obsession and pride—'the kind of pride that lots of us have, which makes him feel that he can manage lives'. And many details of the story, overlooked by Dr O'Brien, show that Greene was not here speaking with hindsight; we can trust the tale as well as the artist. If actions are judged by their fruits, then Scobie's suicide does nothing to protect Helen and Louise, the characters at the centre of what Dr O'Brien calls Scobie's 'pity group'. What to Scobie is the ultimate action of responsibility reveals itself, in the event, as an abandonment. That Scobie is seen by Greene to suffer from the tragic hubris to which good men are most prone is abundantly clear when, after the landing of the responsibility-ridden survivors from the torpedoed ship, he is found musing on the 'responsibility he shared with all human beings, but there was no comfort in that, for it sometimes seemed to him that he was the only one who recognised it'. This kind of responsibility, so unlike the dogged, Conradian fidelity of the ship's engineer, must turn at last—when Scobie's mental endurance has been as stretched as was the physical endurance of the shipwrecked schoolmistress—into obsession and finally hysteria. The distress that leads to Scobie's final act is filled with the hysteric's typical distortion of the 'facts' as we have understood them.

The irony then is abundant. Yet it is repeatedly obscured by what Dr O'Brien calls the hum of approbation around Scobie. Our ears are well tuned to pick up that hum; it is our traditional approval for the Guardian as Philip Mason has depicted him—the responsible and benevolent father-figure of colonial times. To quote Conor Cruise O'Brien once more: 'Scobie's relations to his pity-group are very much those of a colonizer to the natives.' Their pitifulness is necessary to him, it is 'the cheap labour of the heart'. Not surprisingly, the colony in which Scobie serves is in the novel for the most part a backdrop, at best an atmosphere, but never a society. Here surely in the social life of Sierra Leone was the chance for an objectivity that would have resisted our sentimental empathy with Scobie's projection of his emotional needs on the world around him. But Africa had long before presented itself as a blank screen for such projections on Greene's own part, and however solid his understanding of Freetown life may have been in 1942, little of the substance of that life gets into *The Heart of the Matter*.

Whereas Greene found himself in Freetown through the chances of war, his visit to the Congo seventeen years later was a deliberate, writer's choice. He was in search of a locale like Conrad's Inner Station, which might represent by the farthest point of navigation up a great river the limit of an individual's experience. Conrad's tale imparts its sombre resonance to *The Burnt-Out Case;* it is possible to pick up many small echoes such as, for instance, the hard initial consonant in Querry's name which is the same as that in Kurtz—or Korzeniowski. But what is missing is the political dimension of 'Heart of Darkness.' Although Greene had written understandingly about Kenya's agony in the early fifties, he went back for his second African novel to the blank on the map, choosing a Congo leprosarium as a setting 'removed from world politics and household preoccupations' where he might 'best give dramatic expression to various types of belief, half-belief and non-belief'. And the danger of such a social vacuum to Greene is not unlike the temptation felt by his creation Scobie to project his own misunderstood emotions—in Scobie's case, a pity that is really pride—into the whole solar system.

In *The Burnt-Out Case,* Greene has created a hero who has virtually no emotions to project. Querry has come to the end of his vitality—artistic, religious, and sexual—and we must not make Father Thomas's mistake of interpreting this numbness as the darkness before a great spiritual enlightenment. What remains for Querry is presumably a limited usefulness growing from a limited human sympathy; the uncomfortable night spent in the bush beside the injured Deo Gratias has replaced Scobie's frantic bargaining with God at the dying child's bedside. From such self-effacing involvement there may come, not faith, but happiness, the possibility of being (and Greene loves to play on a name) *l'homme qui rit*. In *The Heart of the Matter* Greene imputed and perhaps imparted to his hero a mistrust of happiness: 'Point me out the happy man and I will point you out either egotism, selfishness, evil—or else an absolute ignorance.' The Mission priests who laugh so easily in *The Burnt-Out Case* do not give many signs of possessing these vices. Rather they are aware, whatever their limitations, of what Greene's earlier model Robert Louis Stevenson, called their great task of happiness. For Querry to advance towards such a lightness of heart is achievement enough. Given a hero of this spiritual reticence and humility it looks at first as if Greene also (and the eggs-with-crosses fable is a rather whimsical device for ensuring that Greene both is and is not Querry) has moved within reach of the objectivity he pondered twenty-five years previously in the Liberian heartland.

But the novel ends nearly as catastrophically for Greene as a novelist as it does for Querry. The new objectivity lacks objects; there is not the material here for constructing something upon which to rejoice. To give substance to the lives of leprosy patients from whom one is separated by language and culture might defeat the talent of a Solzhenitsyn, and Greene does little more than sketch in as a background the patients' persistence in quarrelling and making love. In this thin air, the projections, the disturbing signs of subjectivity, begin to recur. The cured lepers provide an analogy for Querry's spiritual numbness which is not easy to accept. Only by virtue of his profession is Dr Colin afforded a map—in his case an atlas of leprosy—to this world of acute suffering. Querry has no such grip on the strange world around him and the life ahead of him. In consequence he becomes the shelterless quarry of the most savage manhunt in Greene's novels. The hunters—the Ryckers, Father Thomas, and Parkinson—are not merely the recipients but the *personifications* of the resentment and hatred, pride and false pity that Querry thought he had left behind him. They are, the novelist revealingly tells us, the flotsam of thirty years as a novelist: their frightfulness out-Greenes Greene. They take over the novel, destroying Querry in their stampede, because there is nothing solid to stop them in this Africa which is for Greene 'the region of uncertainty, of not knowing the way about', a blank space through which to travel in search of a character.

By his own admission, Greene has always been 'fixated' on Africa. His relation with Vietnam, the second country he 'fell in love with', has by contrast been a mature and adult affair. He made four prolonged sojourns there during the years when growing American involvement was turning a colonial war into a confrontation of Asian communism with the West. Just what this ideological conflict meant for the Vietnamese is described in a number of articles that Greene wrote for English, French, and American periodicals. Some of the scenes from the articles are embodied in *The Quiet American,** which was published in 1955, between Greene's two African novels.

Since Fowler, the narrator of *The Quiet American,* is by his own insistence a reporter and not a leader-writer, his purposes are identical with the ones Conrad declared in his preface to *The Nigger of the Narcissus*: 'to make you hear, to make you feel—it is, before all, to make you *see*'. Greene's Vietnam is populated, as his Africa is not, with people whose sufferings are made almost unbearably real to us: the two soldiers in the watchtower, killed because the presence of Fowler and Pyle has drawn the notice of the Vietcong; the fishermen on the sampan dive-bombed in a French raid; the woman caught in a street explosion, covering her dead baby with a straw hat; the river solid with bloodless dead. What gives these scenes a *haecceitas* that is more than journalistic vividness is Greene's objective humility before the beliefs and cultures of the East. 'He could not justify this reluctance to take life: after all, he was a Christian—one of those who had learnt from Nero how to make human bodies into candles.' If the tone is Fowler's, the character of whom this is said, the Goan Catholic, Dominiques, is the creation of a Greene whose Christianity has a less binding option on the truth than it has had in the past, and who cannot enter a Buddhist temple without a prayer.

Dominiques' Christianity has been grafted on to the good stock of Buddhist-Hindu civilization. It is a very different thing from the garish California-style electicism of 'Cadoism', which is the sectarian equivalent of the Third Force conceived of by the dangerously idealistic American, Pyle, as a way out of the choice between communism and colonialism. Pyle's pursuit of a Third

* After *The Heart of the Matter* Greene returned to England for the setting of *The End of the Affair,* in which one once again feels the lack of the 'household preoccupations' dismissed in *The Burnt-Out Case.* It is not the miracles after Sarah's death that are hard to swallow, but those of her earthly life—such as the ease with which she conjures up a dinner for guests in wartime London after a day spent in anguished pacing of Clapham Common.

Force results in a horrific slaughter. Yet he remains as spellbound by the exalted ideas of the leader-writer York Harding as was Conrad's Harlequin by the eloquence of Kurtz. Pyle can even ignore the blood that cries from the ground:

> Pyle said 'It's awful.' He looked at the wet on his shoes and said in a sick voice, 'What's that?'
>
> 'Blood,' I said. 'Haven't you ever seen it before?'
>
> He said, 'I must get them cleaned before I see the Minister.' I don't think he knew what he was saying.
>
> . . . .
>
> He said, 'Thé wouldn't have done this. I'm sure he wouldn't. Somebody deceived him. The Communists . . . .'

Though Greene had avoided re-reading Conrad for many years, such Conradian echoes arise naturally in a novel built around the theme that dominates 'Heart of Darkness', flashes through *Lord Jim*, and underlies the whole of *Nostromo*: the tragic folly of nearly all Western interference in the non-white world.

In witnessing Pyle's actions we are reminded of Marlow's warnings against a 'sentimental pretence', against the egotism that masks itself as philanthropy. Fowler by contrast is insistent on his neutrality, his non-involvement, and his reply to Pyle's 'They don't want Communism' is 'They don't want our white skins around telling them what they want'. Yet Fowler's revulsion at Pyle's interference leads him inevitably to choose sides himself; and though Greene is no more Fowler than Conrad is Marlow, creator and character in both cases share a respect for commitment to a cause that keeps in sight the harshness of the individual human condition.'Heart of Darkness' appeared in book form under the epigraph 'Something human is dearer to me than the wealth of the world'; and Greene has admitted that he finds in communism 'a desire for justice; a preference for the underdog. With all their faults and their mistakes and the wicked men who've come to power, I feel there remains an idealism in communism.' In *The Quiet American* there are suggestions that colonial conquest and rule had once had a cultural dynamism akin to Marlow's 'real idea'. But this has been lost in the war fought for the *colons* whose culture is typified by a collection of pornography; the simple, traditional French patriotism of the bomber pilot Trouin is betrayed when he is dispatched on napalm raids. There is only one side Fowler can take. He informs on Pyle to the Communists.

This is, and is meant to be, politically simplistic. The sceptic Fowler is a man without an ideology, temporal or spiritual, and in the end he is left haunted and guilt-ridden by the impurity of his motives in compassing Pyle's death. Yet the book as a whole has a political substantiality lacking in the African novels and it marks the first stage in the metamorphosis of Greene as a writer which caused him to declare in 1968:'I am more a political writer than a Catholic writer.'

Our Man in Havana, published in 1958, certainly has very little to do with religion and much to do with politics, although in a farcical disguise. Of all Greene's 'Entertainments', *Our Man in Havana* best deserves the name. The novelist's earlier humour sometimes calls to mind the moment in *A Burnt-Out Case* when 'Querry's face was twisted into the rictus of a laugh'. But the Greene who was discovering a lost objectivity in the fifties was becoming capable of genuine comedy; so much was revealed by *Loser Takes All*, a kind of metaphysical romp around the idea of free will, in which the tycoon GOM gives a freedom to his prodigal employee which is the very opposite of Scobie's management of his pity-group in *The Heart of the Matter*. Greene's fantasy of espionage and counter-espionage by East and West in Batista's Cuba is also a hilarious tale. At the same time, it is like *The Quiet American,* a warning against the dangers of psychological annexation, against letting our power-fantasies draw us into neo-colonial interference with a poor and powerless country. Greene on his first venture into the underdeveloped world projected the fantasies of a lost childhood on to the unrealized 'primitive' scene of Liberia. Now, in *Our Man in Havana*, the Great Game played out by East and West in Cuba threatens with disruption and death a rickety society which is yet too real in its suffering to be mocked by these fantasies of dominance. The vulture is a bird at home in the tropical slums; and the Red Vulture, the sinister police chief Segura, turns out to have a humanity lacking in the foreign eagles of espionage attracted by the decoy duck, Wormold—'one of those innocent children', as Segura terms him, 'who set poltergeists to work'. Clearly the theme of the cold war in the Third World is one on which Greene has more to say in 1958 than could be said in an 'entertainment', and after a regression into a blank, apolitical Africa in *A Burnt-Out Case* Greene returns to the Caribbean and to contemporary politics in *The Comedians*.

2

The story of *The Comedians,* as a little homework upon Haitian history shows, takes place in the later months of 1963, although there is some compression into the time-scheme of the novel of events that fall outside this period. Facts are sometimes altered to protect living persons—François Duvalier still tyrannized the country when the novel was published in 1966—and sometimes to underline a theme. Duvalier in his earlier and better days worked in an anti-yaws campaign. But yaws is not a killing disease, and in the novel the campaign is against tuberculosis, the mortal sickness that shadows the ship's cook and the British *chargé d'affaires* as well as the poor of Port-au-Prince.

Since Haiti is a francophone country, Greene can use for his title a term that has different meanings in English and French. In the first part of the book, the English connotations of *comedians* prevail: music-hall jokes, professional funny men. We start with three men in a boat—the dog makes its appearance much later—whose names are inevitably Smith, Brown, and Jones. The three are passengers, idle and irrelevant to the business of getting the ship to port, and irrelevant they are to remain once they reach Haiti. At the same time the ship's progress towards Haiti in this opening chapter ensures a mounting apprehension as Brown and the purser, who already know the country, reveal some of the terrors of Duvalier's rule. And there are other apprehensions, all the more disturbing for being half-defined: we do not yet know Mr Fernandez' avocation, but we guess that this thin black figure who seems to pursue the moribund passenger round the deck, touches the sleeping narrator Brown with a cold hand, and 'unexpectedly' gains on Jones, has something to do with death. When the ship's concert, despite Jones's desperate effort to be the life and soul of the party, ends with Mr Fernandez' tears, the only comedy promised would appear to be one in the Pascalian sense: 'Le dernier acte est toujours sanglant, quelque belle que soit la comédie en tout le reste. On jette enfin de la terre sur la tête, et voilà pour jamais.' Or as Jones has it: 'Shut-eye's the answer to all, isn't it?' (p. 45)

Comparison between this first chapter and Greene's journal of a wartime voyage from which it derives (included in *In Search of a Character*) reveals how skilfully the novelist has re-shaped real-life incidents and people so as to build up not only apprehension but also a complex curiosity. Our awareness that there is more to Smith and Jones than the absurd do-gooder and the con-man recognized by Brown stimulates our interest in the character who can make such partial judgements. The third chapter is given over to satisfying this curiosity about Brown. By this time he is 'home' in his hotel, where the body of the Secretary for Social Welfare lies with its throat cut in the empty swimming pool. The scene could belong to an early Greene thriller but then, in Haiti, life imitates art. Eighteen months after Duvalier came to power a previous presidential candidate, whose election experiences had been rather different from those of Mr Smith in the U.S., staggered in a dying condition into the Cuban embassy, after months of hiding in peasant huts and holes in the ground. Duvalier's men later hijacked his hearse, and the rumour was rife that the President intended to employ his dead opponent as a zombie. The hijacking, too, will follow in the novel. But for the present, Brown's vigil by Dr Philipot's body, while he awaits the arrival of the physician Magiot, offers the novelist a natural pause for retrospection that can satisfy our curiosity about Brown; is he, in Jones's parlance, a tart or a toff?

What we learn puts him firmly among the tarts. Toffs have roots—the Smiths are Smiths of Wisconsin—but Brown is of doubtful legitimacy and doubtful nationality, and behind him stretches a career of deception and gambling up to the time when, summoned by a postcard from the mother he has virtually forgotten, he fetches up in a Haiti hotel and sleeps for the first time in a bed he has not either paid for or failed to pay for. The hotel has become the only home he knows. It is this that makes him ask on this second landing—after he has built up the hotel into a financial success and then seen it abandoned in the rising terror of Papa Doc's reign—'Don't I belong here?'

But the reader finds it less easy than does the journalist, Petit Pierre, to agree: 'Of course you belong here Mr Brown. You are a true friend of Haiti.' (p.48) Brown shows little enough friendship for individual Haitians. From Marcel, his mother's lover and business partner, he recoils with a racial distaste: 'He knelt there in his black suit, looking like some negro-priest at an obscene rite.' (p. 81) Brown relentlessly buys out and dismisses Marcel, whose subsequent suicide is simply bad for business. His mother's physician and friend Dr Magiot he at first treats with similar mistrust. And he makes use of Joseph, on whose skill as barman the hotel largely depends, with a coldness which almost justifies Mrs Smith's tendency to regard him as she would a southern plantation owner. The remarkable thing about the behaviour of all three men towards Brown is that it is without resentment.

Nor does the hotel's initial success really make Brown a true friend of Haiti. The night he looked out at the couple making love in the pool and thought 'I have arrived' marked his success only as a parasite on its host, an *arriviste*. Tourists brought money but—as Dr Philipot's nephew pertinently asks—'who saw the money?' Certainly not the beggars who stood unnoticed at the poolside, holding out their carvings. The life of the Hotel Trianon bore about as much relation to their lives as did that of the original Trianon to the distress of pre-revolutionary France. Like that refuge, the Hotel Trianon once had its cultural pretensions: 'Mingle with the *élite* of the Haitian intellectual life, the musicians, the poets, the painters who find at the Hotel Trianon a social centre. . . .' (p.54) Philipot's nephew Henri was one of those poets, the Haitian Baudelaire; now he speaks out against the new dispensation with all the anger that Aimé Césaire and Frantz Fanon, raised amid the distress of another Caribbean island, have brought to the theme of cultural dependence:

> Henri Philipot said, 'If only we had white mercenaries as Tshombe had. We Haitians haven't fought for forty years except with knives and broken bottles. We need a few men of guerilla-experience. We have mountains just as high as those in Cuba.'
>
> 'But not the forests,' I said, 'to hide in. Your peasants have destroyed those.'
>
> 'We held out a long time against the American Marines all the same.' He added bitterly, 'I say "we" but I belong to a later generation. In my generation we have learnt to paint—you know they buy Benoit's pictures now for the Museum of Modern Art (of course they cost far less than a European primitive). Our novelists are published in Paris—and now they live there too.'
>
> 'And your poems?'
>
> 'They were quite melodious, weren't they, but they sang the Doctor into power. All our negatives make that one great black positive. I even voted for him . . .'. (p.144)

'Wasn't I a comedian with my verses smelling of *Les Fleurs du Mal*?' Henri replies to Brown's reflection that perhaps Jones and himself are both comedians. Here we come to the second meaning of *comedians*: the French sense of 'play-actors'. The Trianon, before Papa Doc, was a stage-set for an imitation of life that accorded well with the Absurdist world-view of Brown as he expressed it on board the *Medea:* 'Life was a comedy, not the tragedy for which I had been prepared, and it seemed to me that we were all, on this boat with a Greek name (why should a Dutch line name its boats in Greek?) driven by an authoritative practical joker towards the extreme point of comedy.' (p.34) An authoritative practical joker sounds very like GOM, and because there is so much that is absurd in Greene's later work we need to keep a firm grip here on his insistence that Brown is not Greene. The jokes of Brown are much nearer to those of the horrible Concasseur than to those of the clown in *Our Man in Havana,* or of Jones in this novel.

Brown is not Greene. Yet he is not called either Jones or Smith, and we may doubt his statement that the three names are 'interchangeable, like comic masks in a farce'. Green can burn out to brown. Greene has always had a talent for self-parody, and in what Martha, Brown's mistress, calls her lover's dark brown view of life we are made to see the book's characters in a manner that repeatedly brings to mind Richard Hoggart's complaint about the 'cartoon art' of Greene's earlier novels. They wear their odd features or carry their properties like figures in Absurdist drama: Smith has his large innocent ears, Jones his toothbrush moustache, the ambassador his cigars. Martha's child is an arrogant midget with a 'small, steely hand'; Brown transfers to Martha's son, as well as to her husband, all his own possessiveness. His affair with Martha, a continual 'interrogation', in a place where that word has sinister overtones, is a sorry farce, a farce rendered the more trivial by the proximity of tragedy:

> She laughed and held me still and kissed me. I responded as well as I could, but the corpse in the pool seemed to turn our preoccupations into comedy. The corpse of Dr Philipot belonged to a more tragic theme; we were only a subplot affording a little light relief. (p.62)

The two remaining chapters of Part I of this carefully structured tale develop the tragic counter-theme. It is the tragedy of the country which became the second republic in the New World at the time that the cry of *Liberté, Fraternité, Egalité* was raised in Europe, and yet was prevented by its legacy of slavery and its subsequent isolation from ever attaining any political realization of those terms. When Mr Smith tries to effect the release of Jones, who has been arrested and beaten up on his arrival (his disguises are seldom well-chosen, and this time he has forged an introduction to an army officer who is *persona non grata*), he fails to make himself understood with terms like 'charge' and 'bail'. What this absence of the rule of law means for the Haitians is made plain in the interrupted funeral of Dr Philipot. The tragic suffering on this occasion is not however all Madame Philipot's. She at least is in a world she knows. A greater trauma is sustained by Mr Smith, who has stepped into a society where his faith in human nature is smashed as relentlessly as the glass around Dr Philipot's coffin. Here the ludicrous becomes the terrible: the top-hatted twin undertakers who lead the Philipot child off to enjoy his *glace à la vanille* are like some nightmarish reduplication of Baron Samedi, holding the future of the New World's poorest country between their black-gloved hands.

Haiti's tragedy has its real-life villain, Papa Doc, whose presence is manifested in *The Comedians* through his bogey-men, the dark-spectacled Tonton Macoutes. His opponent, Dr Magiot, the hero of the Haitian tragedy, is the novelist's invention, though he probably owes much to courageous Haitians of the sixties, notably to Jacques Alexis, stoned to death in 1965, and to Jean-Jacques Ambroise, whose fate it was to be tortured to death some months after the novel was published in 1966; as well as to Jean Price-Mars, who was perhaps protected by his international reputation. But in the novel's antithesis between the genuine and the meretricious, Dr Magiot is reality itself. He belongs as much to Haiti as Mr Smith belongs to Wisconsin—'I'm not sure I wouldn't fight for Papa Doc if the Marines came' (p.253)—and he belongs to an age: his old-fashioned sitting room with its calf-bound volumes of Hugo, Renan, and Marx reflects a personality rooted in nineteenth-century humanitarianism. And under the shadow of these black colossi who confront each other like Good and Evil in a morality play, the European characters of the comic subplot peep about, destined, it would appear, for dishonourable graves. Neither Jones nor Brown has any real calling in the world, and in this first part of the novel we are made to feel that the Smiths' gospel of vegetarianism is absurdly cranky when viewed alongside the real *métier* served by Magiot and betrayed by Duvalier.

3

We return to the three petty men in the book's second part, which concerns itself in turn, though not over-schematically, with the responses of Smith, Brown, and Jones to the Haitian tragedy. There is one surprise here; at the end of this part the Smiths pass out of the comic subplot with a dignity derived from the prime Greene virtues of tenderness and courage. 'Perhaps we seem rather comic figures to you Mr Brown,' Mr Smith remarks before they leave Haiti; and Brown for once replies with sincerity: 'Not comic, heroic.' (p. 209) He has good reason to know, having been rescued from a beating-up at the hands of the Tonton Macoute leader Concasseur by Mrs Smith's righteous indignation thrilling through the phrases of Hugo's Self-Taught French. Her action is a part of the fidelity that the pair show to each other, to their friends, to their mission, and to the truth; a Conradian fidelity deriving from the education of a past age which places them with the Magiots of the world and not with the Browns and Joneses.

The Smiths' finest hour was Nashville. But their non-violent fight for freedom was possible only in a country where the rule of law, however frequently it may be challenged, is constitutionally inviolable. Despite Mrs Smith's moral victory over Concasseur, the Smiths' brand of courage is as displaced in Haiti as is their vegetarianism in a country where ninety-five per cent of the population cannot afford meat, and their philanthropy in a situation where every official demands his rake-off at the expense of the people. Mr Smith finally despairs and withdraws, not because of the flood-lit executions, but in reaction from the Minister's proposals for a discreet share-out of the American money subscribed for a vegetarian centre. The incident makes two points: that there *are* agents of Aid prepared to abuse it in this way; and, more importantly, that the generosity embodied in the Smiths does more harm than good if it operates without political wisdom. By the time President Kennedy suspended economic aid to Haiti, late in 1962, eighteen and a half million dollars had found their way into the pockets of Papa Doc's adherents; a situation Greene neatly sums up in the phrase 'a big Cadillac dating from the days of American aid for the poor of Haiti' and expands, in this second part of the book, in a hauntingly horrific scene at the dusty site of Duvalierville, city of the future.

So far, Duvalierville appears to have only two inhabitants: a man whose house sign shows him to be a justice of the peace ('he must have had a lot of influence to be installed so soon') and a legless cripple who proffers a carving to Mr Smith. It is snatched from him by the Minister, but Mr Smith

> shook off the protecting hand of the Secretary for Social Welfare and ran back towards the cripple. He pulled out a bunch of dollar-bills and held them out. The cripple looked at him with incredulity and fear. Our driver made a motion to interfere, but I blocked his way. Mr Smith bent down and pressed the money into the cripple's hand. The cripple with an enormous effort began to rock back towards the cockpit. . . .
>
> The justice of the peace had risen to watch the transaction outside his box beyond the playground—standing he was an enormous man. He put his hand over his eyes to see better in the hard sunlight. We took our places in the car. . . .
>
> I looked back. The justice of the peace was running fast on long loping legs across the cement-playground, and the cripple was rocking back with desperation towards the cockpit; he reminded me of a sand-crab scuttling to its hole. He had only another twenty yards to go, but he hadn't a chance. When I looked round a minute later Duvalierville was hidden by the dust-cloud of our car. (p. 182)

As a vignette of the neo-colonial world, this is masterly. It is drawn with the same nervous precision that Conrad displays in a very similar scene in *Nostromo,* the moment when Decoud sees, framed in the arch of the town gateway, the steam engine rush past the crowd trudging home from a military spectacle, and hears its 'scream of war-like triumph', its 'tumult of blows and shaken fetters'.

The material interests of capitalism, represented in *Nostromo* by the 'material train' from the silver mines, are presented in *The Comedians* in the form of the vast bauxite concession in the Dominican Republic. Here, treasure is torn out of the bowels of the earth under the management of Mr Schuyler Wilson—a well-chosen name, since it was Woodrow Wilson's imperial ambitions in the Caribbean which led him to plan the 1915 Marines' landing some months in advance of the disturbances which were its pretext. These mineral concessions figure however only in the book's final chapter, at a point in the story when the American ambassador is due to return to Haiti. In Part II of *The Comedians* we are still in the decisive months of 1963, when it was still possible for the United States, in its dealings with Duvalier, to display the idealism and integrity of the Smiths rather than the crass materialism represented by Schuyler Wilson. Throughout October, Haitian exiles were actually trained in the U.S. in guerrilla warfare, a situation that has its counterpart in the novel when Brown brings together the Smiths and Dr Magiot, Duvalier's Marxist opponent, whose basic concern for truth and justice they share despite their political conditioning. But it is too late for the Smiths to learn a new world-view; in South Carolina the guerrilla training soon stopped, and after President Kennedy's death Lyndon Johnson reopened diplomatic relations with the dictator whom the mass of Americans regarded as a bulwark against communism. 'We are abandoned again,' says Dr Magiot; and later, as he waits for the final knock on the door he writes: 'The American Ambassador is about to come back, and Baron Samedi will surely pay a little tribute in return.' (pp. 270, 311)

In himself, Mr Smith is irrelevant to the plight of Haiti and, honestly recognizing his irrelevance, he withdraws from the republic with a near-tragic dignity: 'He had loved people for their colour and he had been betrayed more deeply than are those who hate.' (p. 137) Whereas Smith is irrelevant, Brown is largely, though not totally, indifferent. On two occasions in this part of the novel Brown and Martha come together in a world of which they are no part: 'We—the uncoloured—were all of us too far from home.' (p. 176) On the second occasion they hear the shots of the public execution: ' ". . . you'd better wait for the audience to disperse," I said. "Yes. That's all it means to us. We aren't concerned." ' (p. 206) Martha in fact has her personal bond, her hold on reality, in her child; but as the daughter of a German war-criminal she repudiates all involvement in politics. Brown's detachment has no such excuse. It rises from his determination to possess and not to be possessed. The hotel is his great possession, and any implication in local politics—a dead Minister in the swimming pool for instance—endangers his ownership. Because of his fear of involvement, his attempt through official channels to secure Jones's release from prison is (as the British *chargé* very well sees) elaborate play-acting; it is Mr Smith who goes straight to the Haitians, brushing aside Brown's disingenuous warnings: ' "I don't want to get you into any trouble with the authorities." "I'm not afraid of trouble,'' Mr Smith said, ''with any authorities.'' ' (p. 114)

Against this background of his hesitations and misgivings, the Voodoo ceremony which is the central episode in the book's central movement is for Brown a painful confrontation with the heart of Haitian distress. Henri Philipot, the Haitian Baudelaire, the perfect *evolué,* has said in a previous chapter, 'Perhaps the gods of Dahomey are what we need now.' (p. 188) In the Voodoo rite, the people themselves are in touch with their roots, as the god of their West African ancestors, Ogoun Ferraille, descends upon them. Greene has here brought off a *tour de force* of communication; we sense and share the revulsion of Brown, the con-man and playboy, against this 'savagery', at the same time as we sense and share the appeal that this call to commitment has for the inner Brown, for the *prêtre manqué.* That the attraction seems a worthier response than the revulsion is the measure of how European attitudes, including those of Greene's own Church, have changed. To Mrs Smith, who belongs like many in Wisconsin to the nineteenth century, Voodoo is heathenism; but the double sacrament depicted here, though the baptism is literally of fire, the broken body a cock's, and the wine crude gin, intentionally evokes the same recognition of God's mysterious ways as has inspired the charismatic movement within Catholicism.

Above all there is here brought home to us the change in Greene from the writer of the thirties who found in African religion only the reflection of his own fears and fantasies to a writer whose recovered objectivity makes of this ceremony an allegory of the processes of Third World revolution. Fanon would have disapproved of the religious context; but when the possessed Joseph forces the spirit down Henri's throat he is the representative of the *lumpenproletariat* which, suffering under the post-colonial élite, takes to the country and is there joined by the disillusioned urban intellectuals. As in *Les Damnés de la Terre,* this is the point at which effective action begins; the ceremony over, Henri and Joseph lead a successful attack on a police post and move to the hills. This is based on an actual event of July 1963, described in Greene's article on 'The Nightmare Republic':

> A few brave youths the other day attacked the police station at Kemscoff and slaughtered a couple of TTM and a couple of policemen. Three of them held out in a cave in the mountains for

> more than 24 hours against several hundred police, and they killed more than twenty of their pursuers . . . before they were burnt out with flame throwers.

The leader was the young and embittered Hector Riobo, whose father had been killed in the streets.

In the novel, Brown remains aloof, convincing himself that Henri's participation in the barbaric rite is a *corruptio optimi,* a triumph for Papa Doc as he drags his country down. 'I told myself'—what had 'myself' said?—'that I hadn't left the Jesuits to be the victim of an African god.' (p. 198) This is much the way he fought off faith as a boy. Even then he had great possessions—a gambling gain of three hundred pounds—which were enough to ensure that he could not be possessed, could no more listen to his vocation than he can now respond to Ogoun's drums:

> After a while the rain came. I closed the windows and sat in stifling heat, while the rain fell like an extinguisher over the *tonnelle.* The noise of the rain silenced the drums, and I felt as lonely as a man in a strange hotel after a friend's funeral. I kept a flask of whisky in the car against emergencies and I took a pull from it, and presently I saw the mourners going by, grey shapes in the black rain.
>
> Nobody stopped at the car: they divided and flowed past on either side. Once I thought I heard an engine start—Philipot must have brought his car, but the rain hid it. I should never have gone to this funeral, I should never have come to this country, I was a stranger. My mother had taken a black lover, she had been involved, but somewhere years ago, I had forgotten how to be involved in anything. Somehow somewhere I had lost completely the capacity to be concerned. Once I looked out and thought I saw Philipot beckoning to me through the glass. It was an illusion. (p. 198)

Brown, of course, takes as dark a view of his own behaviour as of everyone else's. He was present at the ceremony because Joseph needed a lift and would have tried to drag his injured leg up the mountain if he had been denied it. When Joseph fails to return after the attack on the police post and Brown is left in the empty hotel he finds that 'perhaps unconsciously I had ached a little with him in his halting process from the bar to the verandah and up and down the stairs'. (pp. 241-2) This admission, so different from the 'hum of approbation' around Scobie, comes late in the story, as a recognition of grace.

There remains Jones, whose response to the reign of terror is the reverse of Brown's. He intervenes. But with his usual uncertainty about his role, his intervention is on the side of Papa Doc and the Tonton Macoutes. Not that his help is any use to them; it is in keeping with Jones's mysterious 'innocence' that the arms he offers to sell the dictator do not exist. He has sufficient confidence in the deal to offer Brown, in the chapter which ends this part of the novel, a share in a swindle that should bring in half a million and allow both men to fulfil their ambitions of running successful luxury hotels in the Caribbean: Jones's is to be a golfers' paradise called Sahib House.

The angry exclamation of Jones's last visitor (he has lost at gin-rummy) hangs over this conversation: *la volonté du diable*! Is Jones offering Brown all the kingdoms of the world? Brown doubts it; Jones seems scarcely to have more in his possession than a cocktail case obtained by false pretences. We doubt it too, and for the stronger reason that the devil's role in this particular morality drama has already been taken. Jones is the tempted, not the tempter. His temptation is a double one. Behind the alluring dream of the Desert Island Bar—'Parakeets on the curtains and a big brass telescope in the window focused on the 18th hole'—lies a farther dream, the hope of the man within. Henri Philipot, who is as much deceived as Concasseur by Jones's military fantasies, has appealed to him for help in training the guerrillas in the mountains: 'I was tempted, oh I was tempted all right.' (p. 213)

We come to the end of this part of the novel knowing a great deal about the pellucid Mr Smith and more about the opaque Brown than he realizes he has told us, but Jones is still an enigma, a crook who believes he has a lot in common with the saintly Smith. It scarcely seems a crime to cheat Papa Doc out of the guns which it was his custom to hand personally to each of his thugs. And for a man of such ambiguity, as Brown comments, Jones has a knack of winning friends. At the end of Part II he appears poised on a tightrope from which he could fall on the side of whichever force exerts the bigger pull: *la volonté du diable*—or *la volonté de Dieu*. He is exactly that ambiguous being defined by Browning in a passage which Greene has said could have acted as an epigraph to all his books:

Our interest's on the dangerous edge of things.
The honest thief, the tender murderer . . .
We watch while these in equilibrium keep
The giddy line midway.

4

No character in Greene's earlier novels treads the dangerous edge of things more precariously than the nameless hero of *The Power and the Glory*—'the drunken priest', in Greene's own phrase, 'who continued to pass life on'. Perhaps this is why Greene himself remains so loyal to a book that some critics have found harshly schematic. To one reader at least the portrayal of Jones, who comes to dominate the last part of *The Comedians,* is artistically far more satisfying than that of the whisky priest, because it has an ending and is complete in itself: the tightrope does not stretch into eternity. Jones topples at last, willy nilly—but other wills are at work—towards the good, and dies fulfilling his farther dream, the dream of the desert leader who strikes water from the rock for his companions.

A man without belongings, Jones gives himself. In the days of his prosperity under Papa Doc, his ability to make the little prostitute laugh had nothing to do with the buying and selling of pleasure. Now in these closing chapters, when his swindle is discovered and he has to be smuggled in woman's disguise into the embassy of Martha's husband (a trick used more than once in Haiti in the Duvalier era), he makes Martha laugh till the tears come; and in the days that follow his presence changes this mansion of a dead marriage into a home. Characteristically, he gives Martha and the ambassador his only possession, the cocktail shaker. But they return to him this symbol of his charisma once he has been trapped by the jealous Brown into joining young Philipot's partisans. For the rest, he relinquishes easily enough, as the whisky priest had done, the things he cannot take on his last journey: 'I travel light, old man.'

Jones is not only without possessions, he is a totally displaced person who yet has an ability to make wherever he finds himself his home. 'I've slept in worse places' is his incredible comment on the cell in the Port-au-Prince police station; and once he has got on the right side of the regime he declares 'I like it here . . . I've landed on my feet.' Yet when he is on the run at last and tries to take refuge on board the *Medea,* which happens to be in port, it becomes clear that he is an adventurer who cannot return to any country in which he has operated. 'He told me', says Henri Philipot at the end of the story, when Jones, unable to limp further on his flat feet, has died covering the escape of the small guerrilla band, 'that there was no room for him outside of Haiti.' Brown's reply is a dry 'I wonder what he meant'. But Henri has no hesitation: 'He meant his heart was there.' (p. 307)

If, by this time, we have veered from Brown's irony to Henri's admiration, it is because we have found Brown as unreliable a reader of Jones's character as he is of Henry James's fiction. On the night that he is waiting for the storm that will be his signal for driving Jones south towards the mountains, Brown is reading James's 'The Great Good Place':

> 'The wild waters of our horrible times,' James had written and I wondered what temporary break in the long enviable Victorian peace had so disturbed him. Had his butler given notice? I had built my life around this hotel—it represented stability more profoundly than the God whom the Fathers of the Visitation had hoped I would serve. . . this might be the last night I would spend in the Hotel Trianon. (p. 274)

The fact that the hero's butler, in James's beautiful tale, does *not* give notice despite much provocation, should alert us to Brown's misunderstanding. The world is too much with James's hero. Worn out by the distractions of a successful writer's life, he falls asleep and dreams he is in some kind of retreat house, an ideally peaceful and ordered community. Like the material dreams of Jones and Brown, this refuge has some of the qualities of a well-run hotel. But the point missed by readers beside Brown who see in the tale only a *fin-de-siècle* yearning for peace at any price is that the hero comes to understand that he cannot stay in his retreat for ever. He returns to his former consciousness and to his own crowded room; but significantly, the room has now become spacious and tranquil, transformed by his knowledge of the great good place into being itself good.

For Jones too the great good place proves to be not a luxury hotel but the bivouac of the warfaring leader. As Brown sees him, he is trapped by his boastfulness into playing a role for which, medically unfit and without experience of active service, he is totally unqualified. Once again he has turned up in the wrong uniform. But Jones sees in the call to action, though it means the renunciation for the present of Sahib House—that symbol of the rich world's battening off the poor world—a chance for him to live out his farther dream. The role becomes reality; as Greene's epigraph from Hardy has it, he who is most kingly is the king. The cemetery where he waits to join the partisans is in truth 'a good place' for Jones. So is the decayed hole among the mountains (Eliot remains a powerful myth-maker for Greene) where he makes his last stand against Papa Doc. It is among such dry rocks, though now set in the arid plain of his own life, that Brown sees Jones in the dream with which the novel ends:

> I said to him, 'Why are you dying, Jones?'
>
> 'It's in my part, old man, it's in my part. But I've got this comic line—you should hear the whole theatre laugh when I say it. The ladies in particular.'
>
> 'What is it?'
>
> 'That's the trouble. I've forgotten it.'
>
> 'Jones, you must remember.'
>
> 'I've got it now. I have to say—just look at these bloody rocks—"This is a good place," and everyone laughs till the tears come. Then you say, "To hold the bastards up?" and I reply, "I didn't mean that".'
>
> The ringing of the telephone woke me—I had overslept. The call came, so far as I could make out, from Mr Fernandez who was summoning me to my first assignment. (pp. 312–13)

Hope and charity Jones has always had, and now faith is added—the knowledge that he has a role, though the world, flesh, and devil have done their best to make him forget it, in the *divina commedia.* The audience's laughter at the phrase 'this is a good place' (we recall the difficulty Brown and Martha have had finding a place to make love in, their brief happiness in the shallow declivity of the hotel garden) is both a misunderstanding and an understanding. They are right to laugh till the tears come, because in dying a death of love Jones is passing on to them the faith that the world itself is a good place.

If Jones's assignment, his role, is to pass life on, then Brown's assignment, now he has fled across the border and found work as an undertaker, is to preside over the rites of death. He is cast, not for Ogoun Ferraille, but for Baron Samedi. But though their ages and their ultimate fates differ, Jones and Brown are exposed to the same appeals and temptations. In a Jones idiom, they are horses out of the same stable. The *Medea*'s purser gets their names mixed. And the scene in Brown's cabin which closes the book's first chapter suggests an affinity of *doppelganger* intensity such as links the captain and the fugitive in Conrad's 'The Secret Sharer'. The unsuccessful con-man Jones is in many ways what Brown might have been if his mother had not left him a hotel in Haiti, and in the cemetery Brown finally acknowledges the bond between them:

> It was like meeting an unknown brother—Jones and Brown, the names were almost interchangeable, and so was our status. For all we knew, we were both bastards, although of course there might have been a ceremony—my mother had always given me that impression. We had both been thrown into the water to sink or swim, and swim we had—we had swum from very far apart to come together in a cemetery in Haiti. 'I like you, Jones' I said. 'If you don't want that half a sandwich, I could do with it.' (pp. 289–90)

Like the captain in 'The Secret Sharer'—a story also recalled when the law-abiding Dutch captain temporarily conceals Jones on board the *Medea*—Brown has helped Jones to escape. But his motives for doing this are suspect. He has cast Jones for the part of his mistress's seducer, and wants him out of the embassy and out of Port-au-Prince. Baron Samedi envies and hates the happiness of the embassy: 'I comforted myself that the days of laughter were numbered.' (p. 263) Whereas Jones has fantasies of water-divining, and dispenses cocktails and bourbon biscuits, Brown dreams that the waters of life are receding from him or that a communion of bourbon biscuits is refused him. Repeatedly he is denied the opportunity to pass on life. There are no guests left at the Trianon to enjoy his *soufflé au grand Marnier,* and after his flight he fails to get work as a catering manager in the Dominican Republic.

As substitutes for the vocation he fought off long ago, these attempts to pass life on in wholly material terms are on a par with his rationalization of his indifference as in itself a kind of commitment—'committed to the whole world of evil and good, to the wise and the foolish, to the indifferent and to the mistaken'. (p. 304) It sounds evasive, and its hollowness reverberates through the succeeding episode, when the remnant of the guerrilla band limp by, followed by Joseph's body on a stretcher. 'He used to make good rum-punches': the stretcher-bearers disapprove of such a trivial exequy, but behind it is Brown's deep envy of the life-givers, of those who in the words of the refugee priest 'would rather be wrong with St. Thomas than right with the cold and the craven', or in the phrase of Dr Magiot's last message, 'would rather have blood on their hands than water like Pilate'. (pp. 309, 312)

Yet the same letter from Dr Magiot reminds us that Brown is not the best guide to his own character, that he can be as unreliable about himself as he is about Jones. 'You won't admit it perhaps, but you are your mother's son and you once took that dangerous journey which we all have to take before the end.' (p. 311) Brown's motives for the dangerous journey are not all egotistical: besides venom against Jones and the desire to revenge himself on Concasseur he is impelled by a hatred of brutality, by fidelity to Joseph. And, mysteriously blended with the 'venom' that he recognizes, by loyalty to Jones as his *alter ego*. Once he has risked his life and lost his possessions in helping Jones, Brown's vision of life clears. He no longer wants to possess Martha, no longer sees her child as a midget security guard but simply as a child. And although he may speak of himself as if he were left with no other vocation than Mr Fernandez' summons to bury the dead, he has played a not disreputable part in the comedy. The butler of 'The Great Good Place' is absurd but faithful, and he also is called Brown. Moreover, Greene's Brown has lived to tell the tale. If we turn back from the last page to the first, as a good novel compels us to do, we find Brown, well established in 'my rather bizarre business', feeling a certain pride that his action helped raise a memorial to Jones. *Exegi monumentum*: the irony remains, but then so does the memorial—a better monument than the hotel of which Brown first used the phrase. Brown's story has put the record right for himself no less than for Jones.

5

To return to the opening paragraphs of *The Comedians* is to be struck afresh with the intensity that marks this novel off from almost every other book of Greene's. The novelist's concentration shows in the smallest details. It produces, for example, the meaningful resonance of the vowels in the first few sentences, as *I—my—pride* begin to contrast with *Jones—stone—home*; it produces too the next paragraph's ironic expectation of 'the *pompes funèbres* they were preparing for me in the parlours of Mr Fernandez', as well as Mrs Smith's prophetic introduction of her husband in the next: 'He's an idealist. Of course, for that very reason, he stood no chance.' (p. 10) At first the significance of such effects is only half apprehended. Later, however, as Greene's driving concerns begin to operate, the means of propulsion perhaps become too obvious. The dreams sound unconvincingly *à propos.* Objects such as Brown's coffin-shaped paperweight are ponderously symbolic. The play with names—'Medea', 'College of the Visitation', 'Angel' (for Martha's child)—oppresses a little by its knowingness. Incidents are needlessly duplicated: Mr Smith's encounter with the beggar in Duvalierville did not need to be buttressed by the frenetic scene at the Post Office, when he casts all his spare cash among the fighting cripples. And characters sometimes embarrass us by becoming explicit on the author's behalf, as Jones does when he talks of getting lost inside himself, or Martha when she delivers her homily on the sexual life as the great test.

It must come as a disappointment that the novel in which Greene achieves such a satisfying objectivity should be marred by this kind of literary overkill. Could Greene not have trusted us to understand him? For two reasons, the answer is no. First there is the difficulty, for a best-selling novelist, that readers are always a few books behind the writer in their expectations. In the most widely-read books of his career, from *Brighton Rock* to *The End of the Affair* Greene established himself as the writer of eschatological thrillers. A large if ageing body of readers on both sides of the Atlantic, many of them Roman Catholics, knew only this Greene when they read *The Comedians*; they had never encountered the political thrillers of the thirties, in which Greene showed many affinities with Malraux, whose political masterpiece, *La Condition Humaine,* is recalled in Dr Magiot's last letter. And the letter itself, with its heavy emphasis on the humanism that is common to Catholicism and communism, is directed to those whose last encounter with the novelist was perhaps in *The Power and the Glory.* Greene's new point of view was unexpected. In the circumstances he could scarcely be other than bald, emphatic, over-obvious.

Secondly, Greene was demanding of his American readers, in particular, something more than a change of viewpoint. He wanted a change of American policy. *The Comedians* is one of the most *engagés* books of its time. *The Quiet American* had attacked an aspect of American liberalism, and the portrait of the Smiths in *The Comedians* in part makes amends for any unfairness in the Vietnam novel. But its prime purpose is to rouse *all* the Smiths of Wisconsin and elsewhere to stop thinking of Papa Doc as a bulwark against communism (and before we smile at the illusion we should ask ourselves if we ever thought much about Haiti at all before we read *The Comedians*) and to campaign for U.S. help to Papa Doc's opponents, among them the *emigrés* priests of *Jeune Haiti.* If Greene sometimes seems to hammer home his points with a relentless insistence, it is because he had to make himself heard against the Schuyler Wilsons; while he was writing the novel, U.S. Marines landed in the Dominican Republic, and all activity there against Papa Doc, including that to which Greene was giving practical help, was brought to a stop.

Chiang-kai-shek lived on to be the darling of the West in spite of Malraux's exposure, and there is still a Duvalier in the Presidential Palace in Haiti. The success of the *engagé* novel is not, however, to be measured by its effect on one generation of the children of darkness. In one dark place Greene listened and responded to the drums of the *tonnelle,* as his own Church was learning to do at the time, and from this attentiveness there has come a genuine novel about the Third World, and not about the white man's self-discovery in a colonial void. The romantic voyage has ended in *une pauvre terre*—a poor country, a pitiable world; but pity now has a human face.

THE DISPOSSESSED

NAIPAUL'S The Mimic Men

1

When Jones, in *The Comedians,* divides the world into toffs and tarts, those with pedigrees and those without, Brown tells him that they are travelling to a country of tarts. Haiti is indeed, like almost every other island territory of the Caribbean, a country of uprooted people, the majority of whom are descended from African slaves. Greene does not however enlarge on Brown's remark, and in spite of passing references to *le roi Christophe,* the historical dimension is lacking in *The Comedians.* The hold, for example, that Voodoo has over the Haitians becomes more understandable when we discover that the black republic was abandoned by the Holy Office for over half of the nineteenth century. In contrast to Greene's novel, V. S. Naipaul's *The Mimic Men*, which was published less than two years later, not only displays the historical awareness we might expect of a novelist writing from inner, indigenous experience of the Antilles' plight; this study of the neuroses induced by a particular form of colonization hinges on the protagonist's discovery of a historical order, on the meaningful linkage of past and present, in his own life as in the life of the society from which he comes.

The Mimic Men is about Trinidad, but because the story culminates in fictional political events, the island has to be renamed Isabella. In our shrunken world, such a fiction is less to our liking than it was when Conrad invented Costaguana. Naipaul has to find a device for rendering it acceptable. His solution is to connect Isabella with real people from outside the Caribbean. J. A. Froude's *The Bow of Ulysses* (1888) is as Negrophobe and Francophobe as it is made to sound in the novel, though one can search it in vain for the 'quotation' from it which occurs on page 92. Sir Hugh Clifford, a friend of Conrad, really was Colonial Secretary for Trinidad and Tobago for four years, and mention of him in the course of the story opens a window on to the globe-encompassing imperialism of Edwardian days. When in the novel Browne returns from his formal reception at Government House as the newly-elected Premier, he relates how he has been shown a painting of a Mediterranean fishing village given to the Governor by first name 'from Winston': 'We shared Browne's admiration: this was an ennobling link with the world, with a great man and great events.' (p. 241) The novel's plantocratic family, the Deschampsneufs, feel no less ennobled by Stendhal's reference to a possible ancestor of theirs, slighting though it may be. For these references to actual people have a double function. On the one hand, they help us to forget the fictitiousness of 'Isabella'; on the other, they emphasize the hunger of the Isabellans for a world which seems more substantial than their own. 'This place doesn't exist', a local novelist keeps saying in *A Flag on the Island,* the zany fantasy that Naipaul took time off from *The Mimic Men* to write. If Naipaul has to coax us to suspend our disbelief in Isabella, he has simultaneously to undermine our belief in Trinidad, to make us understand the conviction of the narrator and of others round him that the real world is elsewhere, and that Trinidad-Isabella is an island of castaways.

History bears out Ralph Singh's presentation of his 'little bastard island'. Trinidad, from soon after its seizure by the British in 1802 until four years before its independence in 1962, was a Crown Colony, the most dependent of dependencies. We may adopt two terms that recur continually in Ralph Singh's narrative and say that historically this country the size of a county, peopled by migrants from four continents, has lacked both *order* and *power.* In Trinidad, even the white planters tended to be refugees; they came to escape the French and Haitian revolutions. Cultural divisions cut across the racial ones in a way that diminished the real or potential force of the racial groupings: a French-speaking landowner had more in common with the patois-speaking slaves he had brought from Haiti than he had with the English planters; the East Indian when he arrived was made to feel an intruder in the old alliance of master and serf. Another refugee group was made up of the *peons,* people of mixed Spanish, Amerindian, and Negro ancestry who had fled from the South American revolutions of the last century. The tradition of Enthusiasm, which in the novel gives scope to the popularist, quasi-religious movement started by Singh's father, was in the real Trinidad a legacy of Negro settlers from the Bible Belt, escaped slaves who had fought against the Americans in 1812. Though they were technically free, their migration to Trinidad can scarcely be called voluntary. There was a strong measure of economic compulsion too in the great post-slavery immigration of Asians, both Indians and Chinese, to work as indentured labourers in the canefields vacated by the ex-slaves. In an afternoon's drive the schoolboy Singh grows acutely aware of the small, racially ambiguous yet self-segregated communities that make up island society:

> The scale was small in time, numbers and area; and here, just for a moment, the rise and fall and extinction of peoples, a concept so big and alarming, was concrete and close. Slaves and runaways, hunters and hunted, rulers and ruled: they had no romance for me. Their message was only that nothing was secure. (p. 146)

Ralph Singh is himself to grow into a self-segregated person, no better able to establish relationships with the individuals he encounters than the mountain communities of 'Spaniards' and 'Caribs' in Isabella are able to fuse into a political entity. But the historical understanding which can unite a society that recognizes the operation of its past upon its present can also mould the individual life. In writing his memoirs in the suburban hotel to which he has retreated at the involuntary end of his political career, Ralph discovers the natural piety that binds his days each to each. At the start of his story, as he recalls his student days in London, the fragmentation of his personality diminishes his self-awareness: 'How could I fashion order out of all these unrelated adventures and encounters, myself never the same, never even the thread on which these things were hung?' (p. 33) But already, as he ponders this fragmentation, he has moved towards wholeness: 'As though we ever play. As though the personality, with all its byways and wilful deviations, all its seeming inconsistencies, does not hang together.' (p. 31)

Because this process of recollection is what the novel is about, its essential action, the physical circumstances in which Ralph writes are evoked with special clarity. A sentence can conjure up a whole straitened way of life: 'I required a folding wooden clothes-airer which I thought I might introduce at nights into the bathroom of the hotel where I now live.' (p.11) Ralph writes on a junkshop table which has been added 'after a little trouble' to the bedroom of a shoddily-built hotel in the brick wasteland of outer London. In the astringency of such descriptions we are made to watch a lonely man writing; in the rhythms of the style we listen to the same man's inner voice as he strives to arrange the fragments thrown up on the coast of memory. It is a demanding style, inviting us to share Ralph's effort to examine these fragments with honesty and exactitude. After an episode has been related, the next section will begin with a sharp spring on its significance, as though Ralph has just read over the previous day's stint and grasped meanings which were not fully present to him as he wrote. Certain key words are used in an exploratory way, gathering connotations as the narrative advances: *taint, violation, frenzy, celebration, withdrawal* are among them. Ralph's effort to stand back from experience and to watch his own behaviour, to be that 'celestial camera' he had felt following him as a child, produces a free use of exclamations and imperatives; the lecturer taps the blackboard, the style is academically demonstrative. At the same time it is emotionally undemonstrative, eschewing alike self-pity and the irony which so easily masks self-pity. 'I was greatly moved', a phrase several times repeated or varied, exactly sets the narrative tone.

The sequence of the narrative, no less than its circumstances and its style, is sufficiently free of chronology to keep the act of composition constantly before us. From the writer's recall of his first winter as a student in London, interspersed with reflections on his present life, it moves onwards to his return to Isabella, 'educated, degreed, travelled', and thence to the success of his business career and the failure of his marriage. At this point Ralph reverts to memories of his childhood and adolescence on Isabella, ending with a lightning recall, like the quick spin-through of a tape we have already heard, of his marriage. The third and last part begins with the narrator, rich and solitary, responding to an invitation to enter politics. It follows him through a political career that ends in his failure to achieve the nationalization of the sugar estates, and his virtual exile as a result of the ensuing race riots. Only at the end does the coherence of this narrative order become clear to Ralph Singh and to us. Then, in a passage which once again vividly evokes his shoddy and straitened surroundings, he recalls how fourteen months previously he had sat a whole day long before a blank notebook, until the right beginning, seemingly *in medias res,* broke through to consciousness:

> Fourteen months have passed since, in a room made over-dry by the electric fire, I re-created that climb up the dark stairs to Mr Shylock's attic to look through a snowfall at the whitening roofs of Kensington. By this re-creation the event became historical and manageable; it was given its place; it will no longer disturb me. And this became my aim: from the central fact of this setting, my presence in this city which I have known as a student, politician and now as refugee-immigrant, to impose order on my own history, to abolish that disturbance which is what a narrative in sequence might have led me to. (p. 292)

Clearly the beginning, the first snow, matters very much, and it is a good place for us too to begin.

2

The tall Kensington house in which Singh lodges as a student offers a paradigm of a fragmented society. Its Jewish immigrant landlord has recently abrogated his responsibility to his tenants by dying. Singh is struck by the secrecy of a London death, so unlike the funeral processions which had—*mot juste*—enlivened afternoons in his native island. The attic in which Mr Shylock spent occasional nights with a young girl is now deserted; in the basement live the Maltese housekeeper and her child; between are the narrow, lonely rooms of alien and ambitious boarders. Lieni runs upstairs, half her make-up removed: 'I thought you would like to know. It's snowing.' To get a better view of the element he has always yearned after Ralph climbs to the fragile attic. There, the coldness and whiteness, the mattress on the gritty floor, the relics of a secret intimacy in the form of Mr Shylock's fuzzed identity card and the girl's blurred photograph, all overwhelm him:

> I thought: let it not happen to me. Death? But that comes to all. Well then, let me leave more behind. Let my relics be honoured. Let me not be mocked. But even as I tried to put words to what I felt, I knew that my own journey, scarcely begun, had ended in the shipwreck which all my life I had sought to avoid. (p. 10)

This terrified awareness of a void, of the final emptiness, also dominates Naipaul's previous novel, *A House for Mr Biswas.* There, the eponymous hero struggles to establish for himself a place on the earth so that he may be spared the fate of living and dying 'as one had been born, unnecessary and unaccommodated'. A whole series of houses plots Mr Biswas's changing positions between the devil and the deep blue sea, between the overcrowded barracoon of his wife's family home and the workhouse-asylum. Ralph Singh's world is more economically emblemed by a single house, the Kensington private hotel. Relegated to its basement, the Maltese Lieni, another islander, tries to relate to imagined social orders, both near and far: she has her illegitimate child baptized, and plans to marry an Indian engineer. But the ceremony which should welcome the child into the social group turns out to be a perfunctory and unintelligible rite in a makeshift setting. And the subsequent party in the hot and crowded basement brings together just such flotsam and jetsam of four continents as Ralph thought he had escaped from when he left Isabella. The guests have found refuge from their inadequacies in role-playing of various kinds: drink, violence, petty thieving, a malicious story-telling which is indistinguishable from the Trinidadian *mauvaise langue.* Now we begin to understand the desperation behind Lieni's make-up, her hunger to become the 'smart London girl'. But Lieni is finally thrust back into this crowd that is not company by her betrayal at the hands of her Indian lover, who is discovered to have a wife and children in India. So there is to be no sailing away to a new life; and Ralph, who has already sailed away and found only forlornness, the conurbation that is no real city, takes himself off alone to a dance at the British Council. Here he performs his own mimesis of betrayal, walking out on a French girl he has encouraged to dance with him. Later, at the boarding-house, the two castaways come together, but Ralph refuses Lieni the consolation of his bed. And when he relents, it is too late. Lieni is asleep.

I have already touched on some of the strategies by which Naipaul focuses our awareness on the imagined procedure of Ralph Singh's writing. A further device for making us feel we are looking over the narrator's shoulder is to provide us with clues to connections that Singh himself does not grasp or grasps only much later in the story. Such a connection may be between minor details: the girl to whom Ralph is gratuitously cruel after the christening, like another in a slightly later episode, is French and so the victim, we realize later, of Singh's resentment at a recent gesture of exclusion by old Deschampsneufs, head of the wealthy French Creole family in Isabella. Or the connection may be between two whole episodes with an identical psychological rhythm. Designers of paperback editions do not often show sharp insight into what is between the covers. It is all the more pleasurable therefore to find that the cover design to the 1971 Penguin edition of *The Mimic Men* makes perhaps the most important connection in the novel, by combining the blurred snapshot of Mr Shylock's mistress, taken in the secure suburban garden of her parental home, with the stingray that is at the centre of an episode in Singh's childhood. Together the two occurrences define the syndrome of Ralph's disordered nature.

Ralph Singh's wealthy relations have built a beach house on the edge of the battering Caribbean surf. From such little security as the exposed building affords the boy walks out one morning, driven by a pariah-like sense of exclusion (it is all an absurd matter of his having used the wrong toothbrush), and suffers a lonely and frightening encounter with sudden death. A brother and two sisters—a family, that is, like Ralph's own—are drowning in the surf, and the groups on the beach are powerless to save them. The Carib fishermen are unconcerned; the popular song from the refreshment shack still fills the air—*Bésame muchos, come si fuere la última vez*; and the child Ralph is overwhelmed by this new knowledge of human vulnerability:

> In my fear I turned away and walked back to the beach house. So private a fear it was, so private a sensation of the weakness of the flesh—those poor arms, those poor feet, this vulnerable head—it was shame for the weakness of the flesh that kept me from telling the story to the women. (p. 131)

Later the news comes and the family go to help pull in the bodies in the fishermen's seine. The net is also full of fish, and people begin to mangle these in a kind of frenzy: 'The stingray, on its brown back, its underside bluish-white, showed a bloody stump where its tail had been hacked off.' (p. 133)

Undermined by this knowledge of death, isolated from the activity that for once—and too late—unites all the non-indigenous racial and social groups, the child walks along the beach which is in its turn undermined by freshets that cause pieces of the shore to crumble away: 'a geography lesson in miniature, with time speeded up'. (p. 133) A passage from Donne's meditations, too familiar and too explicit for Naipaul to quote, will be in many readers' minds: 'every man is a part of the continent, a part of the main. If a clod be washed away by the sea, Europe is the less. . . .' The child Ralph is bent on being an island. He is consoling himself for the deep sense of violation that our first understanding of death, above all the loneliness of death, brings with it, by assuming the pose of being isolated and destined: the camera is in the sky. On his return to the house he finds his cousin Cecil building his own frail defence against obliteration by stamping out his name in huge letters on the sand. Ralph's reaction is different. He leans on the window ledge, 'gritty and sticky with sand and salt' (Mr Shylock's attic has a gritty floor), and teases his cousin Sally: 'I had the pleasure of seeing her stamp.' (p. 135)

My excuse for re-telling these episodes with a clumsiness that can only point up Naipaul's deftness is that I have wanted to bring out fully what they have in common. In each episode something occurs to give the narrator a feeling of isolation and insecurity. In each he protects himself against this insecurity by a kind of Byronic posturing. In each he feels himself compelled to compensate for his isolation by some act, however trivial, of violation. And in this he is not alone: all round him in the city, as earlier on the island, places where the individual is unable to relate to his environment, there rises in others a terror of the void and then, filling the void, frenzy, violence, the gesture of mutilation. Only much later, when Singh has reviewed his life up to the time he enters politics, is he able to grasp the importance of this syndrome in which the child was father of the man:

> For I find I have indeed been describing the youth and early manhood of a leader of some sort, a politician, or at least a disturber. I have established his isolation, his complex hurt and particular frenzy. And I believe I have also established, perhaps in this proclaimed frivolity, this lack of judgement and balance, the deep feeling of irrelevance and intrusion, his unsuitability for the role into which he was drawn, and his inevitable failure. From playacting to disorder: it is the pattern. (p.220)

3

Ralph Singh's insecurity begins in childhood, in the pattern of dominance established within his family by the wealth of his mother's relations. It is typical of the linking of personal and political relationships throughout the novel that this wealth should be in itself a form of colonial subjection: the money comes from bottling Coca-Cola, from economic dependence on American big business. But however insecure this wealth—and Ralph's cousin Cecil eventually loses the licence to bottle—it carries a kind of power. Ralph's sister and to some extent Ralph himself are absorbed into the maternal uncle's household. Already, that is, he experiences the 'colonial' temptation to attach himself to the dominant group and to mimic the behaviour of its members. Yet a painful awareness of his father's bitterness at this defection, and of his mother's guilty self-effacement before that bitterness, is to colour Ralph's adult relationships. He will always need a mother and fear a wife. A schoolroom demand for the feminine of *husband* dredges up horror that is none the less horror for being exceedingly funny:

> An answer was needed, and I knew. I got out of my desk and walked down the aisle to Mr Shepherd's table. He looked puzzled. I went and stood in front of him. He bent down with concern and I whispered into his ear: 'Wife'.
>
> More than thirty years later the man agrees with the child: it is a terrible word. (p.109)

To the child who is already so insecure, his early days at school offer little security. Other pupils appear to know their roles. Deschampsneufs, the descendent of French plantation owners who have traditionally maintained an aristocratic aloofness towards the British presence, plays the Young Master; Browne, the descendent of slaves, unself-consciously acts the Comic Coon. But the sons of later migrants have to search for their roles. While Hok reads Chinese history, Ralph Singh pores over volumes about the Aryan conquest of India and dreams of horsemen among snow-covered peaks. Such dreams bear little relevance to the life of Isabella, as Hok's friends find when he is forced by an outraged schoolmaster to drop out of the school crocodile and talk to his mother, whom he has tried to ignore: she is plebeian and black.

The sharp absurdity of these incidents and the seeming arbitrariness of their recall help to conceal the underlying schematization of this part of the story. Deschampsneufs, Browne, Singh, and Hok typify the racial segments of a totally colonial society that has not yet achieved cohesion into any social order. The education that the children receive does nothing to help them relate to their island community. It only superimposes upon their existing fantasies dreams of yet another landscape, so that they imagine they once took their teacher apples from an English orchard. The masters too are castaways, cherishing their private inner landscapes: snow in the Laurentians, or traffic jams in Liège. Such order as school can give is precarious, and to Ralph's distress this very fragile order is shaken by his own father, who suddenly emerges from obscurity as the leader of a popular protest movement mainly supported by the Negro dockers.

This movement's most dramatic gesture is the slaughter of a racehorse belonging to the Deschampsneufs. Presumably it is killed because the Negro followers of Ralph's father have taken exception to its being named after a legendary hero of emancipation. The carcase is found arranged as an *asvamedha,* a Hindu horse-sacrifice, and to Ralph this is deeply disturbing. Its effect is simultaneously to tarnish his dream of escape and to involve him with the island's affairs; he is now cast for the role of son to the man who has identified with the distressed. On Browne and Deschampsneufs also the movement has a disturbing effect. They are no longer content with their island past. Browne's reading reveals that not only the people but even the trees of Isabella are transplanted from the old world. Deschampsneufs fixes his hopes and ambitions on Quebec, where French culture has survived transplantation as it has failed to do in his own family, who choose to play black. The fragile, tenuous order around Ralph is falling apart, and he becomes prey to an obsessional fear that the parental house will collapse. Only when he has hurried home in fright after seeing a tree fall in a storm—one of those trees whose uprootings supply a *leitmotiv* of the novel—and has found the house untouched and secure does he realize that the wish was father to the fear: he longs for an end to all these broken relationships, for the chance to start afresh and unencumbered. He is ready to leave.

But one traumatic incident takes place before his departure, which is delayed by the 1939 war. He has had his first sexual experience, with his cousin Sally; the union brings the estranged, castaway young man a novel sense of security in a desperately insecure time and place: 'the relationship based on perfect knowledge, in which body of one flesh joined to body of the same flesh, and all external threat was diminished'. (p.186) By the standards of the Indian extended family the affair is incestuous.

Sally's brother Cecil, his moral indignation the greater because he has had a similar affair with one of Ralph's sisters, assumes the role of avenger of the family honour. In the company of his Negro attendant whom it pleases him to call Cecil, and of another Indian, Dulip (who has cast himself for the avenger's role because Singh's father, after taking to the hills, has co-habited with Dulip's mother), Cecil drives Ralph to a lonely beach for what appears to be merely a drunken outing. The production of a revolver implies that there is in fact a plan to execute the taboo-breaker. The scene becomes a powerful emblem of colonial dereliction. Four near-naked figures prance drunkenly among the bleached and stranded tree-trunks on a sunless beach, linked only by inbred fear and hatred. Their hostility is prevented from erupting into violence by the arrival of a white family; under their uncomprehending gaze, the would-be executioners become happy, boisterous islanders gambolling in the surf, and Ralph is saved. But a new compulsion has asserted itself: the compulsion to persist in playing a role, no matter how irrelevant that role may be to the danger of the player's situation.

For the present, this scene enacted by frenzied castaways represents the shipwreck of Ralph Singh's early life. He is rejected, adrift, unrelated. He consoles himself for his isolation by further withdrawals, retreating from the offered gifts of friendship; he fails to appear at his farewell dinner and leaves for the greater dereliction, the experience of finding himself totally adrift in London. Here he assumes a role that offers some alleviation to his complex hurt, one encouraged and in part devised by the equally hurt Lieni: the role of Don Juan. But the seduction of *au pair* girls in no way destroys his isolation. The participants have nothing to share but bed; they are separated by their different languages and their different basic images. And Naipaul implies that Ralph, introverted to the point of narcissism, wants things that way. Yet on at least one occasion an encounter with an *au pair* girl seems to hold the promise of a real relationship, just as on occasion the assemblage of people in Mr Shylock's boarding-house, though they are brought together by nothing more than the rapacity of their landlord, shows signs of becoming some kind of community. The house, however, is bought and the boarders evicted in order, Ralph later discovers, that it may be turned into a brothel; and as if to match this decline Ralph's casual affairs are replaced by visits to prostitutes. From this arid existence, he is rescued by his marriage to Sandra. Or so at least it appears at the time.

In name and in nature Sandra is socially 'placed' with a skill that is not, as with so many minor contemporary novelists, an end in itself, but is made to serve the main concerns of the novel. Ralph and Sandra are well matched; too well matched. Like him, she is an intensely self-regarding personality; like him she has totally repudiated her background, which could be characterized by her favourite term of abuse, 'common'. Marriage for both is a defiant rejection of their origins, and for Sandra the celebratory mood is heightened by a sense of having escaped a drab and restricted existence. Sharing this celebratory mood, Ralph returns with her to Isabella and embarks on the energetic business career that makes him a rich man in five years. This life as the most successful in a group of prosperous young Indians with expatriate wives seems to Ralph a total escape from his London existence; only later does he see that both modes were alternative reactions to

> the injury inflicted on me by the too solid three-dimensional city in which I could never feel myself as anything but spectral, disintegrating, pointless, fluid. The city made by man but passed out of his control: breakdown the negative reaction, activity the positive: opposite but equal aspects of an accommodation to a sense of place which, like memory, when grown acute, becomes a source of pain. (p. 61)

Accommodation to Isabella takes the form of a determined repudiation of his roots: 'I hadn't, I must confess, informed my mother of my marriage.' (p. 62) Those round him have made a similar repudiation, and the outward and visible sign of their withdrawal is the one-class and luxurious housing estate that makes Singh's fortune.

But the building of Crippleville is more than withdrawal, it is violation. Island society, where traditionally the rich have lived alongside the poor, is disturbed by this new pattern of suburban housing, and it is emblematic of such disturbance that the builders, in their landscaping, have to blow to fragments the stump and roots of a giant tree, leaving 'a monstrous wound in the red earth'. Characteristically Ralph Singh, the disturber, wishes he could have preserved this relic of the pre-Columbian world. Within their own social group also the loftiness of Ralph and Sandra is a withdrawal that disturbs. They build a 'Roman' house, a building turned in on itself and made the more narcissistic by the substitution of a swimming pool for the *impluvium.* The group has its own *mauvaise langue,* and exercises it at the couple's expense. At the house-warming, words become deeds. Under the guise of behaving with drunken exuberance, the guests begin to break the place up. Singh drives out to the ruins of a famous old slave plantation, now the haunt of 'rapists and others seeking social revenge', and weeps—not for the destruction of what is replaceable, but for the disorder, the 'lack of sympathy between man and the earth he walks on', to which there seems to be no end.

Sandra should have protected him from this desolation. But the satisfying match has not ripened into a real marriage; the parade of intimacy, like the flirtations in the Oxford excursion train in Singh's Don Juan days, conceals a loneliness *à deux.* On account of her sexual initiative and her social aggressiveness, Ralph thinks Sandra a much more self-sufficient character than she in fact is. Already in London the reader has been made to detect the vulnerability of her nature under the rough tongue and the grubby mackintosh. In Isabella, she experiences again and again the syndrome of isolation, hurt, frenzy, from the moment of her mother-in-law's histrionic rejection of her on the quayside to the moment she is cut by her last friend, Wendy Deschampsneufs. With Sandra the frenzy takes the significant form of her stereotyping her victims as racial inferiors: a Latvian expatriate wife is 'the sub-Asiatic', a Swedish acquaintance is dubbed a 'common little Lapp'. Wendy's rejection is revenged by the island vulgarism that corresponds to 'a touch of the tarbrush': 'the Niger is a tributary of that Seine'. By such small racial violences she compensates for her own rejection and isolation; they are to have their greater counterparts later in the novel. For the present, they herald the end of the marriage, a union that could have filled the void in both lives were it not for Ralph's wilful withdrawal, his refusal of the proffered gift. Once again he is shipwrecked. Once again he must act, lonely and self-sufficient, before the celestial camera. The role this time is imposed on him by Browne, who calls at the Roman house from which Sandra has departed with an invitation to Singh to join the party that is working for independence.

4

Browne needs Ralph's capital. He also needs his name, which the disruptive movement initiated by Ralph's father, now regarded as the first gesture towards independence, has made a 'name of peculiar power'. And the careers of father and son are linked by more than political activity. From a number of incidents recalled in the second part of the novel we have discovered that 'Gurudeva's' political acts were the culmination of the sequence of isolation, hurt, frenzy, that we have been observing in the son. As with the son, the hurt comes to Singh *père* from those who are closest to him. When Ralph gives his cricket bat, a gift from his father, away to Cecil, his father goes to the nearest café and systematically breaks up ninety-six bottles of Coco-Cola. Later on, he tries to assert himself as head of the household, presiding over an unhappy Sunday dinner and a subsequent outing which, in the face of his family's indifference, turns to a frantic display of bad driving culminating in a crash. At another time he invites Ralph to ride, illegally, on the crossbar of his cycle to reach home through a downpour, but once they are there the boy slips silently away from this intimacy; and this is to be their last contact, for shortly afterwards Ralph's father leads the distressed and disaffected to the hills in order to settle them on crown land. The lawlessness inherent in the various ludicrous episodes of family life now spreads: 'Calm in the hills, he offered disorder and drama.' The Deschampsneufs' racehorse is killed.

> After that deed our island changed, though change was not to show for fifteen years. It was like the loaders' insulting of Cecil's father, the gesture which suddenly reveals society as an association of consent and teaches, dangerously for the future of all, that consent can be withdrawn. (p. 169)

The incident with Cecil's father goes back to Ralph's childhood and is yet another manifestation of the syndrome: the uncle has spoken to Ralph sentimentally of a group of Indian sugar-cane loaders as 'my people' and is hurt to the point of frenzy when, after an attempt by his chauffeur to pass their lorry on a wet road, they shout obscenities at him. The incident epitomizes the fate of the disturber in a fragile social order, and it is this role of disturber that Ralph, at the end of his marriage and the culmination of his business career, is now invited to play.

A disturber is also the central character of *A Flag on the Island,* which stands in the same relation to Naipaul's major novels that Graham Greene's 'entertainments' stand to his; in fact echoes, perhaps unconscious, of *Our Man in Havana* can be detected in it. So too can the underlying seriousness of Greene's book. Frank, the G.I. narrator ('generous' or, someone suggests, short for Frankenstein), is as insecure as Ralph—'I feel the whole world is being washed away and that I am being washed away with it.' And though he brings his insecurity from outside the island, it is expressed in an image that recalls Ralph the castaway child: 'The child, testing his courage, steps into the swiftly moving stream, and though the water does not go above his ankles, in an instant the safe solid earth vanishes, and he is aware only of the terror of sky and trees and the force at his feet.' On the island he plays the double role of exploiter and benefactor, as if he were Greene's Smith and Jones rolled into one. Disastrously, his first intervention occurs at a moment when, as the local philosopher Henry has observed, people are beginning to relinquish their racial nostalgia and to merge into a community of sorts.' "Some people corporate in one way", Henry said. "Some people corporate in another way."' As Achebe's Ibo characters might put it, Frank puts his knife on the things that hold the islanders together, and they fall apart. Even a seeming philanthropy, the urge to relieve distress, can be an aspect of the frenzy that hides an inner insecurity. 'This is part of the excitement; money became paper over which other people fought.' Henry is rightly wary of such Aid, even in the days when it takes the form of purloined army stores: 'Some people look at black people and only see black. You look at poor people and you only see poor. You think the only thing they want is money. All-you wrong, you know.'

A Flag on the Island is of course something of a squib, and lacks a political argument such as underlies *The Mimic Men.* That argument, sustained through the third and last part of the novel, is that the economic weakness of small ex-colonial territories compels their politicians to betray the connotations of order implicit in their very title, and to create disorder. And this disorder replaces order of a kind, the paternal structure of a Crown Colony: a shabby order, as Ralph sees, and one that must be relegated to the past, and yet one within which an undignified figure like his grandfather, as nominated member of the legislative council, had benevolence and service imposed upon him. That this is Naipaul's argument as well as Ralph's is made clear in an article by him published in 1970 and included in *The Overcrowded Barracoon*

> These Caribbean territories are not like those in Africa or Asia, with their own internal reverences, that have been returned to themselves after a period of colonial rule. They are manufactured societies, labour camps, creations of empire; and for long they were dependent on empire for law, language, institutions, culture, even officials. Nothing was generated locally; dependence became a habit. How, without empire, do such societies govern themselves? Where is now the source of power? The ballot box, the mob, the regiment? When, as in Haiti, the slave-owners leave, and there are only slaves, what are the sanctions?

A party of self-determination, such as is led by Browne and Ralph Singh, gains its support by holding out to the deprived a hope of alleviation which cannot be fulfilled. 'They play with incurable distress.' Just how incurable, they discover when responsibility suddenly falls upon them; it is as if the other side in the tug of war had suddenly let go. The unrealities of post-colonial industrialization supply some of the sharpest satire in the novel for any reader who has watched the same processes at work elsewhere. A Czech adventurer makes plastic buckets that stink. Imported margarine is put into imported tins in a factory employing five operatives, who are photographed in their white overalls, looking grave and professional; the margarine is a little more expensive than the ready-tinned imported variety. To those below the poverty line, this play-acting of the mimic men is betrayal, and they react with what Singh calls 'the negative frenzy of a deep violation which could lead to further frenzy alone'. (p. 245) The frenzy takes the form of racial violence: Indian against Creole on the sugar estates, Creole against Indian in the towns.

Ralph is at the centre of this political play-acting, but we are given to understand that it is not hindsight alone that reveals him to us as a man who sees the best and does the worst. His education has given him an ideal of order. The Roman house represents something more than his temperamental narcissism; it stands also for his longing after Roman decorum and proportion, the ideals of the City. For a time the Roman house serves as the party headquarters, accommodating a group that gives itself the dedicated air of a religious community. This too is play-acting. The group, like Ralph himself, lack the Roman *virtus,* and this incompleteness, this lack of integrity in Ralph, prevents him from dropping the role of friend to the oppressed and using his real gifts—he is a trained economist, a successful and experienced businessman—for constructive action: 'I could have drawn together sufficient of the elements of our island to make my power certain and to restore calm.' (p. 263) But instead:

> I struggled to keep drama alive for its replacement was despair: the vision of a boy walking on an endless, desolate beach, between vegetation living, rotting, collapsed, and a mindless, living sea. No calm then: that came later, fleetingly. Drama failing, I knew frenzy. Frenzy kept me silent. And silence committed me to pretence. (p. 264)

In this state of mind, Ralph's journey to London to negotiate the sugar nationalization is not initiative but withdrawal. He is quickly informed of what he knew already, the hopelessness of his mission, and escapes by an instinctive regression into the kind of celebratory existence which had eluded him at his first coming to London. The city is now transformed from its post-war drabness; Lady Stella, daughter of the sugar magnate, replaces the socially discontented L.S.E. student, Sandra. The affair does not last long, since withdrawal is as inevitable a part of Ralph Singh's sexual behaviour as of his political; and after a stopover encounter with a prostitute which represents the total failure of all relationship, an abomination of desolation, Ralph finds himself back alone in the Roman house while race riots flare through the island. From there only one further flight is possible: exile in England.

I have spoken of the novel's political argument. It is of course debatable whether or not a novel should have a political argument as distinct from a political subject, and it is possible to see in Ralph Singh's somewhat bald theorizing in this final segment of *The Mimic Men* an indication of Naipaul's own shift of interests: his next book was to be a study in depth of two phases of colonial history. Certainly there is some failure in reader psychology in these political chapters. The demands Naipaul makes of his reader are always exacting but they are justified as long as the skills demanded are those relevant to reading of fiction. But here, at the point where, in most novels, the curve of the story would flatten out a little and our concentration be allowed to relax, we find ourselves shifted to a different field of discourse, one demanding a different type of reading skill, and a redoubled concentration.

Moreover, our acceptance of this political narrative is hindered by real obscurity in the action: it is never made plain just how and why the racial violence occurs. Perhaps the reason for this is that in the third part of the tale Isabella ceases to be identifiable as Trinidad. Plenty of resemblances remain. Eric Williams's People's National Movement became a force in 1956 and in 1959 it achieved cabinet government, together with the control of the police which so much exercises Ralph Singh in the novel. But no prominent East Indian played the role of Singh in Eric Williams's cabinet, although a few half-identifications are possible; and Trinidad, despite its many sub-groups, has mercifully never experienced the kind of race frenzy which erupts in the novel. For the political alliance of Negro and East Indian and for the breakdown of such an alliance in race riots, Naipaul had to go to Guyana, to the history of the People's Progressive Party under the dual leadership of Jagan and Burnham. In Guyana, however, the disturbances of the sixties were the outcome of historical and geographical factors which did not operate, or operated only on a smaller, less menacing scale, in Trinidad. And a further complication seems to have arisen from the fact that the novelist completed the book in Uganda, at a time when the East African army mutinies created an atmosphere of total political disorder; a time too when the Indian minorities in these countries, the scapegoats of every political and economic failure, were feeling exceptionally insecure. Browne's wholesale deportation of British civil servants, for example, is based on the notorious 'Tank Hill Party' episode in Kampala, and does not correspond to any conceivable behaviour by a West Indian politician. Of course there is more to this mingling of political incidents than political discretion, or caution regarding the laws of libel. Naipaul wants to enlarge the applicability of his fable. But in a novel as concerned with cause and effect as *The Mimic Men,* this blurring of historical causality weakens the tale at its most vital point.

There is also blurring of another kind. I have quoted a passage written by Naipaul in 1970 which could have come from the imagined pen of Ralph Singh. In the last part of *The Mimic Men* this most sophisticated novelist, usually so alert to the need to maintain a distance between himself and his narrator, seems to me to use his protagonist as a mouthpiece and so lay himself open to the charge of 'colonial-mindedness' so often levelled at him by West Indian critics. In examining this accusation we need to keep a distinction between Singh's past and present attitudes—he is writing with hindsight—and also between Singh's economic and his political views, in so far as these can be separated. Ralph Singh is not being colonial-minded when he writes about his own successful re-negotiation of the bauxite concession. He is showing up the inevitable dependence of the men without power of whom he was once one. Although the concession seems a more tangible achievement than the production of smelly plastic and costly margarine, it still is a *concession* to foreign capitalism such as had repeatedly to be made, despite Eric Williams's avowed Marxism, in the early days of P.N.M. rule in Trinidad. Here, then, Naipaul's satire is directed against the real dependence inside the pretended independence. But in political, as distinct from economic matters, Trinidad has shown itself a country to be reckoned with, and here it might be said that Naipaul joins with his narrator in a needless despondency. Ralph Singh's failure to achieve the nationalization of the sugar industry in the novel is not a failure in bargaining power, but a failure in timing: it appears to take place at the intermediary stage in political evolution which existed in the real island of Trinidad between 1959 and 1962, years in which Britain retained the right to disallow Trinidadian laws. After independence, Eric Williams resisted with remarkable success America's pressure on him to agree to the retention of her wartime bases on the island; and there is no explanation in the novel of why Singh could not have stood up equally firmly to the sugar magnates and nationalized the industry in an independent—as against a semi-independent—Isabella. Political emotion has here fouled the lines of political reasoning to do real injury to the novel as an artifact.

But Naipaul's political critics overstate their case. They pay no heed to the theme which is abundantly clear in *The Mimic Men* as in all his other books concerned with the West Indies: the primal *wrongness* of Caribbean colonialism in all its phases—the creation of a slave society and economy, the prolongation through indentured labour of a form of serfdom long after black slavery ended, and the relegation of the islands for many decades to the status of slums of empire, a relegation culminating in an ill-prepared 'granting of independence'. This was the violation the novel never lets us forget, as it traces out the pattern of rejection, impairment, alienation, in individual lives as well as in the groups that compose this heterogeneous society. The novel is a *nosce teipsum*: without an understanding of his own nature and of the nature of the culture he has inherited, the West Indian intellectual may involve himself in action that is only dangerous mimicry: an alliance with the distressed that is a sharing of nothing more than resentment, a bestowal of the gift of drama that is ultimately irrelevant to their plight.

5

Ralph Singh's father also bestows the gift of drama on his adherents. But he is not left to play the role of disturber for very long; the authorities intern him for the duration of the war, and on his release he becomes a religious figure, the *sanyasi*. He completes in this way the Hindu cycle of life: student, householder, man of affairs, recluse. And in this last phase, which is both moving and embarrassing to Ralph, who is on the point of leaving for England, he displays that charisma which Ralph learns about years later from Lord Stockwell:

> These simple people came and told him their troubles. The usual sort of thing. Job, sickness, death. While they were talking he was always doing something else. But at the end he would always speak a word or two, sometimes a sentence. It was marvellous. And sitting down, witnessing this, you felt immensely comforted. I couldn't leave. (p.273)

The scene is the fulfilment of what his missionary mentor had seen in Ralph's father as a young boy. In his son's life it has its counterpart not long after Ralph's meeting with Lord Stockwell. Ralph has returned to the Roman house on the deeply troubled island. A man brings him a stone sticky with blood and a child's hair, and Ralph leads him outside and makes him drop the stone so that he may 'destroy the images of vulnerable flesh'. It is a highly ambiguous scene; it reveals to Ralph Singh and to the reader his gift of a real leadership, but only at the point where the disorder caused by his disturbance has brought profound suffering to the man he is now able to influence. This ambiguity is worth pursuing, since it leads to an awareness of an extra dimension to the novel; a dimension which more than compensates for the weaknesses in political veracity that we have already noticed.

Ralph repeatedly withdraws, and often the withdrawal brings disastrous consequences for those round him. But withdrawal can represent virtue as well as the absence of virtue. The contradiction is illustrated when Ralph the schoolboy, out of a sense of futility, withdraws from a race he is really too old to run in, and is praised for his sportsmanship. Such a sense of the vanity of vanities is described by Ralph as the beginning of religion or of neurosis. That it operates throughout most of his life as the beginning of neurosis is clear from the frenetic consequences of his various withdrawals; in the same way, his father retreated into the hills and spread disorder through the island. But the other possible outcome of withdrawal is postulated early in the narrative, when Ralph recalls how he was asked, in the days of his greatest success, what he would do if that success were suddenly to end:

> Relief: this was my first reaction, and it was a reaction to the man in front of me. Not in any unkind way, for with the word there came a picture of myself in some forest clearing, dressed as a knight, dressed as a penitent, in hermit's rags, approaching a shrine on my knees, weeping, performing a private penance for the man in front of me, for myself, for all men, for whom in the end nothing can be done. (p.47)

There is of course plenty of self-dramatization here; the vision is tarnished with the mimicry of Ralph's role-playing existence. But behind the posturing we recognize the deep and Indian drive towards non-attachment, that acceptance of the human condition which Ralph can bestow upon the man holding the bloodstained stone. It involves a renunciation of all compensatory violence, an acceptance such as Simone Weil (herself influenced by Sufi mysticism) has expressed of the vacuum created in us by violation, an acceptance of *le vide*: 'Aimer la vérité signifie supporter le vide et par suite accepter la mort. La vérité est du côté de la mort.' Such acceptance is not inactivity but the prelude to activity. Yet in the Roman house Ralph's vision can no longer lead to activity because his own previous filling of the void by role-playing has created a disorder which renders action impossible for him or for those he might have led. Browne too is caught between an acceptance of the void and a frenzied rush to fill it. There are times when he feels violation is violation and cannot be undone; slavery is the history that must be endured. But either he lacks the will to go forward from that position or his followers force him into the role of the racial avenger, the man who must hurt to compensate for the historical injury inflicted on his race.

When Ralph and perhaps Browne as well have yielded their places to the 'faceless men', Ralph can look back like his father on a life that has followed the traditional Aryan pattern. But each phase, for reasons that have been traced in his childhood, has ended in neurosis. The student could not relate to the fragmented society of either Isabella or London and when Sandra put her startling question: 'Why don't you propose, you *fool*?', he was on the edge of breakdown. The married man lived in isolated ascendency over another kind of society, that written with a capital S, until his marriage ended in marital indifference and extra-marital frenzy. The man of affairs, after a brief reign over the diversity of interests that constitute a new political party, threw away his political career in a mixture of criminal inactivity and irresponsible action. Now, at the age of forty, he is totally withdrawn into his suburban hotel where, if there is order of a sort, it is 'rooted in nothing, linked to nothing'. In eighteen months, which are virtually unrecorded because their emptiness leaves nothing to record, he has come to accept the vacuum: 'My present urge is, in the inaction imposed on me, to secure the final emptiness.' (p.13) There is no means left of filling the void; like his father wrapped in his *sanyasi* silence, he can no longer speak the words that wound, and the void must be endured for the truth's sake. So he repudiates in the writing of his memoirs not only self-pity but the equivalent luxury of guilt; and a phrase such as 'my aching love for Sandra' comes as a shock to us long after the story of the marriage has been dispassionately told.

When Ralph begins to write in quest of the final emptiness he does not realize, as he does fourteen months later, that 'the recording of a life might become an extension of that life'. These fourteen months of composition are the book's extra dimension. They not only supply the need we feel in all first-person narratives for information about how and where the narrative is being written, and what the narrator feels as he writes it. They reveal to Ralph an order where he believed there was only futility and disorder. The career which, as he began to write, seemed to him to have been interrupted by parentheses, now reshapes itself as a continuous whole; the sense of having in his time played many parts is replaced by an awareness of the persistence of personality.

It will be seen that I am taking Ralph's narrative at its face value. There are difficulties here. Singh himself insists that his view of his life has changed in the course of writing about it. On what compulsion then must we accept the perspective with which the book ends as either final or truthful? Now that Ralph has taken to the forest (only it is a forest that has been cut down to make way for suburban pubs and putting greens) can we be sure that this phase is not one more piece of play-acting that will issue in disorder? Has Naipaul failed to foresee the reader's doubt in this matter, because he is too deeply involved with his narrator? Alternatively, is the doubt part of Naipaul's plan, so that the book shall remain ironic at Singh's expense to the very end?

The answer to these questions is in the hands of a character who appears in the closing pages. In fact nothing but his hands appear, the rest of him being concealed behind a pillar in the hotel dining room. He is nicknamed 'Garbage' by Ralph Singh, because at each meal his hands work vigorously on the dinner plate, separating the eatable from the uneatable. When that operation has been completed, the food eaten, and the little mound of garbage handed to the waitress, the hands take a decisive grip on the cheese:

> . . . the cheddar shifts about on the oily slaughter-board; there is a struggle; thumb and finger release their hold, but only to press down more firmly; instantly, then, the knife falls in a strong, clean stroke that continues until the cheese is truncated and still. And I almost expect to see blood. (p. 295)

There is no mistaking Garbage's meal as an emblem of Ralph's life; Ralph too sits behind a pillar, and Garbage is a kind of mirror image of himself. But so ludicrous an emblem has an effect similar to that of Brown's transformation into an undertaker at the end of *The Comedians.* It disinfects but does not destroy our sense of an ending. Ralph Singh, during his months of writing, has extracted and assembled the meaningful elements in his life, and the resultant self-knowledge has made it possible for him at last to act rather than perform. But the self-knowledge comes when his great future is behind him and there is little left for him to do: the ferocious assault on the cheese can be as much of a waste of talent on trivia as the promise of fresh and decisive action.

Garbage's dexterity with the cheese knife cuts Singh's fate down to size and controls the sentimentality that a sight of the end engenders in the most sober reader. His presence helps us to balance loss against gain, and the gain is very much there, solid and unrhetorical as a slice of cheese. Singh's discovery of order in his past is not his narcissism in a new guise. It is something more fruitful. It issues in the discovery of order in the present, represented by that standard property of philosophical argument, the table:

> . . . when I first sat at it I thought it rough and too narrow. The dark surface was stained and scratched, the indentations filled with grit and dirt; the drawers didn't pull out, the legs had been cut down. It had been provided specially; it was a junkshop article, belonging to no one, without a function. Now it feels rehabilitated and clean; it is familiar and comfortable; even the scratches have acquired a shine. This is the gift of minute observation which has come to me with the writing of this book, one order, of which I form part, answering the other, which I create. And with this gift has come another, which I least expected: a continuous, quiet enjoyment of the passing of time. (p. 294)

When he contrasts this subdued life, with its recognizable social order, its decorum, its small rituals, to the desolation of his first few weeks in exile, Singh can truthfully say in his island patois, *je vens d'lue*; he has come from far, from the brink of madness to a recognition of order. This surely is achievement, not a prolongation of self-deception. And there is a second course in the repast. Of the two means open to him of becoming a builder rather than a demolisher, a business career or the writing of history, Ralph's natural bent seems to be for the historian's task. Even in his political days he found time to write to Browne about Roman history and to Deschampsneufs about Hindu philosophy. These letters, though, were evasions, pseudo-history. Now that he has discovered, in the writing of his memoirs and in the attitudes the act of writing has evoked, the nature both of the Roman *virtus* and the Hindu *dharma,* Ralph Singh can become a historian rather than one who plays at being a historian. What he could now assume is not a fresh role but a responsibility: to bring to verbal order and understanding the disorder of the imperial past.

CONCLUSION

Novelists of the Colonial Experience

In the foregoing essays I have not deliberately avoided cross-references. To have done so would have been disingenuous, since a network of relationships so clearly exists between the six novels discussed. But I have tried to leave the initiative in comparison and contrast to the reader, in order that he or she may be the better able to audit my final account. For what I want to attempt now is literally a summing up: the brief reconsideration of these six novels in their possible groupings of twos and threes and as a set of six. Such small samples cannot of themselves be the bases of generalization, but I hope to be able to suggest the wealth of other evidence that lies to hand, over and above the half-dozen novels considered here, on the novelist's response to the colonial experience.

1

To draw a racial line between three novels by expatriate and three by indigenous writers is to invite trouble; but it is trouble of a kind that needs to be confronted for the sake of critical accuracy. A racial alignment inevitably gives rise to a stereotyping of each group by the other. Because writers such as Conrad, Forster, and Greene belong by birth to the dominating side in the colonial experience, critics who themselves belong to the once dominated, ex-colonial world have claimed that such European novels are a kind of literary exploitation. Bloke Modisane speaks of the literary scramble for Africa. Richard Wright fulminates about the 'psychologically crippled white seeking his own perverse personal salvation' in Africa. And though we could perhaps write this off as the self-compensation of an Afro-American who was deeply hurt to find Africans regarded him as an expatriate, we must take seriously the not very different judgement of such a sober critic as M.J.C. Echeruo:

> Most European novels of Africa in which European characters play a major role have one common theme: the re-education of the white man in the jungle-purgatory of Africa. It is with the anxieties, expectations, frustrations and fulfilment of European man in the alien world of Africa that these novels are concerned.

The Victorian allegedly worked off his frustrations by shooting lions and tigers in the tropics; and in Third World eyes, his descendant is doing much the same when he sets a novel in any part of that tropical world. This legend, like all the other confusions that have resulted from the colonial encounter, calls for some patience in its disentanglement. We may start by conceding that the expatriate writer often is a man or woman with a psychological wound. But pain can sharpen the traveller's insight: when Mary Kingsley 'went down to Africa to die' she wrote the most vivid and understanding account of West Africa hitherto published by a European. Significantly, such a wound (to keep Edmund Wilson's image) can help the writer to understand the trauma of conquest. All three expatriate writers with whom we have been concerned knew in their childhood the experience of being dominated, of being at the mercy of some kind of arbitrary power. Some of Conrad's earliest memories were of exile to Russia under conditions which killed his mother and hastened the death of his father. This childhood passed in the shadow of imperial oppression was appallingly lonely; the adult Conrad was to value highly the comradeship of a ship's company. Forster and Greene had in their childhoods the contrary experience, scarcely less traumatic, of oppression inside the small, potentially vicious world of an English public school. 'Sawston' is the powerful image of mindless cruelty in Forster's novels. Major Callendar must be a distinguished old boy. And Berkhamsted School was to Greene 'a savage country of strange customs and inexplicable cruelties'. Baron Samedi walked through the early lives of all three writers.

In their actual experience of the countries in which their stories are set, Conrad, Forster, and Greene were well placed to study the colonial presence as at best an intrusion and at worst a violation. Whatever disturbances of mind they brought with them, they did not suffer the childhood trauma of rejection experienced by writers who belonged by long residence, and often by birth as well, to the dominant group inside a colonial society: an experience skilfully evaded by Kipling in *Kim,* less skilfully confronted by Doris Lessing in *The Grass is Singing,* and movingly evoked by Jean Rhys in *Wide Sargasso Sea.* Nor were they ever implicated in the colonial system as officials. Leonard Woolf and George Orwell knew very little of what they were letting themselves in for when they went to the East, the one as a magistrate in what was then Ceylon, the other as an officer in the Burma Police. When they came to write fiction their problem was to control their feelings of guilt. In *The Village in the Jungle,* Woolf succeeded in this better than did Orwell in his frenetically angry *Burmese Days*; though in the end, in 'Shooting an Elephant', Orwell conveyed more eloquently than any other writer has done the intolerable position of the individual trapped in the colonial system. Guilt is also a recognizable element in Joyce Cary's *Mister Johnson,* a fine novel of the colonial experience of which I have written at length elsewhere. Cary, however, found relief from guilt, not in kicking against the pricks with Orwell and Woolf, but in developing a historical perspective that allowed him to see the colonial intrusion as an inevitable disturbance in a world of continual change.

Neither poor white waifs nor imperial overlords, Conrad, Forster, and Greene are thoughtful travellers who were careful in their journeys to dissociate themselves from the master race. In the Congo, Conrad was set apart as 'the English captain'. He believed himself to be exploited by the company that employed him and nursed a lifelong resentment against its local manager, Camille Delcommune. Forster, in his first voyage to the East, found that he and his Cambridge friends were looked at askance by the Anglo-Indians. And when Graham Greene revisited Hispaniola in the late fifties and early sixties he had already made plain, in *The Quiet American,* his feelings about United States intervention in the Third World.

'Heart of Darkness', *A Passage to India,* and *The Comedians* all appeared several years later than their writers' first travels in the countries in which they are set. Such intervals, during which 'the compost of the imagination', as Greene terms it, has time to ferment, commonly precede major works of literature. But in the case of these three writers there was also an important sequel: each of them, it would appear, was imaginatively awakened some years after his first visit by a virtual cry of distress from the country concerned. We have seen that Conrad was aware of the agitation about the Congo Free State which arose in the eighteen-nineties; though it was at first directed against those who executed an English trader, it quickly turned to an exposure of atrocities done to the Congolese. When the Amritsar massacre occurred six years after Forster's first visit to India, he heard more about it and was more profoundly shocked by it than most English people; the articles he wrote as a 'special correspondent' on his return to India in 1921 are very largely concerned with the aftermath of the Punjab disturbances. For Graham Greene the cry of distress possibly took the form of revulsion at the slaughter, in July 1963, of the group of young partisans who had raided Kemscoff police station, near Port-au-Prince. Another of Conrad's novels offers an interesting parallel. *Nostromo,* the story of the domination of a South American country by Western material interests, would seem to have gained its imaginative impetus, not from any news from the New World, but from events in Africa. Conrad regarded the Anglo-South African War as the suppression of an agricultural people, devoted to the land, by those who sought to join with Rhodes in the exploitation of South Africa's mineral resources.

Attuned to the dominated, distanced from the dominators, and reminded by events of the inherent wrongness of all domination, our expatriate novelists inevitably see the colonial encounter as a painful disruption. Their vision is not very different from that of Chinua Achebe, who not only called his first novel *Things Fall Apart,* but used as its epigraph the whole of Yeats's passage about the 'mere anarchy' that has been loosed upon the world. Disturbance is the subject of 'Heart of Darkness' from the moment Marlow sees the French man-of-war firing into the bush to the point at which an immense darkness descends upon the listeners to Marlow's disturbing tale. At the heart of the story the arch-disturber Kurtz terrorizes the Congolese with his rapacity and terrifies the reader with the shock of recognition. This theme of disturbance was to reverberate through Conrad's subsequent novels—in, for example, the oppression felt by Mrs Gould when she sees the San Tomé mountain, rich in silver, hanging over Sulaco 'more soulless than any tyrant, more pitiless and autocratic than the worst government, ready to crush innumerable lives in the expansion of its greatness'. The same crushing weight of material interests is behind Greene's disturbers in Vietnam and in Havana. In *The Comedians* the disturbers appear at first sight trivial, irrelevant, without real power. Yet when Brown returns to Haiti to claim his possessions—a hotel and a woman—his arrival causes Dr Philipot to walk out to the pool and cut his throat; in nourishing their egos at the expense of a *pauvre terre* the comedians are living out the pattern of colonial dominance. Forster is perhaps less sensitive than Conrad and Greene to the strictly political aspects of the colonial intrusion. But he is the most perceptive of the three in his insights into the impulse to disturb and dominate. Adela's curiosity about India, which wrecks several careers, is part of her intellectual arrogance, the ultra-rationality of an enlightened and emancipated English lady. Mrs Moore on the other hand belongs to the dominated and not to the master race. She is an old lady everyone ignores; a good situation from which to enter the world of the punkah wallah and the Sweepers' Band.

Each of these three novelists then, far from using colonial society as a convenient setting for a self-exploration, engages with that society through, in the first place, a natural sympathy with the plight of the disturbed and, in the second place, his own experience and knowledge of the colonial encounter. In 'Heart of Darkness' the engagement may be less tenacious than in the other books, for in the concluding episode the self-explorer moves to the centre of the stage and attitudinizes a little. But Conrad keeps a wider distance between himself and Marlow than is always recognized by critics for whom the story is primarily a voyage into the unconscious. Conrad's two subsequent novels are able to deal less subjectively, if also less compellingly, with the colonizer; Forster and Greene are perhaps helped towards the objectivity of *A Passage to India* and *The Comedians* by the fact that each novel was preceded, in *Maurice* and *A Burnt-Out Case* respectively, by a highly confessional work. And though 'Heart of Darkness' has its hesitations, all three novelists, in the major works we have considered, are as innocent of emotional exploitation of the colonial scene as they are critical of its political and economic exploitation.

The white reader is no less ready with his stereotypes than the black. If the expatriate novel is misread as an indulgent self-survey, the indigenous novel is often misread as nothing more than the revelation of what lies (to use a title from the colonial past) At the Back of the Black Man's Mind. Of course there is plenty of writing to meet this expectation, especially in Africa; plenty of shapeless reminiscence thinly disguised as fiction. But the indigenous writer who takes his *métier* as seriously as does Achebe or Narayan or Naipaul is in no position to make this kind of revelation, for what it is worth. He is usually quite as distanced from the dominated side in the colonial encounter as the best expatriate writers are distanced from their dominating compatriots. In the first place he is set apart by his education. Westernization begins early. The line *etru bo pi ale a she e anando we aquandem,* which we suddenly encounter in a poem by Christopher Okigbo, is not some piece of Ibo ancestral wisdom, but the attempt by a class of Ibo infants to recite 'Little Bo-Peep'. And the later stages of this education tend to be thorough and bookish, with a higher admixture of Mediterranean-based philosophy, theology, history, and literature than would be found in any Western school curriculum of the present day. In this it still pursues the goal set before it by Macaulay in his famous Minute. Macaulay also insisted that English should be the medium of instruction; and in his adoption of standard English the Third World writer is again setting himself apart from the society he depicts. There may be social loss involved in this distancing, but there is almost certainly aesthetic gain; the Third World writer sees the cultural suppression or, in the case of the Caribbean, the cultural deprivation suffered by his society all the more clearly because his own disturbance has been profound. In these circumstances, his writing becomes, to take Philip Mason's term, primarily a search for a pedigree: a quest shared by Achebe, Narayan, and Naipaul and indeed by every other writer of like distinction from what were once the tropical colonies.

This pedigree is likely to be something very different from what the reader might expect. Bloke Modisane has a short story about a black South African who is first humiliated by a white street crowd and then, when he reaches the shelter of his local shebeen, further intimidated by his half-drunk companions, who force him to recite Shakespeare. Ashamed of his servility in the earlier encounter he launches into Hamlet's musings on the dram of 'eale' that corrupts individual virtue. This does not please his hearers. All they want from him is Mark Antony's version of 'Burn, baby, burn'. The episode tellingly sums up the quandary of the Third World writer. His audience, whether black or white, attempts to impose on him roles of acceptance or protest; at the same time he knows that his proper task is to search deep in his own experience and the experience of his community for the self-knowledge which is a true pedigree.

Time and again, the Third World writer is praised for the wrong thing. Narayan's *The Bachelor of Arts,* a seemingly artless tale that is as much concerned with truth and reality as anything he has written, is taken as a realistic portrayal of Indian marriage customs, and as such lumped together with the wearisome number of Indo-Anglian novels in which a young man reluctantly accepts the bride chosen by his parents, only to find that she is for him the one woman in the world. With similar misunderstanding, Aimé Césaire's fierce parody of Harlem-style exoticism is taken *au grand sérieux*; white critics nod benignly and uncomprehendingly over his cries of deprivation, much as the English family in *The Mimic Men* reacts to the antics of the execution party on the beach. *Not waving but drowning.* At least Narayan and Césaire are two writers who do not yield to their audience's demand for stereotypes. Others have not been able to hold the line. It is saddening, in reading Camara Laye's *L'Enfant Noir* or George Lamming's *In the Castle of my Skin,* to reach the point when the clear Wordsworthian recall of childhood experience begins to be scribbled over with the attributions of the dominators: to founder on Laye's unconvincing stress upon a pastoral communality, or on the adolescent race-consciousness ('my people'), apparently without ironic overtones, of Lamming's Barbadian narrator.

Role-playing, of the kind typified by Modisane's 'Situation', is a defence against disturbance. But the individual and the group who have been disturbed by the colonial intrusion themselves need to trouble the waters of the collective memory; the analogy with psycho-analysis holds quite as much—and as little—for the indigenous writer as it does for the expatriate. The process can be painfully difficult and carry the writer beyond the threshold of obscurity: an obscurity of form in a work such as Ngugi Wa Thiongo's thoughtful but involuted presentation of Kenya's immediate past in *A Grain of Wheat;* a verbal obscurity in 'Wole Soyinka's discovery of inglorious ancestors in *A Dance of the Forests*; a narrational obscurity in Wilson Harris's search for a pedigree among the myths of the Guyanan jungle. The distinctive skill of the three indigenous novelists we have been concerned with shows itself in their navigation between the whirlpool of facile role-playing and the hidden rocks of an incomplete cultural self-realization.

As a child, R. K. Narayan learned to love the Hindu gods because the chaplain of the Christian mission school that he attended in Madras chose to ridicule them. 'I was thinking the other day why it is that I can't write a novel without Krishna, Ganesa, Hanuman, astrologers, pundits, temples, and davedasis, or temple prostitutes. Do you suppose I have been trying to settle my score with the old boy?' The idiom, reminiscent of Nataraj's Queen Anne chair and rolltop desk, suggests the cultural pressures that disturbed India for a century and a half; the amused tone conveys the security that Narayan feels in India's power to withstand these pressures and 'go on'. The South Indian does not have to search far for a pedigree. Sastri is quietly working away behind the blue curtain, guardian of the traditional values that are affronted but not shaken by Vasu's intrusion. Chinua Achebe's search has had more deliberation about it. Though he emphasizes that he has never 'had to do research as such' for his novels, a Nigerian graduate of his generation is likely at some time to have looked at the major studies of Ibo social life. That way of life was preserved in the memories of his father's generation, but because the family had become Christians a certain distance maintained itself between them and their neighbours, making it possible (Achebe has remarked) for him not to take things for granted. If the search was more deliberate for him than it was for Narayan, the motivation was also stronger; the value systems of African traditional life have suffered a far greater dislocation through the colonial impact than has the Hindu ethos. For V. S. Naipaul, the disturbance is greatest of all and the search for a pedigree most arduous. The West Indian has to examine and reject a number of false pedigrees, grand with armorial bearings: 'nous n'avons jamais été amazones du roi de Dahomey' . . . nor, one might add, Aryan horsemen either. But Ralph Singh's search into his past does not end in negative findings. To sit reading Martial in a pseudo-Roman house may be as pantomimic as the ritual of taking up one's begging bowl and walking off—in Trinidad!—in the direction of Benares. Yet these absurd mimic flourishes are nourished by roots that go down to the ancient cultures of the Mediterranean and the Ganges, roots which it has become the business of Ralph Singh's life to discover.

2

So far we have been moving among broad generalizations. Our three expatriate writers belong to three different generations, each with its own distinctive set of attitudes towards the fact of colonial rule, and all we can safely say they have in common is the sensitive awareness of the disturbance that rule has caused. Our indigenous writers come from three countries with widely differing colonial pasts, and the common factor in their work is little more than their determination to get the past right. If we are to achieve any sharper definition, we need next to look at these novels in the pairings already suggested by the arrangement I have given these essays: the stories set in equatorial Africa, those set in India, and those with a Caribbean setting.

The surprising discovery we then make about 'Heart of Darkness' and *Arrow of God* is that, although nearly a lifetime separates their dates of composition, and though Achebe's novel is in part a riposte to Conrad's, the books have a strong affinity of theme and attitude. Both are virtually (to make use of Conrad's phrase) 'about a man who went mad in the centre of Africa'. Both, as Conrad claimed for his story, go far beyond their anecdotal origins. Both explore the ultimate cause of their hero's alienation in the imperial intrusion into Africa and develop the theme that a man who cuts himself off from his natural community ends by serving dark gods. Or as Conrad put it in a rare interpolation of his own point of view into *Lord Jim*: 'we must fight in the ranks or our lives don't count'.

The two novelists have, however, arrived by quite different routes at their common theme of man as a social animal for whom isolation spells moral and mental disaster. 'Heart of Darkness' stemmed from Conrad's own intensely isolating experience in the Congo in 1890 and we have already seen the complexity, sometimes bordering on confusion, which results from his reflecting on that experience, now as the pragmatic English sailor, now as the sceptical European intellectual. By comparison with the wound of genius that brought Conrad's tale into existence, the origins of *Arrow of God* appear to lie in a singularly extroverted and even impersonal concern with a whole past way of life. It follows that each novelist is strong in the area of the other's weakness. What is lacking in Achebe as a storyteller is that Ancient Mariner-like power of compulsion which ensures that we cannot choose but hear all Conrad has to say. What is lacking in Conrad is an affirmation or tangible presentation of the values by which men live in society: the values that Kurtz has presumably abjured.

The few glimpses we are allowed of organized society in 'Heart of Darkness' suggest that man, though a social animal, is primarily, as Conrad told Cunninghame-Graham, 'un animal méchant', restrained in his gracelessness only by respect for the policeman round the corner and fear of what the neighbours may say. It is not surprising that the darkness which hangs over London at the beginning of 'Heart of Darkness' should deepen into a Dickensian murk in *The Secret Agent*. Conrad, we have seen, is evasive about the 'true belief' which enables man to withstand the dark gods. The only truly cohesive society, to Conrad's way of thinking, is a ship's company; a body which Achebe, to judge by his satiric picture of the European reservation at Okperi, would hold to be no society at all. It is true that a ship's survival in the face of the elements calls for a collective endeavour such as Achebe recognized in the village groups of Iboland. For the Nigerian writer, however, society means very much more than restraint in the fear of internal censure or determination in the teeth of external danger, whether human or natural. A recognition of the positive values that bind a society together counterbalances the individual disasters in all of Achebe's novels, much as it has prevented the communities of West Africa—in contrast to some in other parts of the continent—from falling totally apart under the pressure of colonial annexation.

The difference is one between the generations as well as between the races. Conrad wrote out of a situation of communal confidence, indeed over-confidence; he felt that the tribal euphoria of the Diamond Jubilee and Omdurman needed to be checked by something more sobering than the organ-notes of 'Recessional'. Achebe wrote out of the reverse situation. In the years immediately before and immediately following Nigeria's independence, the Ibo people were feeling insecure and in need of reassurance about their own values. Something not dissimilar was achieved by the novel in England early in George V's reign; a time when the pattern of dominance was sharply defined, though it was not a vertical and regional pattern, but the stratification of social class. In consequence, Achebe, by his social affirmation, has brought back into the English novel something that it had in Lawrence but has notably lacked since the death of Orwell. And at the same time this social affirmation in no way impedes Achebe's handling of that dominant theme of the Western novel, 'the darkness of man's heart'.

Conrad and Achebe not only belong to different generations but they set their novels in two countries that have had very different colonial histories; whatever the follies and wrongs of British conquest in West Africa, they never matched the depths touched in the early exploitation of what is now Zaire. Forster and Narayan both write about the same country; and when, in order to complete his tale, Forster moves his scene from the Ganges to a Hindu festival in a small princely state on the edge of the Deccan, he carries us into the same world as Narayan portrays in the temple rites and subsequent procession of *The Man-Eater of Malgudi.*

As private secretary to the Maharajah of Dewas State Senior, Forster in 1921 was deeply involved in the Gokul Ashtami ceremonies. In some ways this was a dynastic rite: a dozen years earlier the young Maharajah had written his own account of the festival to his tutor, Forster's friend Malcolm Darling:

> . . . Well it was altogether a splendid show I think. Everybody did his duty very well. The Bhajans of Dewansahib, Rajarangi and the old Fadnis were well sung, specially it was very striking to see the Dewan singing them with his austere but devoted face and an attitude of absolute unity with the Deities in front of him.
>
> Every day the hall where the Gods were enthroned was decorated by different people according to their different tastes. . . . The Dewansahib wrote out on the walls beautiful and instructive mottoes from old Holy Books and decorated the place with fine shawls, bunting, and plantain tree arches. The typewriter worked on till 9.0 p.m. bringing out leaflets which declared mottoes of victory to Sri Krishna God and so on.
>
> . . . .
>
> At 12.0 p.m. on the sixth the whole army fired salvoes and the guns blew forth and present arms were done. The whole hall was thronged by people and amidst the great and devoted excitement the God Krishna was born. (*The Hill of Devi,* pp. 113–14)

The fascinating thing about this letter is that it so exactly corresponds, in mood and tone, to the account of the temple ceremony given by Narayan's narrator. Nataraj is almost as proprietorial as the Maharajah, since the temple was 'built by public subscription in the days when my grandfather and a few others had come here as pioneers'; and he feels a similar satisfaction in the splendid show for which he is largely responsible: he has worked even harder than the Maharajah's 'typewriter'. He too, amid all the hubbub, can distinguish and delight in a particular musical offering: 'The piper was blowing his cheeks out, filling the air with "Kalyani Rag", a lovely melody at this hour.' He takes the same uncritical pleasure as the Maharajah in the decorations: the God 'wore a rose garland, and a diamond pendant sparkled on his chest'. And like the Maharajah, Nataraj knows he is present at a miraculous event: 'The priest was circling the camphor lights before the golden images, and the reflections on the faces made them vibrate with a living quality. God Krishna was really an incarnation of Vishnu, who had saved Gajendra; he would again come to the rescue of the same animal . . . .' (pp. 181-3)

In *A Passage to India,* Forster used the Maharajah's account, as well as his own direct experience of the ceremony in 1921 and his subsequent research into the origins of the festival. Accordingly the 'lump' which he added to his tale is made up of various ingredients and in comparison with the two Indian narratives it could be called, in the strict sense of the word, sophisticated. As a participant, Forster's feelings were mixed. The Quaker in his blood was grieved at the extravagance and the tawdriness of the rites. One of his jobs was to help choose adornments worth a very large sum for the Krishna image; in his letters home he compensates for this enforced idolatory by calling the image Dolly and describing it as having the face of an ill-tempered pea. 'There is no dignity, no taste, no form,' he writes, 'and though I am dressed as a Hindu I shall never become one.' The incessant din brought him to a state of collapse: 'It is the noise, the noise, the noise, the noise which sucks one into a whirlpool from which there is no re-emerging. The whole of what one understands by music seems lost for ever.' And the novel keeps the rhetorical figure of repetition: 'Music there was, but from so many sources that the sum total was untrammelled. The braying banging crooning melted into a single mass which trailed round the palace before joining the thunder.' (p. 296)

Nor were the beliefs of the worshippers any more satisfying than their rites. What did it mean to believe in the *birth* of a god who was, had been, and ever should be? Forster's account of the miraculous birth moves uneasily between a less than happy inflation of the Maharajah's simple profession of faith—'and in the rosy dust and incense, and clanging and shouts, Infinite Love took upon itself the form of SHRI KRISHNA, and saved the world . . .'—and an ironic deflation of such fideism '. . . All sorrow was annihilated, not only for Indians, but for foreigners, birds, caves, railways and the stars; all became joy, all laughter; there had never been disease nor doubt, misunderstanding, cruelty, fear.' (pp. 299-300) From this 'muddle (as we call it), a frustration of reason and form', Forster takes refuge, again as his Quaker forebears must have done, in the mystery of the individual's experience. When he contemplated the religious feelings of the Maharajah, as distinct from his rites and his beliefs, Forster felt at home. For he recognized in 'Baput Sahib' the fruits of the spirit, a capacity to extend the delicacy of his *bhakti* to daily human relationships: 'He is always thinking of others and refusing to take advantage of his position in his dealings with them: and believing that his God acts similarly towards him.' This too is Godbole's achievement in his hallowing of Mrs Moore. It is a miraculous achievement; yet one feels that for Forster it can only be thought of as being attained in spite of rather than through the utter confusion of the festival.

Uneasiness shows itself also in the narratorial comment on the crowd round the shrine in the novel: 'a most beautiful and radiant expression came into their faces, a beauty in which there was nothing personal, for it caused them all to resemble one another during the moment of its indwelling, and only when it was withdrawn did they revert to individual clods'. (p. 296) The last word shocks more than it was meant to do; it sounds like a relic of Forster's exasperation with the 'half-witted menials' of the Old Palace who had been rather more hindrance than help to the private secretary in his preparations for the great event. Both the aesthetic bemusement of the narrator and the holy rapture of the Minister of Education are forms of detachment very different from Nataraj's involvement in his temple rite in the Indian novel. To Nataraj's seeing, the crowd is anything but impersonal and he rejoices in its variety much as Forster's real-life Maharajah delighted in decorations 'by different people according to their different tastes': 'men bearded, cleanshaven, untidy, tidy; women elegant, ravishing, tub shaped and coarse; and the children, thousands of them, dressed, undressed, matted-haired, chasing each other between the legs of adults, screaming with joy and trying to press forward and grab the fruit offerings kept for the gods.' (pp. 181–2)

One of the many individuals known to Nataraj in this crowd is the dancer Rangi. A female figure also detaches herself from the crowd in *A Passage to India,* at the point when the palanquin of Krishna reaches the lakeside. 'On either side of it the singers tumbled, a woman prominent, a wild and beautiful young saint with flowers in her hair. She was praising God without attributes—thus did she apprehend Him.' (p. 327) Her prototype, in Forster's letters home, is less romantic:

> A lady fanatic was in the Dewan's group. She was gaudily yet neatly dressed in purple and yellow, a circlet of jasmine flowers was round her chignon and in her hands were a pair of tongs with which she accompanied herself. We could not discover whether she was praising God with or without attributes. Her voice was too loud. She nodded and smiled in a very pleasant way.

Again we feel Forster's determination to cross, in the novel, from the near-ridiculous to the sublime. He does not quite make the jump and is left slithering on the slope between religion and religiosity. Whatever the infelicities of Narayan's prose, his imaginative vision in his temple scene is much steadier than is Forster's. Rangi, wrapped in faded brocade and 'agitating herself' before the images, is neither risible nor romantic because for Nataraj she is so completely *there,* someone he must communicate with; and he is in a turmoil of confusion since he does not want to be laughed at for talking to a prostitute—rite or no rite, the crowd is in the mood 'to enjoy anything at anybody's expense'. (One is reminded how Forster, a week after his festival, wrote home that it was a great misfortune that art in India was associated with prostitution.) The real religious event in Narayan's temple is not a flight to the inane but Nataraj's liberation from his prim and complacent and secretly concupiscent self. And this is achieved through the cry to the god which is also a cry for help to all those who are prepared to act to defend Kumar against the demon. Where Godbole achieves detachment, Nataraj achieves engagement and becomes part of the dance of life.

The more we look at the essential differences between the two episodes, the more it becomes evident that Forster, for all his sensitive recognition of the central place religion held in Indian life, was subject in his understanding of that religion to the limitations of his time and place. He was an Edwardian Englishman of evangelical origins, who appreciated order and doubted if Indians could ever achieve an ordered government of their own; and chance placed him in a minute princely state whose ruler believed that 'India generally has not in any way shown its fitness for a popular government'. He came too from an environment where the only respectable alternative to agnosticism was a refined, Dean Inge-style mysticism. Given this background, his receptiveness to Indian beliefs and practices was remarkable. No present-day English traveller would have to make a tithe of Forster's efforts of imagination. British rule of India is too much a thing of the past for the traveller to be much disturbed by the itch for making everything shipshape. (V. S. Naipaul's genuine distress with the muddle of India is an interesting exception, and by his own admission it is a 'colonial' response—as, he maintains, was Gandhi's.) Moreover, the English passion for ranging things coldly on shelves died out when there were no longer servants left to range them. And an awareness of new forms of worship and new emphases in doctrine inside Christianity would render it unnecessary for our traveller, at rites such as Forster and Narayan describe, to struggle to transmute muddle into mystery. Like Nataraj and 'Baput Sahib', he would go prepared to pick up the melody in the uproar or the action of grace in the confusion of mundane concerns. But it would be a pity if he forgot Forster's imagination and courage in opening a way to the shrine.

There is virtually no time-gap between *The Comedians,* published early in 1966, and *The Mimic Men,* finished in July 1966. By then, direct colonial rule was past history for Trinidad, as for nearly every territory in the former British Empire; in Haiti it had ended with the eighteenth century. Yet these two novels about the post-colonial world bring home to the reader as nothing else does the tragic legacy of the colonial past. In tropical Africa, in the mid-nineteen-sixties, few scars of exploitation remained outside of the Congo, and colonial trusteeship had left many real achievements. If, in the dark seaward passages of a West Coast fort, the traveller could suddenly feel overwhelmed by the outrage of the slave trade, outside the ramparts the busy and thriving market women, descendants of those who stayed, seemed remarkably free from memories of racial injury. In India too, by the same date, the hurts of imperialism had been largely forgotten, while the administrative and cultural institutions introduced by the last wave of Aryan invaders remained, as positive and monumental as the Victorian buildings that housed them. Distress was still there, and in the succeeding decade it has reached horrifying proportions but it is a distress that rises more from the callousness of man and nature than from any legacy of colonial rule. But to travel in the sixties to Jamaica or Haiti was to be confronted with a living reproach. These island communities were the bastard offspring of European mercantilism: long forgotten, disabled, and excluded from any inheritance. Colonial rule affected the societies of Africa and Asia for better or worse, but they have outlived it and can, if they so wish, repudiate the memory of imperial conquest. But in the Caribbean the societies are themselves the creations of colonial power, and will never escape their history.

I give an outsider's response. Graham Greene's response to Caribbean distress in *The Comedians* is also an external one. Haiti in the novel awaits the landfall of three voyagers who between them represent the successive but overlapping approaches of the European world to the chain of islands that have for centuries lured the adventurer with *la magie antillaise.* Three centuries earlier, Jones would have been a buccaneer of the Spanish Main. Significantly, his previous gun-running has been in the Congo basin, which, in Lumumba's day as in Conrad's, offered a free field of activity for the latter-day buccaneer, or exploiter. Smith is the very reverse of this, the man with a mission. He has seldom been given much scope on the Caribbean scene, but in the whole history of imperialism he came to the fore early in this century, at a time when exploitation was being exposed by a new generation of economists and a new generation of anthropologists was abandoning cultural Darwinism for cultural relativism. With the end of colonial rule the benevolence of the Western world's Smiths was channelled into aid and development. Brown in his turn stands for a yet later phase in Europe's relations with the ex-colonial world, the stage of indifference. His line is a familiar one—'I'm just here as an expatriate'. So, for the first half of this century, Europe virtually closed its eyes to the destitution of the Caribbean.

The first impression that comes from setting *The Comedians* alongside *The Mimic Men* is that Greene's technique as a novelist is old-fashionedly simple. The conventions are those of the adventure story. Secondary characters are very good or very bad; characters in the foreground are more complex but with a complexity controlled by the moral absolutes to which they can be related. Save for a chapter of the narrator's recollections the narrative moves forward in steady sequential order. At its climax it meets the expectations of a 'Western': the hero, his goal almost reached, falls into the villain's clutches—and is rescued by timely marksmanship. And the storyteller is in the old yarning tradition: he has total recall and virtually no hindsight. But it is wholly unfair to Greene to see in this well-worn conventionality the slickness of the popular entertainer. His technique perfectly accords with the object of his tale, which is to say to the reader: 'Look *there*'. We, the outsiders approaching Papa Doc's domain in the company of Greene's three adventurers, are forced to feel its full shockingness much as we might respond to a gifted documentary on the large or the small screen. For reality lies 'out there', in Joseph's injuries; not in the performances of the three comedians as each begins to act up to his private fantasy of a Caribbean island.

The Mimic Men, its title makes clear, is also concerned with the substance and the shadow. But the fantasy is here an indigenous one and must be explored by introspection. Greene makes us see, and in the process makes his narrator see. Naipaul's narrator is in quest of understanding and his task is to make us, too, understand. The book's method is therefore aimed at achieving a self-realization which is also the self-discovery of colonial man: a historical creation, unable, unlike colonized man, to return to his own 'reverences'. Ralph Singh's life story has no suspense to rivet our attention, because it is necessary that our curiosity should move freely, shuttling under the past and over the present, till a tight web of relationships has established Ralph's personality for us. Self-knowledge must be thus confirmed before any moral judgements can be made. For this reason, the complaints of critics that Ralph Singh is an unpleasant character are as irrelevant as would be remarks on the niceness or nastiness of Freud's more complicated patients. What is discovered matters less to the story than does Ralph Singh's gain of the ability to make discoveries about himself. Accordingly the actual writing of the narrative is the most important thing in the book. It represents the quest for a pedigree not only for Ralph but for all those marooned as a consequence of the migrations that have occurred in the past, in response to the material demands of Europe and white America.

Each book concludes with a wry profit-and-loss account. If Brown has lost the dream behind the dream, which was no mirage but a vocation, his *alter ego* Jones has managed to achieve it. And Ralph Singh may discover as historian the embryonic structure of the society he so much disturbed as a politican. The Caribbean is not the place for larger hopes.

3

It would appear that the novel of the colonial experience needs for its creation a certain kind of *moment,* in a sense that is almost the opposite to Taine's; its appearance is aided, not by the build-up of the past in the present, but rather by a repudiation of the immediate past. The novelist is a delicate barometer of the winds of change. His temperament and his experience of the colonial encounter enable him to anticipate those changes of theory and policy that cause an empire to be built, transformed, and relinquished.

The British have experienced a series of such moments ever since they began, late in the last century, to reflect on their great possessions. Writers in what was once the British Empire experienced the moment of decision shortly after independence, at the very time they had begun to turn to the novel in English as a means of expression. For both expatriate and indigenous novelists, the point of departure is a disturbance of the old civilization-barbarianism dichotomy on which imperial rule was once based. It follows that our six novels are all political works, not in the superficial, corridors-of-power sense (Brown, on his voyage to Haiti, is not making much progress in reading this kind of political novel) but in the essential sense that they are concerned as much with the *polis*, with man in his group relations, as they are with his intimate and familial relationships.

The partition of Africa was the major imperial concern of the late nineteenth century, and the almost Roman confidence of the imperial generations best showed itself in their attitude to equatorial Africa. Here surely, in the heart of darkness, barbarism had to give way to civilization. Colonial rule was defended by the idealists as a civilizing mission and by the 'realists' as the survival of the fittest. But in 1902 J. A. Hobson asked the question: fittest for what?—and exposed the circular illogic of the defence with the answer 'the fittest to survive'. Hobson's book on imperialism is the breaking of a wave. Behind him were the mounting criticisms of European activities in Africa which since the middle of the previous decade had been voiced not only by radicals such as Cunninghame-Graham but also by such sober researchers as Holt and Morel; while the more open-minded missionaries and such scientifically-inclined travellers as Mary Kingsley were indicating that tribal life had restraints that the disturbers of it themselves all too often lacked. Roger Casement—ex-missionary, trader, and investigator—embodied the new doubts about the dispossession of the technically unadvanced peoples by the technically advanced. And Casement's friend Conrad wrote 'Heart of Darkness' in the turmoil of feeling that arose through his own involvement in imperial actions. He had a strong loyalty to the British Merchant Marine, the life-line of Empire. He had also seen, in the Congo, the kind of thing that happened some way beyond the port of unlading, 'There was in him', wrote Orwell, 'a sort of grown-upness and political understanding which would have been impossible to a native English writer at that time.' Conrad was deeply disturbed and sought to disturb his readers in 'Heart of Darkness', but we do not need to impose the allegory of a psychological night-journey upon the tale to explain its febrile quality. It arose out of a hectic moment in European political thinking, the first great shock to the cultural self-assurance of the master-race when it realized the barbaric acts performed in its name in central Africa.

Imperial confidence was by no means overthrown. But the challenge from economists and anthropologists caused it to assume a new form in the Liberal era that began in 1906. The myth of indispensable overseas markets was replaced by the idea of the dual mandate which at least conceded that colonies should be governed for the benefit of their inhabitants as well as that of the metropolitan country. The myth of the civilizing mission gave way to the notion of indirect rule aimed at allowing subject peoples to develop in their own way. Trusteeship, a concept that went back to Burke, was now in vogue. Whatever the attitude of the capitalists who exploited the mystique of the white man's burden, the idea was not cant to those who assumed it. The new imperialist could be genuinely high-minded. Unfortunately, he could also be ill-mannered. Lugard, in evolving his policy of indirect rule for Africa, drew heavily on British experience in India, where a high indigenous culture made the doctrine of trusteeship particularly tenable. He also derived from India the protocol that hedged round his administrators: because they had to be seen to be incorruptible, they had to be rendered unapproachable beings, god-like in their confidence. As late as 1936, Nehru was struck by 'something of the religious temper' about the British assumption of always being in the right in their colonial dealings.

When Forster went to India in 1912, he was appalled by the bad manners of English officials and the even worse ones of their wives. Benevolence, trusteeship worked well as long as degree was observed; the 'toiling ryot' was the object of a kindly and often highly beneficial paternalism. But the Raj was abrasive in its dealings with the new nationalists, and much coldness and rudeness were directed towards the educated Indian. A confrontation, a new crisis in Imperial thinking, was becoming inevitable. By the time of Forster's second visit, this confrontation had taken place not only between O'Dwyer's troops and the nationalist movement to which O'Dwyer, Dyer, and other elements in the Raj so grossly over-reacted, but also at home between those who believed Britain should rule India in perpetuity and those who acknowledged, in the spirit of the Morley-Montagu reforms, that nationalism must in the end lead to *swaraj*. Forster shared Rabindranath Tagore's repugnance for the vulgarity of modern nationalism; and circumstances placed him, as the private secretary of a minor prince, in an odd position from which to observe this new turn in the colonial dialectic. But the very confusion that arises from Forster's oblique view of the new developments imparts a richness to the texture of *A Passage to India* which is perhaps lacking in such a novel as Cary's *Mister Johnson*, published some sixteen years later. Cary's experience of the colonial scene was contemporaneous with Forster's, but he waited till the conflict between trusteeship and devolvement had been clarified before he tried to expose the failure of indirect rule.

Mister Johnson appeared early in the Second World War; by the end of that war, there was no longer any doubt that colonial rule was a dying institution and that the imperial task was now to prepare a cadre of educated people—soon, in the next shift of thinking, to be stigmatized as an élite—to lead their countries into independence. It is from this élite, largely as a result of the metropolitan-aided expansion of education in the forties and fifties, that the Third World novelists have chiefly come.

Narayan, of course, belongs to an earlier generation. But he too gains in authority as a writer from the new political *moment* of the nineteen-sixties. This time the crisis is in the thinking of the once-colonized, instead of that of the colonizers; but like those previous crises, it leads to a questioning of the old civilization-barbarism distinction. With the first upheaval in imperial thought, the pendulum swung towards the recognition of an indigenous culture. With the second, it swung back towards the absorbed Western culture of the élite. Now, in the post-independence world, new questionings arise. Narayan looks at the disruption of Indian *mores* caused by Nehru's attempts at Westernization and by the wish to emulate the Chinese technological advance. While he recognizes the salutary aspect of the disturbance, he seeks stability in the underlying continuity of Hindu culture as it persists in rural India. The narrator of Chinua Achebe's fourth novel, *A Man of the People*, also has to go to the country, literally as well as figuratively, to find among the rural people some vestiges of those elementary decencies that were missing from Nigerian public life on the eve of the Civil War. Achebe writes as a member of the ethnic group that most whole-heartedly assimilated Western ways in the belief that they were 'civilized', and then woke sharply, around the time of independence, to their loss of cultural roots. Of his first three, interrelated novels, *Things Fall Apart* deals with what has been lost from Ibo life, *No Longer at Ease* with how it was lost, and *Arrow of God* with why it was lost; the answer is found to lie deep in Ibo experience, in that very confusion between eager change and rigid constancy which also produced the post-colonial crisis of identity.

The conflict in these novels is between positive value systems. No such positive choices existed at the other end of the Middle Passage. *The Mimic Men* is, by Naipaul's own definition, 'a book about a vacuum'. Its hero, like many of the new colonial élite, begins by believing that civilization lies in the metropolis. But he finds in London only emptiness, a non-society from which he returns to the non-society of the Caribbean élite who are expatriates in their own islands. No voyage home is possible. Ralph

Singh has to put down his roots into the here and now. The culture that replaces as a value system the colonial dichotomy of civilization and barbarism has always been there for Narayan and needed only to be rediscovered by Achebe; but for Naipaul it has to be created through a process of historical definition.

Over the past century, the approach of the technically developed societies to the technically undeveloped has been, first to exploit; then to protect; then to assist; and then to ignore. By the sixties, the wish to ignore, in which governments have fortunately not always followed the inclinations of their electorates, was widespread. The ex-colonies now had their independence: it was up to them to make what they could of it. Haiti, because it gained this independence long before any other ex-colonial country of the Third World, moved without any intervening stages from exploitation to neglect—a neglect broken in 1915 in the name, once again, of civilization against barbarism. By the nineteen-sixties these terms had been conscripted into the cold war between the Western democracies and the Communist bloc. Spheres of influence now replaced the coloured patches on the map, but the motives of neo-colonialism were no more altruistic than were those of the powers that drew up the Treaty of Berlin three quarters of a century earlier. *The Comedians*, no less than *Nostromo*, is a novel of the colonial experience despite its having been written about a country that became theoretically independent several generations ago. Once the buccaneers were forerunners to the colonizers. Now, in the persons of mercenaries, gun-runners, property 'developers', and industrial adventurers, they inherit their kingdom.

Each of these six novels could be said to owe its birth, as distinct from its conception, to the pressure of a particular political moment. But as Dr Magiot has it, there is a *mystique* as well as a *politique*. One of the most striking facts that emerges from setting these novels together is that all six authors are deeply concerned with the non-material beliefs that shape political ends. This is true even of *The Mimic Men*, which at first reading might seem to be as unconcerned with religion as its author, writing in *An Area of Darkness*, maintains himself to be:

> I came of a family that abounded with pundits. But I had been born an unbeliever. I took no pleasure in religious ceremonies. . . . With my lack of belief and distaste for ritual there also went a metaphysical incapacity, this again a betrayal

> of heredity, for my father's appetite for Hindu speculation was great. What, then, survived of Hinduism in me? Perhaps I had received a certain supporting philosophy. I cannot say; my uncle often put it to me that my denial was an admissible type of Hinduism.

This uncle's view is surely very relevant to *The Mimic Men*, a book which establishes its affirmations, much as Donne in a great lyric establishes his, upon 'the quintessence even of nothingness'. The image of the *sanyasi*, ascetic of the woods, gains substance as the story progresses. From being an image of evasion it becomes, in Lord Stockwell's recollections of the spiritual authority exercised by Ralph Singh's father, the image of something that has itself evaded Ralph. Yet he is to experience, though too briefly and too belatedly, something of his father's authority when he prevails upon the man with the blood-stained stone to lay it on the ground. To say that Ralph Singh, at the end of the book, has lost his life to save it would be to make Mrs Moore's mistake of thinking that Krishna must come in another song. The acceptance of the void is total. But not only is Ralph Singh not without faith, in Hindu terms of the way of negation; the ordering of experience represented by his narrative itself expresses a *mystique* that owes something to Mediterranean stoicism but a good deal more to a supporting philosophy that is fundamentally Indian.

A previous difficulty over the relationship of narrator and novelist inevitably recurs at this point. Does Ralph abjure disguise as the story ends, or has he merely found a new role for himself? He thinks he is at last being sincere, but is he? The uncertainty suggests that in examining the mystique of any political novel we need perhaps to distinguish, though the distinction is not always clear-cut, between novels about fidelity and novels about faith. Fidelity, because it can be a means without an end or with only an unworthy end, often issues in tragedy. Faith, because its end is the novelist's ultimate good, issues in *la divina commedia*. The 'type' of fidelity is Abraham placing Isaac on the sacrificial stone: a story which would end tragically if it were not narrated from the viewpoint of faith.

'Heart of Darkness' and *Arrow of God* are stories about fidelities that are independent of the worth or even the existence of their objects. Marlow's fidelity is to his work as a steamboat captain. In so far as he takes pride in work well done, this is fidelity to an ego-ideal; but it is at least an ego-ideal that serves the welfare of those closest to him and is dependent on their approval. As such it is far removed from Kurtz's fidelity to his great intentions: self-delusions which mask the appetite that is all he gratifies in the end. *Arrow of God* makes the same distinction within a single character. When Ezeulu officiates at the feast of pumpkin leaves, his pride in his role is nourished by the people's belief that their welfare depends on his propitiation of the god. But when Ezeulu refuses to call the feast of the new yam he is serving nothing but his own vengefulness under the name of Ulu. Discriminations are made between fidelities according to their fruits, but not according to their absolute truth. Conrad knows, as in the end Marlow is made to know, that there is no sacred fire for the lightbearers to carry into the dark continent. Achebe knows, as in the end do the people of Umuaro, that once Ulu has ceased to be the repository of the collective will of the tribe, he is useless. In both tales we have witnessed *ragnarøk*: an eclipse of the gods to whom the characters were faithful according to their lights but in whom the writers have no faith.

Narayan and Greene are associated with one another through Greene's long-standing admiration for and promotion of Narayan's writings. And they are both novelists with a faith. In Narayan's long career as a novelist the faith has been as self-renewing as it is in the society he depicts. Faith, Kumar, painted afresh in honour of Krishna, walks unharmed at the head of the procession, with the children round his feet and the god on his back. But Greene, I feel, wrote many novels of fidelity before he achieved a novel of faith in *The Comedians*. It is true that the numinous does not quest through that book as the hound of heaven, in a way it does in *The Power and the Glory*, nor guard as a jealous watchdog in the way it does in *The End of the Affair*; but then both these manifestations have the air of authorial self-persuasions which leave the reader unsatisfied. In *The Comedians* the numinous is as present as the air we breathe. Jones, though full of grace, must apprehend it 'without attributes', since he acknowledges no beliefs. Nor does he perform any propitiatory rites: the sacrament that dominated *The Power and the Glory* and *The Heart of the Matter* is here a supply of bourbon biscuits for the small boy Angel—Greene's self-parodying reduction of his previous theme of divine possessiveness. So it is possible to read

The Comedians without consciously recognizing it as a religious novel at all. But it is not possible to read it without experiencing the sense of light in darkness: the darkness of a poor and forgotten country, and the darkness of Brown who begins at the end to comprehend the light.

Serenity and illumination, the temper of those late Shakespearean comedies which both Narayan and the later Greene often bring to mind, are conditions most of us know better by report than by experience. This may be the reason why, out of these six books, the one to which the reader finds himself or herself most often returning is likely to be *A Passage to India*. It is a book which contemplates, in the friendship of Fielding and Aziz, fidelity to the holiness of the heart's affections. It does this without the sad irony of Conrad or Achebe, though with a strong awareness of how vulnerable such fidelity must be. It acknowledges too the power of faith, as represented by Mrs Moore and Professor Godbole, to come to the help of fidelity. The happiness that illumines Aziz in the mosque, his acquittal at the trial, and the renewal of his friendship with Fielding all involve Mrs Moore in some way. But the way is not very obvious. Faith here comes by gleams and not as the constant light it is for Narayan. The horses swerve apart, the earth says 'not yet', and the sky says 'not there'; and this is the experience of most of us whether under a tropical or a temperate sky.

Many other changes could be rung. What brings our six novels together in the end however is not this or that common ingredient as much as the common seriousness of the writers before the fact of colonial conquest. 'The empires of our time were short-lived, but they have altered the earth for ever: their passing away is their least significant feature.' So Ralph Singh, a little pontifically, near the beginning of *The Mimic Men*. Later, the Churchillian phrases give way to a testing and reshaping of political and philosophical attitudes. Ralph changes as he writes. Moreover the world changes round the writer. Since I began this study, the United States has abandoned its military intervention in Indo-China, Portugal has relinquished the last colonial empire, the sugar producers have exacted a fair price for the commodity that once peopled their countries, and the prices exacted for oil have made some people rich in underdeveloped countries and have pauperized some industrial nations. In such ways, the critic can learn something of the problem of the political novelist: to give a permanently satisfying form to his or her changing awareness of a world in continual change. The problem is one of the hardest in fiction, and the six novelists studied here have all had their failures. In these six novels, I believe them to have succeeded.

APPENDIX

CONRAD'S LOST LETTERS ABOUT THE CONGO

In *Joseph Conrad: a Personal Reminiscence* (1924), Ford Madox Ford states that during the First World War he came across a large body of political letters written by Conrad, during his sea years, to a compatriot. He goes on:

> Before that one of Conrad's relatives had showed the writer a number of letters that Conrad had written to the *Indépendance Belge*. These were quite another matter—admirably written, intensely emotional. As if Pierre Loti had had some heart! They had, in fact, as is to be expected, a great deal of the body and substance of *Heart of Darkness*.
>
> At both of these documents, however, the writer did no more than glance. The lady had treasured up as cuttings her nephew's correspondence and, when Conrad was out of the room, presented the bundle to Conrad's *ami le poète*. He read them for perhaps half an hour before Conrad came in again: then their author exhibited so much perturbation that the writer desisted. The probability is that Conrad burned the bundle.(pp.95–96)

If these letters about Africa were in manuscript, they have certainly gone for good. But the word 'cuttings' suggests they had been printed. If so, there is good hope that they will eventually come to light, provided Ford did not make up the whole episode. My experience of Ford's reminiscences is that there are always some grains of truth in his wildest fantasies. His account of how he helped Conrad to get the right prose rhythm for the ending of 'Heart of Darkness' is a whole nugget, as the manuscript reveals. And he is fairly circumstantial about the missing letters, telling us that Conrad 'would declare that the articles in the form of letters were remarkable productions. He would remind the writer of his aunt's expressed opinion that those letters formed magnificent prose . . . .'(p.97)

Although the letters could have been written at any time between

1890 and 1918, the likeliest date for the incident described by Ford is April 1899, when Marguerite Poradowska visited the Conrads at Pent Farm. The *Indépendance Belge* was a royalist newspaper, unlikely to publish anything defamatory about the Congo State. Moreover it did not publish letters in the earlier nineties. I have searched the files for 1891 and 1895 through 1898 without success. Ford could have assumed that the paper was a Belgian one, because Marguerite Poradowska lived in Brussels; but she was in fact French-born, spent much time in Paris, and contributed to French journals. If Conrad wrote his letters in the first heat of his bitterness about the Congo, they could have appeared in a left-wing Belgian paper during the early weeks of 1891, when he was in Brussels, or in a Swiss paper during his stay at Champel-les-Bains in the spring of that year, or in a French paper following his brief stay in Paris, where he met Marguerite Poradowska around midsummer. If he was stirred to write his letters of protest at the time of the agitation over Stokes, or any of the subsequent Congo scandals, the possibilities grow correspondingly wider. There is, in fact, a very large haystack round a needle which may or may not exist. But the search is worth pursuing.

NOTES ON SOURCES

HEART OF DARKNESS

Page references to the story relate to the volume called *Youth: A Narrative and Two Other Stories* in the Collected Edition (Dent, 1946–1954) of Conrad's works. I have also made use of the numbers of *Blackwood's Magazine* in which the tale first appeared in 1899, of the modern editions by Leonard F. Dean and Bruce Harkness (both 1960), and, by courtesy of the Beinecke Library at Yale University, of a microfilm of the manuscript. Other quotations are from 'An Outpost of Progress' in *Almayer's Folly and Tales of Unrest*; 'An Observer in Malaya' and 'Well Done' in *Notes on Life and Letters*; 'Geography and Some Explorers' and 'The Congo Diary' in *Tales of Hearsay and Last Essays*—all in the Collected Edition. Quotations from *The Inheritors* come from the 1901 New York edition.

Of the various collections of letters, I have drawn upon G. Jean-Aubry's edition of Conrad's *Lettres Françaises* (1929); William Blackburn's edition (1958) of his letters to William Blackwood and David S. Meldrum; Edward Garnett's own edition of the letters to himself (1928); René Rapin's edition of the letters to Marguerite Poradowska (1966); and above all, C. T. Watts's *Joseph Conrad's Letters to R. B. Cunninghame-Graham* (1969), supplemented by 'To Conrad from Cunninghame-Graham: Reflections on Two Letters' by Eloise Knapp Hay and Cedric Watts, in *Conradiana*, 5 (1973). Lawrence Graver's *Conrad's Shorter Fiction* (1969) reprints Conrad's important letter to *The New York Times* on the subject of *The Inheritors.* Other letters are quoted from G. Jean-Aubry's *Joseph Conrad: Life and Letters* (1927) and from Jocelyn Baines's authoritative 1959 biography.

Biographical facts about Conrad's Congo experiences also come from Baines and Jean-Aubry, as well as from Zdzisław Najder's *Conrad's Polish Background* (1964), Otto Lütken's 'Joseph

Conrad in the Congo' and Jessie Conrad's subsequent letter, both in *The London Mercury*, 22 (1930), from L. Guébels' 'Joseph Conrad, marin d'eau douce' in *La Renaissance de L'Occident*, 31 1929), and from J. Stengers's 'Sur l'Aventure Congolaise de Joseph Conrad' in the *Bulletin des Séances de l'Académie Royale des Sciences d'Outre-Mer*, 1971-4 (1974). By my main debt is obviously to Norman Sherry's *Conrad's Western World* (1971). Conrad's friendship with Casement is documented by John Powell's article, 'Conrad and Casement Hut Mates in Africa' in *The New York Evening Post* for 11 May 1923; by W. R. Louis in 'Roger Casement in the Congo', *Journal of African History*, 5 (1964); and by Brian Inglis in *Roger Casement* (1973).

My historical sources include H. M. Stanley's *The Congo and the Founding of its Free State* (1885), Mary Kingsley's *Travels in West Africa* (1897), Alain Stenman's *La Reprise du Congo par la Belgique* (1949), Roger Anstey's *Britain and the Congo in the Nineteenth Century* (1962), and Ruth Slade's *King Leopold's Congo* (1962). Exposures of abuses in the Congo State include E. J. Glave's 'Cruelty in the Congo Free State', *Century Magazine* (1897), S. L. Hinde's *The Fall of the Congo Arabs* (1897), E. D. Morel's *King Leopold's Rule in Africa* (1904) and the same writer's *History of the Congo Reform Movement*, edited by W. R. Louis and J. Stengers (1964), and Alfred Parminter's interview in *The Standard* for 8 September 1896. S. J. S. Cookey's *Britain and the Congo Question 1885–1913* (1968) is a full treatment by an African historian. Beyond making use of Lionel Declé's 'The Murder in Africa' in *The New Review*, 12 (1895), I have relied for knowledge of Stokes on W. R. Louis's 'The Stokes Affair and the Origins of the Anti-Congo Campaign' in the *Revue Belge de Philologie et d'Histoire*, 43 (1965).

The Times and *L'Indépendance Belge* have been my main newspaper sources for the period. In addition to *The Times*'s reports of the controversy that broke out in 1889 and 1890 over the Emin Pasha Relief Expedition, I have made use of Stanley's *In Darkest Africa* (1890), J. S. Jameson's *Story of the Rear Column* (1890), Herbert Ward's *My Life with Stanley's Rear Guard* (1891), J. Rose Troup's *With Stanley's Rear Column* (1890), A.-J. Wauters's *Stanley au secours d'Emin-Pasha* (1890), and H. R. Fox Bourne's *The Other Side of the Emin Pasha Relief Expedition* (1891). Jerry Allen, in *The Sea Years of Joseph Conrad* (1965) connects Conrad's tale with the cruelty of Barttelot, but not with the alleged demoralization of the whole group. She was anticipated by Jakob Wassermann, whose biography, *Bula Matari*, was translated in 1932 as *H. M. Stanley—Explorer*. Iain R. Smith's *The Emin Pasha Relief Expedition 1886–1890* (1972) has a valuable chapter on the rearguard. Hugh Clifford's review of 'Heart of Darkness' is in *The Spectator* for 29 November 1902; it reveals the Victorian horror of 'going native' upon which Christine Bolt has some interesting comments in *The Victorian Attitude to Race* (1971). Though I cannot agree with much in K. K. Ruthven's 'The Savage God: Conrad and Lawrence' in *The Critical Quarterly*, 10 (1968), this article supports my belief that there is a connection between 'Heart of Darkness' and the Benin Raid. I have made use of three eye-witnesses' accounts of the raid: R. H. Bacon's *Benin, The City of Blood* (1897), Alan Boisragon's *The Benin Massacre* (1897), and Felix N. Roth's 'A Diary of a Surgeon with the Benin Punitive Expedition', *Journal of the Manchester Geographical Society*, 14 (1898).

Dilke's article 'Civilisation in Africa Today' can be found in *Cosmopolis*, 3 (1896) and Mille's story 'Le Vieux du Zambèse' in Volume 5 (1898).

A number of critics have made helpful studies of Conrad's views on colonization; notably Eloise Knapp Hay in *The Political Novels of Joseph Conrad* (1963), Avrom Fleishman in Conrad's *Politics* (1967), and Jeffrey Meyers in *Fiction and the Colonial Experience* (1973). Jonah Raskin's *The Myth of Imperialism* (1973) is unfortunately as politically biased in one direction as Robert F. Lee's *Conrad's Colonialism* (1969) is in the other; but I have profited very much from Raskin's article 'Imperialism: Conrad's *Heart of Darkness*' in *The Journal of Contemporary History*, 2 (1967) as I have also done from the relevant chapters in Alan Sandison's *The Wheel of Empire* (1967) and G. D. Killam's *Africa in English Fiction* (1968). Graham Greene's comments on 'Heart of Darkness' can be found in *In Search of a Character* (1971). The significance of 'Try to be civil, Marlow' I learnt from an article by Kenneth A. Bruffee, 'The Lesser Nightmare: Marlow's Lie in *Heart of Darkness*' in *Modern Languages Quarterly*, 25 (1964).

ARROW OF GOD

My quotations from *Arrow of God* are from Heinemann's 1965 paperback edition which has the same pagination as the original 1964 edition. Significant changes introduced in the second edition (1974) have been noted in my text. I have also quoted from 'The Role of the Writer in a New Nation' which appeared in *Nigerian Magazine*, 89 (1966) and has been reprinted in *African Writers on African Writings*, edited by G. D. Killam (1973).

Chinua Achebe's other novels are *Things Fall Apart* (1958), *No Longer at Ease* (1960), and *A Man of the People* (1966). Other novelists referred to in this chapter are Nkem Nwankwo (*Danda*, 1964; *My Mercedes is Bigger than Yours*, 1975) and Elechi Amadi (*The Concubine*, 1965; *The Great Ponds*, 1969). 'Wole Soyinka is also well known as a novelist and a poet, but my references are to his plays, of which a collected edition appeared in 1973–4.

I give my informants on Ibo history and social life in chronological order: A. G. Leonard, *The Lower Niger and its Tribes* (1906); G. T. Basden, *Among the Ibos of Nigeria* (1921) and *Niger Ibos* (1938); C. K. Meek, *Law and Authority in a Nigerian Tribe* (1937); M. M. Green, *Ibo Village Affairs* (1947); Daryll Forde and G. I. Jones, *The Ibo and Ibibio speaking Peoples of South-Eastern Nigeria* (1950); R. G. Horton, 'God, man and land in a Northern Igbo village group' in *Africa*, 26 (1956); J. S. Boston, 'Some Northern Ibo Masquerades' in the *Journal of the Royal Anthropological Institute*, 90 (1960); Simon Ottenberg, 'Ibo Receptivity to Change', in *Continuity and Change in African Cultures*, edited by W. J. Bascom and M. J. Herskovits (1959); V. C. Uchendu, *The Igbo of South-East Nigeria* (1965); J. C. Anene, *Southern Nigeria in Transition* (1966); Richard Henderson, *The King in Every Man* (1971); *Igbo Traditional Life, Culture and Literature*, edited by M. J. C. Echeruo and E. N. Obiechina (1971), an admirable symposium forming a special number of *The Conch* (I am particularly indebted to the articles by D. I. Nwoga, M. S. O. Olisa, B. I. Chukwukere, and Obiora Udechukwu); and E. N. Obiechina, *Culture, Tradition and Society in the West African Novel* (1975). I have also gleaned a good deal of anthropological information from the novels of Onuora Nzekwu.

There is much disagreement among these scholars, beginning from their different spelling and uses of the name of the people they are writing about. I have kept to 'Ibo' instead of the more correct 'Igbo', which an English reader is likely to pronounce 'Igg-bow'; and when I have had to use the word substantively I have preferred the linguistically barbarous 'Ibos' to 'the Ibo', which suggests a much more homogeneous group than the Ibo people actually comprise. The word itself, Dr B. E. Obumselu informs me, probably means 'neighbour'.

The area in which I have had to tread most warily, partly as a result of the diversity within unity of the Ibos, is my interpretation of the way Achebe presents Ibo religious ideas. In his collection of essays, *Morning Yet on Creation Day* (1975), Achebe himself discusses '*Chi* in Igbo Cosmology' and one passage in this essay is particularly relevant to *Arrow of God*:

> The Igbo . . . postulate the concept of every man as both a unique creation and the work of a unique creator. . . . All this might lead one to think that among the Igbo the individual would be supreme, totally free and existentially alone. But the Igbo are unlikely to concede to the individual an absolutism they deny even to *chi*. The obvious curtailment of a man's power to walk alone and do as he will is provided by another potent force—the will of his community.

In the novel I find this tension represented by Ezeulu's devotion to a unique deity in contrast to the community's recognition of the need to live in harmony with natural forces. I find significance in the fact that when M. S. O. Olisa calls village priests 'the genuine philosophers of Igbo life' he is writing about Eze*alas*, or priests of the Earth Goddess, not about devotees of such an anthropomorphic being as Ulu. There is perhaps also significance in R. G. Horton's report of the existence, in a community near Enugu, of a cult of *Uluci*, 'evil luck', similar to the Yoruba and Egba veneration of a trickster spirit who works against the common will of men and gods.

Chinua Achebe's books have attracted more critical comment than those of any other African writer. David Carroll's study (1970) seems to me to be far and away the best.

A PASSAGE TO INDIA

The manuscripts of *A Passage to India* are now owned by the University of Texas, who have deposited a microfilm at King's College, Cambridge. A transcript has been photographed and published as *The Manuscripts of 'A Passage to India'*, edited by R. L. Harrison (1971). My page references are to the 1947 'pocket' edition published by Edward Arnold.

Forster's first visit to India is documented by the diary he kept at the time, which is still at King's College; he extracted the most interesting passages for 'Indian Entries' in *Encounter,* 18 (1962). G. Lowes Dickinson's reactions to India on the same journey are discussed by Forster in his biography of Dickinson (1934). Forster's stay in Egypt is reflected in *Alexandria: A History and a Guide* (1922), in a review 'Two Egypts' in *The Athenaeum* of 30 May 1919, in letters about forced labour to *The Manchester Guardian* (29 March 1919) and *The Times* (13 November 1919), and in the 'Notes on Egypt' appended to *The Government of Egypt, Recommendations by a Committee of the International Section of the Labour Research Department* (1920). *The Hill of Devi* (1953) fully documents Forster's sojourn in Dewas State Senior on his second visit to India. Other impressions from this visit are recorded in four articles for *The Nation and Athenaeum*: 'Reflections in India. I.—Too Late?' (21 January 1922), 'Reflections in India. II.—The Prince's Progress' (28 January 1922). 'The Mind of the Indian Native State' (29 April and 13 May 1922), and 'India and the Turk' (30 September 1922). Forster wrote many other articles and reviews on Indian subjects. I have quoted from one of them. 'The Nine Gems of Ujjain' (1914), which is reprinted in *Abinger Harvest* (1936). I have also quoted from P. N. Furbank's introduction to *Maurice* (1971).

Books by Forster's friends and contemporaries which I have drawn upon and quoted include: G. Lowes Dickinson's *Appearances* (1914), J. R. Ackerley's *Hindoo Holiday* (1932), Virginia Woolf's *Roger Fry* (1940) and *A Writer's Diary* (1953), J. M. Keynes's *Two Memoirs* (1949), D. H. Lawrence's *Collected Letters* (1962), and Leonard Woolf's *Sowing* (1960). Forster himself commented on the structure of *A Passage to India* in an interview for *The Paris Review,* and this has been reprinted in *Writers at Work,* edited by Malcolm Cowley (1958).

My sources for the Punjab troubles of 1919 are: *The Times* of that and the following year; B. G. Horniman's *Amritsar and our Duty to India* (1920); Edward Thompson, *The Reconstruction of India* (1930); Brian Bond, 'Amritsar 1919' in *History Today,* 13 (1963); Rupert Furneaux, *Massacre at Amritsar* (1963); Arthur Swinston, *Six Minutes to Sunset* (1964); V. N. Datta, *Jallianwala Bagh* (1969). Forster refers briefly to the massacre in 'Notes on the English Character' reprinted in *Abinger Harvest.* Among many general studies of the British Raj I have found Francis G. Hutchins's *The Illusion of Permanence* (1967) outstanding for the illumination it both derives from and gives to literary works.

Comments by Indian readers that I have found of special interest are those of N. C. Chaudhuri ('Passage to and from India' in *Encounter,* 2, 1954) and J. A. Ramsaran ('An Indian Reading of E. M. Forster's Classic' in *Ibadan Studies in English,* 1, 1969). I have received encouraging confirmation of some ideas in my chapter from two unpublished theses by Indian scholars. G. K. Das in his Cambridge doctoral thesis on *E. M. Forster as an Interpreter of India* draws detailed parallels between the novel and the events in Amritsar; Dabjani Chatterjee in a University of Kent dissertation on *The Role of Religion in E. M. Forster's 'A Passage to India'* sees Forster's awareness of the Upanishads in Mrs Moore's 'darkness'. My quotation is from Max Müller's translation of the Isa Upanishad (1879). Among previous treatments of the novel's political aspects are A. Shonfeld's 'The Politics of Forster's India', *Encounter*, 30 (1968), Lionel Trilling's *E. M. Forster* (1944), Arnold Kettle's *An Introduction to the English Novel* (1953), Andrew Rutherford's introduction to *Twentieth Century Interpretations of 'A Passage to India'* (1970), and a very good chapter in Jeffrey Meyers' *Fiction and the Colonial Experience.* Barbara Hardy in *The Appropriate Form* (1964) stresses the 'mystical' element in the novel, but does not like it; Denis Godfrey does (*E. M. Forster's Other Kingdom,* 1968). The religious and political aspects of the book are brought together by June Perry Levine in *Creation and Criticism: 'A Passage to India'* (1971).

THE MAN-EATER OF MALGUDI

Although all R. K. Narayan's novels have been published in England, they are not always easy to come by. The page references in this chapter are to the 1968 paperback edition of *The Man-Eater of Malgudi,* published at Mysore by Indian Thought Publications. Other novels of Narayan that I have referred to or quoted from are *The Bachelor of Arts* (1937); *The English Teacher* (1945); *Mr. Sampath* (1949); *The Financial Expert* (1952); *Waiting for the Mahatma* (1955); and *The Guide* (1958). Biographical material has been drawn from Narayan's autobiography, *My Days* (1975) and his 'English in India' (in *Commonwealth Literature,* edited by John Press, 1965), from Ved Mehta's 'The Train had Just Arrived at Malgudi Station' (in *John is Easy to Please,* 1971), and from V. Panduranga Rao's 'Tea with R. K. Narayan' (*Journal of Commonwealth Literature,* 6, 1971).

The critical comments which I have found most helpful are those of V. S. Naipaul (*An Area of Darkness,* 1964), V. Y. Kantak in 'The Language of Indian Fiction in English' (*Critical Essays on Indian Writing in English* edited by M. K. Naik *et al.,* 1968), William Walsh (*A Manifold Voice,* 1970), and Shirley Chew in 'A Proper Detachment: The Novels of R. K. Narayan' (*Readings in Commonwealth Literature,* edited by William Walsh, 1973).

The mythological element in *The Man-Eater of Malgudi* is discussed by Edwin Gerow in 'The Quintessential Narayan' (*Literature East and West,* 10, 1966), V. Panduranga Rao in 'The Art of R. K. Narayan' (*Journal of Commonwealth Literature,* 5, 1968), K. R. Srinivasa Iyangar in 'Indian Storytelling in English', (*Two Cheers for the Commonwealth,* 1970), and Meenakshi Mukherjee (*The Twice-Born Fiction,* 1973).

In attempting to grasp the mythological dimension to Narayan's work I have found the largely anthropological accounts of popular Indian religion, such as L. S. S. O'Malley's *Popular Hinduism* (1935), Alain Daniélou's *Le Polythéisme Hindou* (1960), and J. Gonda's *Visnuism and Sivaism* (1970) enlightening, as well as the more philosophical attempts to interpret Indian thought for the West, such as the books of R. C. Zaehner. My own unplanned explorations of Indian stories have naturally included the re-telling of classical tales by Narayan himself, in *Gods, Demons and Others* (1965) and *The Ramayana* (1973).

THE COMEDIANS

Bodley Head are the publishers of the first (1966) edition of *The Comedians,* from which my quotations are taken. I have tried to set the book against the background of Graham Greene's whole *oeuvre.* Works by Greene which I actually allude to or quote from in this chapter are, in chronological order, *Journey Without Maps* (1936); *The Power and the Glory* (1940); *The Heart of the Matter* (1948); *The Lost Childhood and Other Essays* (1951); *The End of the Affair* (1951); *Loser Take All* (1955); *The Quiet American* (1955); *Our Man in Havana* (1958); *A Burnt-Out Case* (1961); *In Search of a Character* (1961); *Collected Essays* (1968); *A Sort of Life* (1971). Although I have made use of the Collected Edition which began to appear in 1970, my quotations are taken from the individual first editions. I have also quoted from Greene's preface to the 1962 American edition of *The Power and the Glory.* Use has been made too of Greene's article on Haiti, 'The Nightmare Republic' in *The New Republic* (16 November 1963), and of his articles on Vietnam, especially 'Indo-China' in *The New Republic* (5 April 1954), 'Before the Attack' in *The Spectator* (16 April 1954), and 'An Indo-China Journal' in *Commonwealth* (21 May 1954). An interview published in *The Listener* (21 November 1968) as 'Graham Greene takes the Orient Express' is full of important statements.

Other works referred to in this chapter are Conrad's *Lord Jim* (1900), *Nostromo* (1904), and 'The Secret Sharer' ('*Twixt Land and Sea,* 1912); Henry James's story, 'The Great Good Place' (in *The Soft Side,* 1900); Barbara Greene's *Land Benighted* (1938); and Frantz Fanon's *Les Damnés de la Terre* (1961).

Three books—*Haiti and the Dominican Republic* by R. W. Logan (1968), *Papa Doc: Haiti and its Dictator* by Bernard Diederich and Al Burt, with an Introduction by Graham Greene (1969), and R. I. Rotberg's *Haiti: The Politics of Squalor* (1971) have been my chief guides to the recent history of Haiti. I have supplemented them with Francis Huxley's *The Invisibles* (1966) and Rémy Bastien's 'Vodoun and Politics in Haiti', in *Religion and Politics in Haiti* (1966), as sane studies of Voodoo. Jean-Pierre O. Gringas's *Duvalier, Caribbean Cyclone* (1967) concludes interestingly with a translation of the quotation from Pascal which I have used in this chapter.

Few of Greene's many critics pay much attention to his politics, and those who do appear not to like *The Comedians*. For A. A. De Vitis ('Greene's *The Comedians*: Hollower Men' in *Renascence*, 18, 1966), it is 'the gloomiest of his novels to date'; David Lodge ('Graham Greene's Comedians' in *Commonwealth*, 83, 1966) thinks there is a lack of intensity in the way that negative and sceptical attitudes are 'characteristically filtered through the consciousness of a disillusioned narrator'; Martin Turnell (*Graham Greene: A Critical Essay*, 1967) holds the book to be basically a study of indifference, while Gwenn R. Boardman (*Graham Greene: The Aesthetics of Exploration*, 1971) feels that its ambiguities are too explicit and its jokes too old. Jeffrey Meyers (*Fiction and the Colonial Experience*, 1974) declares it the weakest of Greene's long novels. I am glad to have Conor Cruise O'Brien on my side in the matter. Dr O'Brien's essays on earlier Greene novels can be found in the second edition (1963) of *Maria Cross*. An older essay on Greene to which I have referred is Richard Hoggart's 'The Force of Caricature: Aspects of the Art of Graham Greene' in *Essays in Criticism*, 3 (1953).

THE MIMIC MEN

Besides *The Mimic Men*, the first edition of which (Andre Deutsch, 1966) I have used for quotations in this chapter, most of V. S. Naipaul's novels are set in Trinidad: *The Mystic Masseur* (1957), *The Suffrage of Elvira* (1958), *Miguel Street* (1959), *A House for Mr Biswas* (1961), *A Flag on the Island* (1969), *Guerrillas* (1975), and also the second section—'Tell me Who to Kill'—of *In a Free State* (1971). Trinidad is also the setting of Shiva Naipaul's novels, *Fireflies* (1970) and *The Chip-Chip Gatherers* (1973), and those of Michael Anthony (*The Games were Coming*, 1963; *The Year in San Fernando*, 1965; *Green Days by the River*, 1967).

I have supplemented Naipaul's historical work, *The Loss of El Dorado* (1969), and his essays in *The Middle Passage* (1962) and *The Overcrowded Barracoon and other Articles* (1972), with such general histories as Gordon K. Lewis's *The Growth of the Modern West Indies* (1968), with more particularized ones such as Donald Wood's *Trinidad in Transition: The Years after Slavery* (1968) and Eric Williams's autobiography *Inward Hunger* (1969), and with such sociological works as Martin Klass's *East Indians in Trinidad: A Study of Cultural Persistence* (1961). *The Bow of Ulysses*, to which Naipaul refers in *The Mimic Men*, is the subtitle of *The English in the West Indies* by J. A. Froude (1888).

There are several monographs on Naipaul's work. I have found that by Landeg White (1975) the most informative and interesting. Kenneth Ramchand has written a penetrating essay in 'The Theatre of Politics' in *Twentieth Century Studies,* 10, (1974).

My quotation from Simone Weil is from *La Pesanteur et la Grâce* (1948).

NOVELISTS OF THE COLONIAL EXPERIENCE

'The Literary Scramble for Africa' is the title of an article by Bloke Modisane in *West Africa,* 30 June 1962. My quotation from Michael Echeruo is from *Joyce Cary and the Novel of Africa* (1973) and that from Orwell is from 'Conrad's Place and Rank in English Letters' (1949) in *Collected Essays,* IV (1968). Paul Theroux explains Christopher Okigbo's mysterious English nursery rhyme in an article contributed to *An Introduction to Nigerian Literature* edited by Bruce King (1971).

The literary works I have referred to in this chapter are Kipling, *Kim* (1901); Doris Lessing, *The Grass is Singing* (1950); Jean Rhys, *Wide Sargasso Sea* (1966); Leonard Woolf, *The Village in the Jungle* (1913); George Orwell, *Burmese Days* (1934) and 'Shooting an Elephant' (1936) in *Collected Essays* I; Joyce Cary, *Mister Johnson* (1940; see also my *Joyce Cary's Africa,* 1964); Bloke Modisane, 'The Situation' in *Black Orpheus: an Anthology of African and Afro-American Prose,* edited by Ulli Beier (1964); Aimé Césaire, *Cahier d'un retour au pays natal* (1956); Camara Laye, *L'Enfant Noir* (1954); George Lamming, *In the Castle of my Skin* (1953); Ngugi Wa Thiongo, *A Grain of Wheat* (1967); 'Wole Soyinka, *A Dance of the Forests* (1963); Wilson Harris, *The Palace of the Peacock* (1960) and subsequent novels; Conrad's *The Secret Agent* (1907). Since this book was written, the contrast I have tried to make between Forster's and Narayan's Indias has been made with all the force of fiction in Ruth Prawer Jhabvala's *Heat and Dust* (1975).

Finally, I list the works which have helped me to build up some idea of the changing forms of Imperialism during the past hundred years: J. A. Hobson, *Imperialism: a Study* (1902); V. I. Lenin, *Imperialism, the Highest Stages of Capitalism* (1916); Lord Lugard, *The Dual Mandate in British Tropical Africa* (1922); Leonard Woolf, *Imperialism and Civilisation* 1928); Frantz Fanon, *Peau Noir, Masques Blancs* (1952); R. Maunier, *The Sociology of Colonies* (1949); George Bennett (editor), *The Concept of Empire, Burke to Attlee* (1953); Philip Woodruff (i.e. Philip Mason), *The Men Who Ruled India* (1953–4); O. Mannoni, *Prospero and Caliban* (1956); A. P. Thornton, *The Imperial Idea and its Enemies* (1959); R. Robinson, J. Gallacher, and A. Denny, *Africa and the Victorians* (1961); Peter Worsley, *The Third World* (1964); Kwame Nkrumah, *Neo-colonialism, the Last Stage of Imperialism* (1966); Richard Faber, *The Vision and the Need* (1966); Colin Cross, *The Fall of the British Empire, 1918–1968* (1968); B. Porter, *Critics of Empire* (1968); V. G. Kiernan, *The Lords of Humankind* (1968); Philip Mason, *Patterns of Dominance* (1970); Philip D. Curtin (editor), *Imperialism* (1971); Edward Grierson, *The Imperial Dream: The British Commonwealth and Empire, 1775–1967* (1972).

INDEX